The Year of Miracles

What the Living Do

Johnny, the kitchen sink has been clogged for days, some
utensil probably fell down there.
And the Drano won't work but smells dangerous, and the
crusty dishes have piled up

waiting for the plumber I still haven't called. This is the
everyday we spoke of.
It's winter again: the sky's a deep, headstrong blue, and
the sunlight pours through

the open living room windows because the heat's on too
high in here, and I can't turn it off.
For weeks now, driving, or dropping a bag of groceries in
the street, the bag breaking,

I've been thinking: This is what the living do. And
yesterday, hurrying along those
wobbly bricks in the Cambridge sidewalk, spilling my
coffee down my wrist and sleeve,

I thought it again, and again later, when buying a
hairbrush: This is it.
Parking. Slamming the car door shut in the cold. What
you called that yearning.

What you finally gave up. We want the spring to come and
the winter to pass. We want
whoever to call or not call, a letter, a kiss – we want more
and more and then more of it.

But there are moments, walking, when I catch a glimpse
of myself in the window glass,
say, the window of the corner video store, and I'm gripped
by a cherishing so deep

for my own blowing hair, chapped face, and unbuttoned
coat that I'm speechless:
I am living. I remember you.

Marie Howe

The Year of Miracles

(recipes about love + grief + growing things)

Ella Risbridger

with illustrations by Elisa Cunningham

for Tash, of course,
on fire with wonder

BLOOMSBURY PUBLISHING

LONDON · OXFORD · NEW YORK · NEW DELHI · SYDNEY

Sixty-Seven Recipes

Notes

This is a memoir, which is to say, it's a kind of fiction. It is what happened, as it happened to me; not as it happened to anyone else.

Some events have been compressed. Most names have been changed. All oven temperatures are given for a standard electric fan oven.

Meals mostly serve 4 generously (2 hungry women, plus leftovers for tomorrow's lunch); but occasionally 1, and sometimes 2, where noted. Cakes, breads and baked goods tend to be made in a 450g loaf tin, a 20cm or 22cm round cake tin, or a 23cm skillet: slice them up however you want. I also use a 35cm x 25cm baking tray with a little lip; and a 30cm x 23cm roasting tin with high sides, like for brownies or lasagne. Things like pickles usually fit into a recycled 370g jam jar, washed in very hot water and dried in the oven – but I wouldn't keep them for longer than a few days in the fridge.

Eggs are unrefrigerated; butter is mostly salted; and milk is mostly semi-skimmed.

But honestly? Do your best with what you have, and it will probably be fine.

It will probably be fine in the end.

Winter, Before

This is a story about grief.

It wasn't meant to be, but what can you do? It gets into everything. It changes everything. It changes you, the way people say birth changes you: it made me live differently, made me love differently. It made me better, and deeper, and bigger.

This is a story about grief, and so it starts – of course it starts – with a carcass.

A chicken carcass; a cold plate in a cold fridge in the middle of the night; and Jo – all her pink hair shining in the fridge-light, the ends of her stage makeup smudgy around her eyes – picking at it like a hungry crow.

I hadn't seen her in a year. It was four in the morning, and we were both broken-hearted, and we had been out dancing because of it.

'We should live together,' Jo said, partly into the fridge.

It was four in the morning, and I knew she was being flippant, as a compliment to the cold chicken, and I hoped so much that she wasn't. The thing was that the fridge – in fact the whole flat – was already up on some estate agent's website; and everything was in piles marked TO SELL or TO BIN or TO KEEP. The person I loved had died; and had died after a long, desperate struggle; and died without a will; and those three things combined had broken our home in half.

It was an aftermath of a flat, as if an earthquake, or other cataclysm, had cracked it right down the middle. So much had already gone: my saucepans, a yellow dress, the good Japanese knives. All our paintings. Our bed. Anything that had been *ours* had gone, as – of course – had anything that was his. I had retained the sofa, which was solely mine; about three thousand books; the ends of the crockery; and the will to live.

It would have been nice to have a plan.

'You could eat the leftovers,' I said. I didn't want to think too much about how nice it would be to have a plan, and so I was talking too fast and flippantly myself. 'I hate leftovers. I always have to do something with them.'

'Like what?'

'Like soup,' I said. 'Or pie.'

'You could make *this* into a pie?' She gestured at the bones and the scraps.

'I could,' I said. 'If I could be bothered.'

She eyed me critically, as if she was summing me up.

'Let's live together and eat a lot of pie.'

'Are you serious?' I said.

'I think it would be nice. Nice house. Nice life. Nice chicken pie with my name on.'

'With your name on?'

'Initials will do,' she said. She went over and put the kettle on, as if it were her kettle, as if we already lived together. 'Milk, no sugar?'

I nodded.

'You do the pie, I'll do the tea,' she said. 'Easy. Nice easy life.' She looked around at the wreckage of the flat, at the places where Jim had been; and then I looked at her, and all the places where her own life had come apart at the seams. None of it had been very easy.

'Nice easy life,' I said. 'Easy as pie.'

'Leftovers pie,' she said. And she made the tea, and then – as easy as that, as easy as pie – we lived together.

When someone you love is dying, you think a lot about miracles. People talk to you a lot about miracles. You *hope* for miracles; and – sometimes – they are granted to you. Because it's true that in the presence of the dying, small miracles happen all the time. Practical miracles.

A sudden response to treatment; a sudden burst of energy; a rally strong enough to get you home, to the chip shop, to the sea. Miracles. A birthday party; a year you didn't know you'd get.

A moment for a coffee alone. Two hours' sleep, three hours' sleep, precious rare four hours' sleep. Being on the bus back from the ward before the late-night supermarket shuts, in time for a fish pie ready meal or butter for toast. A brownie in a café together. Pizza on the steps. A roast chicken in the old black roasting tin. Time to roast a chicken at all. More miracles.

The miracles get smaller the closer you are to the end.

Some genius on the therapy staff remembers where they saw that missing wheelchair part: *miracle*.

The pub on the corner has easy, built-in wheelchair access: *miracle*.

The pub on the corner sells seaside-style chips and little hot pies with pastry all the way round, top and bottom: *miracle, miracle, miracle.*

I had always been good at finding miracles, but proximity to dying made me a prodigy. Everything that wasn't death was life, and everything that was life was miraculous, bright as a dropped penny among all the tubes and wires.

And I saw, too, that miracles were not born, but made. The doctors, the nurses, the therapists and healthcare workers. The scientists and technicians and machinists. The architects and bartenders and cooks. The bus driver who waited; the woman who held the bus up on purpose. The friend who, in the endtimes, left a chicken packed in ice outside my door. 'I knew you'd want to do it yourself,' said the note, and I did want to; and that was a miracle, too. It was a miracle to have been left a chicken; it was a miracle to make a chicken; and it was a miracle to know that I could take the chicken, and rosemary and mustard and butter, and make it into something perfect; but it was mostly a miracle to have been known. The cooking was a miracle; and the friends were a miracle. Dependable, reliable miracles.

I know now that it's no use waiting for miracles; you have to make them. You have to choose to find them from what you have, and where you are.

And so you start with a carcass. You start with the scraps; you start with what you have.

Leftovers Pie

The ingredients are, mostly, optional; these are mostly just
guidelines for pie. Leave out what you don't like; add in what you
do. Buy pastry. Shove in sweet potato or squash or chickpeas. If
you have no leeks, up the onions; or if you have no onions, up the
garlic. If you have no wine, use water. If you have no cream, add
cheese and a splash of milk; or if you have no cheese, leave it out.
God, if you have no chicken, leave it out. Don't worry. Be sensible;
bring what you have, and it will work out just fine. I promise.

For 1 large pie (3 meals for 2 people)

For the pastry

500g plain flour

200g cold butter

100g Parmesan

1 tbsp iced water

Milk or a lightly beaten
egg yolk, to glaze

For the filling

2 tbsp butter

2 leeks

1 white onion

4 garlic cloves

1 x 250g punnet of button
mushrooms

$^1/_2$ rotisserie chicken, or a
huge handful of cooked
chicken-y scraps

1 chicken stock cube
or stock pot

2 tbsp plain flour

6 sprigs of fresh thyme
or 1 tsp dried

100ml white wine

1 tbsp miso

Whole nutmeg, for grating

Black pepper

1 Parmesan rind

2 tbsp double cream

- - - - - - - - - - - - -- -- -- - - - -- - - - - - - -- - -

So first make your pastry. Weigh out the flour into a large bowl.
Grate in the butter and Parmesan, then rub in with your fingertips
until it resembles breadcrumbs. Add the iced water, slowly,
and bring the dough into a ball. Try not to work it too hard, but
honestly? You're probably fine. You're making your own pastry.
Wrap it in cling film and chill while you make the filling.

Put a tablespoon of the butter into your biggest frying pan over a low heat, and let it melt.

Top and tail the leeks, then slice them in half vertically and rinse well under the cold tap. Chop roughly into half-moons, then press out into half-rings. Tip the leeks into the melted butter and stir to coat.

You can ignore the leeks while you chop the onion finely. Add that to the leeks and stir, then cook for 10 minutes. Grate the garlic in, and stir again. Cook for 15 minutes, or until everything starts to soften. (Don't worry: we will keep cooking everything for ages yet and then it's going in the oven – everything will get soft!)

Wash the mushrooms, then break them into pieces with your hands. Cutting mushrooms is a fool's game: uneven chunks taste better. Chuck them in too. Stir.

Shred the chicken and set aside.

If you're using a stock cube (not a pot), you'll have to crumble it into the pan as if it were seasoning. That's fine. Do that bit now. Stir. Sprinkle over your flour and stir again. Add the thyme leaves (fresh or dried). Stir.

Using a spatula, make a clear space in the centre of your frying pan. Shimmy all your floured veg to the sides. In that clear space (spotlight!), melt the remaining tablespoon of butter, and add the stock pot, if that's what you're using – let the stock pot and butter melt together, without stirring.

When they are melted, slowly add the wine, and slowly, *slowly*, stir. Add the miso and let everything simmer and reduce. This is a cheat's way of making a sauce (or velouté, really). Grate in the nutmeg (about half) and *a lot* of pepper. I mean really, do not stint on the nutmeg or the pepper. Chuck in the Parmesan rind and fold in the shredded chicken. Dollop in the cream and stir. Let the sauce reduce still further, to a sticky wine-y syrup, while you do the next bit.

Take your pastry from the fridge, and divide it into two not-quite-equal halves. Take the bigger half, and put it between two sheets of baking paper about twice as big as your pie dish. $\longrightarrow$

⟶ Lightly grease your pie dish.

Roll your pastry out to about the thickness of a pound coin; remove the top sheet of baking paper, and use the other one to kind of flip the thin pastry sheet into the dish. Look how it doesn't tear! Look how easy that was! Press the pastry lightly into the corners of the dish and all the way up the sides, leaving a little overhang. Trim, reserving the offcuts.

Repeat the rolling process with the smaller half, but leave the pastry sheet between the baking paper for now.

Check your filling: is it reduced enough? You don't want it to be too wet, like you want it to be a homogenous pie-type filling not a bunch of disparate soggy parts.

Let it cool, if you can, so it doesn't make the pastry soggy. At this point, you might want to pre-heat your oven to 180°C.

Spoon the filling into the pastry-lined pie dish. Flip the other sheet of pastry over the top, and press down the edges with a fork. Trim the edges.

With your reserved pastry trimmings, make little balls to go around the edge of the pie – and of course, save enough to cut out your initials. Dot the pastry balls around the pressed-down edges of the pie, and lay the initials in the middle. Stab the centre of the pie with a fork, then brush the top lightly with milk or beaten egg yolk.

Bake for 25 minutes or until the pie is golden and glossy and cracking all over. Serve with peas, and be praised for your leftovers pie, and how you made something out of nothing.

Cooking, and the people who love you: the two greatest and most practical miracles of all.

I am writing this, now, in our narrow kitchen: mine and Jo's. It's snowing outside, maybe the last flurry of the year. There are already green shoots coming up in the park and in the little garden I planted the year I wrote everything in this book. The book and the garden grew together, putting tentative little tendrils out into a new world. It felt like a new world to me: a new bad world, where everything was changing, and every word felt like a missive into an uncertain future, like a message in a bottle, an engraving of a body on the side of a spaceship. I was writing to remember; and I was growing things to hope; and I was cooking for both of those reasons.

The snow swirls past the kitchen window. The wall is patched with experimental pink (Confetti, Hellebore, Sulking Room) and there's chicken stock (carcass and scraps, golden and shining in the old faithful cast-iron casserole) simmering on the stove. Steam creeps up the glass of the French windows that lead out onto the fire escape, now blanketed in fine, powdery snow. Beneath the snow, everything sleeps. Somewhere under there are last year's bulbs, the deep roots of rosemary and thyme. Somewhere under there is the deep dark earth I carried all the long walk home last summer, too afraid to take the train; the compost I dug with all the things we couldn't eat, the eggshells, the potato peel, the carrot tops.

Things are coming to life again. They always do. Lazy mornings turn into hurried lunches and cosy evenings. Days turn into weeks into months into seasons; into a year, and round again. Each morning Jo and I eat breakfast together; each evening we eat dinner together. We are the joint tenants of this patchy little kitchen, and joint owners of a large and beautiful pine dining table and six white chairs. We are – per the government – a household. The law of the land says that if we eat together, we are counted together; if we 'share cooking facilities' or 'one main meal a day' we are legally entangled for census and other administrative purposes. This is true, and I find it beautiful: more than beautiful. I find in this quiet corner of the legal system something that at last feels like home.

It has mattered more than ever, in the year in which I have written most of this story, to know who your household is: to know what it means to be a household, to be counted as one. This book comes from a year where we had to know who our people were, and where we were coming from; where we had to remember what mattered, and weigh up love, and sacrifice, and grief, and pain, and all those things that make up our ordinary lives. Ordinary lives are always full of love, and pain, and grief, and joy: that's what it is to be alive. That's what it is to be human. This is not a big story. This is not a story about the world, but about my world, and – maybe – about yours too. It is (a little bit) about the time in which I wrote it, but really it's about the things that outlast, the things that stay.

The word 'household' is old (fourteenth century, I think?); and what is older still (as ancient as we have stories to tell it) is that it is what we eat, and how we eat it, that holds the world together. Persephone and her pomegranate; Circe and her herbs; the old stories. Break bread with me and we are bound to each other.

We eat a lot of chicken, and a lot of eggs, and a lot of vegetables; some fish, but not so much; almost no red meat. We eat quite a lot of treats, and more butter and olive oil than I would dare to tell you. An almost constant supply of carbs, one way or another. Pesto pasta for at least one meal a week; ready meals for one more. We cook, we shop, we eat. We drink a lot of tea and a lot of orange squash. Almost every morning we chat about dinner; almost every afternoon I figure it out, read the barometer of our moods, the weather and the season, and the contents of the fridge. We find a harmony: one that takes into account my need to make stuff up, and her need to eat at eight every night, what I like, what she likes, the nights we stay out late and the mornings we wake too early and the people we both bring home. Our friends. Their friends. Family.

I cook; she washes up.

These are the miraculous constants of our life together: the meals we eat, the way we eat them, the days spooling out into weeks and into months and into seasons and into a year, and another one.

All cookbooks are love stories, in one form or another, and this one's mine. Or maybe, more accurately: this one's ours.

But let's begin at the beginning.

January, a new house, a new household, a new year, and the seasons all before us.

January

Douglas says, 'Well, I think – I think we're done?' He puts the blue IKEA bag of books – the last of 29 – down on the floor, and we look around.

The 29 IKEA bags – which had taken up the whole of the last flat, and eight car journeys to ferry here – are stacked against one wall, and the floor is enormous and empty. Annie sets a box – the toaster, the mugs, the butter – down on the kitchen counter, and comes through with us, to look at the emptiness.

In the centre of the floor Jo flips herself up onto her hands, like a circus performer, and over again onto her feet. 'So much space,' she says. There is so much space, and now all we have to do is fill it.

We mark out spaces on the floor with masking tape where things will be; and Douglas and Jo put the ancient sofa – the last survivor of the Tiny Flat, the last survivor of the Jim years – back together.

'Thank you for this,' I say, inadequately, to Annie, and to Douglas. They had never really known Jim – Annie only slightly, Doug not at all – and they had never known me before I had loved a person who died. They had never known the person I used to be, never known the person who drank real coffee and had panic attacks every day and didn't know about death, or miracles.

'Thank you,' I say again, and look out of the big bay window. The window overlooks a road, and on the other side of the road, some green space. Or, at least, what will be green in a few months. It is brownish now, trees bare and sparse, but the church tower behind it is like something from my childhood; something from the not-city, or a city I'd imagined when I was a little girl, all winding streets and leafless trees and Narnia lampposts. It is nothing like the London I lived in before. But then, I am nothing like the person who lived there.

'Tea before you go?' I say, to Douglas, and to Annie. I say it to sort of stop thinking things, but I mean it. The sofa is nearly back together, shabbier than I remember, and smaller than it had ever looked before. It took up the entire living room floor of the Tiny Flat. Here it takes up one corner.

In the kitchen I find the kettle, and put teabags into mugs. Green for me; purple for Jo; yellow for Douglas; grey, flecked with pale blue and white and silver, for Annie. I am fussy about mugs: I like them to be used by the right people in the right combinations. It's lucky, I think, that Douglas (yellow) and Annie (grey) had both offered to help; and it's lucky that Jo packed the mugs in pairs, nestled in tissue and folded tea towels. No, not lucky. It's the kind of thing Jo knows without being told, which is to say, it is the kind of small, unspoken intimacy that makes us a household: the knowing, and the doing, and the making of the tea.

The kitchen is narrow and plain, with a five-hob gas stove that sold me on the house in the first place. *I could cook*, I think, in a kitchen like this. *I could really* cook *here*. There is a big window, and a door onto a set of fire-escape steps, leading down to a little patio. The steps are black iron, twirled with dead ivy, and the patio is concrete and spare and covered with old leaves and broken bits of shed.

It's winter, and nothing is growing: nothing has been planted. I open the kitchen door and look at the drab nothing below. *This could be a garden*, I think. *This could be a garden*. And then I go back into the sitting room with four cups of tea, to start sorting the books.

Annie goes home; and after a while, the sofa *finally* put together, so does Douglas. And it's just me and Jo, and we sort books, and make more tea.

'I should cook,' I say to her, and she shrugs and goes: 'Do you really want to? Aren't you knackered? Because we can get takeaway.'

And I don't know what she means. I always cook. Cooking for people is how I love them; cooking for people is why I'm here. I've got this kitchen; don't I need to earn it?

'You wanted pie,' I say, lamely; and now I think about it, I don't want to cook at all. I am knackered, and I don't want to cook. 'You wanted pie, didn't you?'

'Only metaphorically,' Jo says, and pulls out her phone and orders Nepalese.

And while we're eating our dumplings and curry and rice, surrounded by space and books, Jo says: 'It's easy if you let it be easy,' and I'm thinking about that, and how good the dumplings are, and I'm thinking: *this is going to make a very weird cookbook*.

Dippy Eggs

The first non-takeaway thing we eat, in the new house, is dippy eggs. I make the eggs, Jo makes the toast; the tea is a combined effort. One puts the kettle on, one finds the teabags, one finds the milk and washes up the mugs, and so on. We don't talk about it; it just sort of happens this way, as if it has been happening like that forever. Which feels like a sign.

So then hot sweet tea, in the right mugs (green for me, lavender for Jo); there are no egg cups, so the eggs balance precariously in those glass ramekins that you buy puddings in, padded all around with the tissue paper that the mugs were wrapped in. The tissue paper is neon green and hot pink – itself leftover from birthdays – and this gives the eggs, grey January though it is, a sort of Easter-ish feeling.

The whole thing, really, has a sort of Easter-ish feeling: a celebration, something risen, something against all the odds very much alive. Magic, or – a miracle.

It's the morning and the light through the bay window is cold but clear.

The best dippy eggs – by which I mean soft-boiled, the greatest eggs on earth – are like this:

Bring the water to a rolling boil, with big bubbles
breaking on the surface.
Eggs in. One minute exactly.
Lid on, heat off. Six minutes exactly.
In the six minutes, make and butter the toast;
cut it into soldiers.

'The thing about death,' Jo says, bursting the yolk with a buttered crust, 'is that it's exactly as terrible as an egg is perfect.'

And the golden yolk spills down the brown shell and onto her fingertips, and the year is just beginning and the light catches all her pink hair and makes it glow. And I take a sip of my tea, and a breath, and cut the top off my own egg, and know exactly what she means.

Pigeon Days, American Pancakes

January is my worst month – bad dreams and grey rain – but even in January, there are moments worth hanging on for. Not many, maybe, but enough. Enough bright cold days, sun clean and icy, that you can believe that it's worth getting out of bed. Enough perfect moments – five? – that you can get through the rain.

They have done these experiments on pigeons. The pigeons live in a box. The box has a lever in it. At the end of the lever is a treat dispenser. It's very simple, to start with: hit the lever, get a treat. When the pigeons always know when the treat is coming, the pigeons are lever-neutral. If the lever never, ever does anything, the pigeons are also lever-neutral. But then the scientists make the lever dispense treats at random. Sometimes the pigeons peck a dozen times and get nothing; sometimes a single peck dispenses more joy than they know what to do with. There's no method, no system. And the pigeons become obsessed with trying to get treats. The lever is their life.

This, basically, is me in January. Jo is at the theatre all day with Max and Charley, making weird magic, and I'm on my own in the new kitchen, opening and shutting the door as if by doing so I too might make magic. I obsess over the weather, as if by hoping I might summon either real snow or cold sunshine, birds singing in the bare branches. Most days it doesn't work. Some days – some mornings – it does.

'Pigeon days', let's call them: as close and as far as a wood pigeon calling down the chimney, the smallest hint of spring in the air. There are snowdrops in someone's garden a little way up the road, tucked into the shadow of the wall. I crack the kitchen door open, just for a little while, and put on an extra jumper and some socks. And I make pancakes.

Pancakes – pouty, plump American-esque pancakes – are not my thing, not really. But they are Jo's thing. Which is the whole thing, isn't it? Sometimes – when there's a hint of spring in the air, and a little cold sunshine through the kitchen door – you just make the thing for the people you love, for the joy of making the people you love the thing they love. And these are pretty great: fluffy and fat and stacked, with melted butter in the batter, and bacon done to a crisp under the grill, and extra maple syrup. People want pancakes that feel like pancakes. Here they are.

For 4

Streaky bacon	1 tbsp golden caster sugar
50g butter + more to serve	200ml milk
200g self-raising flour	3 large eggs
1½ tsp baking powder	Maple syrup

- -

Put your bacon under the grill, now, before you forget.

Take a big non-stick frying pan and melt your butter over a low heat.

While it's melting, whisk together the flour, baking powder and caster sugar in a big bowl.

Measure out the milk and beat the eggs into it with a fork. Tip in half of the melted butter and beat again.

Pour one into the other and whisk until smooth (an electric whisk makes it easier, but I don't have one, so!).

You can let the batter stand now for half an hour, if you feel like it, but honestly don't feel obliged. (Obviously, turn off the bacon and the butter if you're doing this.)

Shake the butter in the pan to coat the base. Use a big spoon (like an old-fashioned, real tablespoon-tablespoon, not a measuring spoon-tablespoon) to dollop batter into the pan. Don't crowd the pan. Start with two pancakes: cook for 2 minutes, then flip. (If you can't flip, it's too soon; don't worry).

Once you've flipped them over, put two more dollops in the pan: basically, the rule is to have two pancakes cooking on any given side at one time. You'll know when they are done, because they will be golden on both sides, pick-uppable with a spatula (not doughy and sticky!), and also because they will obviously be cooked pancakes.

Serve with the crispy bacon and plenty of maple syrup, and probably more butter. Because why not?

Cardamom Buns

If you go out of our house and up the hill, then down the hill, and up another hill, you get to the heath. It's the kind of wide, flat open space you don't usually get in London: the sky is vast, and grey-white clouds skim across it the way they do above the sea. I am always getting lost on the heath, which should be impossible, but it's too flat for me to ever know which way I'm supposed to be going; I have to navigate by the distant silhouettes of Canary Wharf, and – before them – the shapes and spires of St Margaret's, All Saints', and Our Ladye Star of the Sea.

Across the heath, beyond the high park walls, is the cricket pitch. I see Beezle first, a little smudge of white and brown racing for the tennis ball, and behind her, Nancy, big headphones and Otto's tan jacket. Beez bounces into focus, jumping up at my coat, and I shake her paw with my hand, like we're civilised people.

'Hello, small friend,' I say to Beezle the dog; and then, to Nancy, coming up behind her, 'Hello, bigger friend!'

We walk most days, the three of us. Ten thousand steps, ninety minutes.

Weeks become months become seasons become years, and round we go again: the earth moves from brown to speckled to high green, snowdrops, crocuses, vast sweeps of daffodils, cherry blossom, horse chestnuts (white, then pink, then conkers), drifts of leaves, swathes of mud, parakeets in bare branches, sticky buds, catkins, green again.

'Isn't it amazing?' I say to Nancy, kicking through a mulchy pile of leaves, 'Isn't it amazing that we saw all these leaves in bud, and then they were here, and now they're becoming earth, and then more will grow – and we get to see it all?'

She ignores me, which is the privilege of our years of friendship: she has no obligation to respond to the maybe-twee things by which I am sometimes overcome. We throw the ball for the dog, and walk, and talk. We talk about work, mostly; about how to phrase something, how to say something, a plot or a puzzle or a difficult email. This is how we both work best: outdoors, under a big sky, letting the depth of the dark earth and vastness of the grey clouds put everything into perspective.

'Time for a coffee?' Nancy says, which one of us always says; which means, really, *which way should we walk?* ⟶

No time for a coffee means two loops of the park itself, one loop to discuss her work, one loop for mine. But *time for a coffee* means down through the park, and along the river; across the bridge, up the road, and into the bakery.

Time for a coffee means time for a chat with the baker; time to make small talk with a stranger in the queue, or fall briefly in love with the blue-tattooed girl drawing in the window seat, the builder buying buns, two teen boys in battered donkey jackets brushing hands over the sugar bowl and pretending it's by accident. *Time for a coffee* means time to eavesdrop on the NCT mums, dungaree babies and iPad entrepreneurs, the Queer Liberation students and the squatting hippies from the under-threat communal garden on Ink Street. *Time for a coffee* means time to flick through the stack of leaflets about neighbourhood zine festivals and tai chi classes and adverts for bedrooms and bicycles, Help Wanted and Help Given. *Time for a coffee* means the long table, Nancy at one end, me at the other, laptops out, occasionally trading a word. (*What's the name of that thing where they put the pigeons in the box and give them treats?*) *Time for a coffee* means decaf for me, Americano for her, same every day, with a crust for Beez, lying under the table, gnawing. *Time for a coffee* means, more than anything else, cardamom buns.

The cardamom buns at this bakery, our bakery, are twisted knots about the size of a fist. The yeasted dough is white and close-crumbed, somewhere between tender and chewy: not cakey at all, and just begging to be dipped in coffee, like this was Europe or somewhere. They are barely sweet. Or, at least, they would be barely sweet if they weren't drenched in cardamom-scented syrup, tiny flecks of seeds suspended in the sugar. The glaze sets hard into a kind of fine sticky lace around the base of the bun. In the seam of the knot, the syrup meets the spiced butter between the layers, and makes a kind of caramelised ribbon running the full length of the twist. They are perfect: the reward for a long walk, for a day when there's time to go all the way down through the avenue, along the great brown river, and up the road to the bakery.

The trouble, of course, comes from the fact that the day you most need a bun is always the day when you don't have time to walk to the bakery. The day you (I) most need a bun is the day when there's no time for any walk at all; the day of one hundred and six steps total, all of them between the fridge and my desk, mugs accumulating around me like frost forming on a window. The sky behind my back changes through the kitchen door, and I see it only in the reflection in my screen.

I need a bun – and more than that, I need to make something with my hands: I need to knead. I need to knead and braid and make something tangible out of my evening. When you spend a lot of time in your head, and at your screen, there's something satisfying about making something in the real world. And there is nothing more real than a bun.

Just the word 'bun' is soothing, and so is the process of making them: with a stand mixer it's easier, but by hand it's more fulfilling (dealer's choice). They take a minute, but they aren't difficult; the knotting is a little fiddly, but that's part of it, the focus on your fingers and the stretch of the dough. In the middle of January, they make me think of Christmas mornings, of having something small and true to celebrate, of clean snow instead of gritty, icy mud. They make me think of wide skies and warm fires; and when you give people these buns, wrapped in a twist of brown paper, they look at you like you've hung the moon. Cardamom and cinnamon have that effect on people, especially when combined with butter and yeast.

I would never claim to be a better baker than a professional, but I'm pretty good for a girl in her own kitchen. Plus, Georgie, a professional caterer and cookbook writer, gave me this recipe, and these are – for my money – the best you can get (outside of the bakery through the park). $\longrightarrow$

Makes 13 buns, a baker's dozen

For the dough

12 cardamom pods

200g plain flour + 200g strong white bread flour (*use 400g of either if you don't have both, but it is honestly best to use both*)

1 tsp flaky sea salt, pinched to a powder (*or just regular table salt, which I never remember to buy*)

75g light soft brown sugar

7g yeast (*1 sachet or 1 tsp*)

75g butter

250ml milk

Pinch of saffron

1 tsp ground cinnamon

For the filling

100g butter, at room temperature

100g light soft brown sugar

2 tsp ground cinnamon

2 tsp ground cardamom (*or 12 pods, bashed and seeds extracted*)

For the glaze

70ml water

50g light soft brown sugar

3 cardamom pods, bashed but basically whole

- -

For the dough, bash the cardamom pods with a pestle and mortar (or a rolling pin and a sturdy bowl) to get the seeds out, saving the empty pods to infuse the milk later. Grind the seeds finely, then put them into a large bowl – probably the bowl of a stand mixer, honestly, but if you love to knead by hand, please knock yourself out. Add both flours, salt, sugar and yeast and stir, then set aside.

In a reasonably sized saucepan, melt the butter and pour over the milk. Bring to a simmer, add the cardamom pods and saffron. Take off the heat, and set aside for half an hour or so, still in the saucepan. The infused milk and butter should be at room temperature before you use it: is a drop on the inside of your wrist too hot? too cold? If not, then it's grand. You could also use a kitchen thermometer, but it might just be one step too far for this recipe, so if that's what's making you give up, don't bother even thinking about it.

Slowly, with the motor running and the dough hook on, pour the milk and butter through a sieve into the flour mixture. You want it to come together into a smooth dough, so knead for about 5 minutes (10 by hand, but see how you go). You may wish to keep the butter dish to hand here – if the dough just doesn't seem... supple enough, or smooth enough (you'll see what I mean if this happens to you), add a teaspoon of butter and keep kneading. It is the nicest dough in the world, honestly, or one of them.

When it's ready – lovely and smooth and supple – let it rise in a warm place until doubled in size, about an hour and a half. I have never cracked the overnight rise with these buns, but I hear it can be done: many people I trust leave this dough for half an hour in the warm, and then overnight in the fridge. I'm telling you this because I think the problem is me, and maybe you'll have better luck, but also in case you end up having the same problem and think you are just a bad baker.

While the dough is rising, make something so delicious it feels like you should eat it with your head under a napkin. For the filling, beat together the butter, sugar and spices. OH NO. Do not eat it all with a spoon. You are not six. (Because you are not six, you can eat it with a spoon if you want to, but please imagine how nice it will be melted into buns, so try not to eat it all yet.)

Back to the dough again, also the filling. Take the doubled dough out of the warm place. (Fridge-risers, you've made your own cold bed.) Hold it in your arms like a lovely baby, except one that smells of spices. Delicious, spicy baby. Dump the spicy baby onto a floured surface, and roll it out into a large rectangle, about 5mm thick, with a short side of the rectangle nearest to you. This is actually quite thick, thicker than you think. Rectangle here is an approximate term, but you're going to fold the dough into thirds, and anything that is an odd shape won't get folded properly – so it either won't get buttered with the spicy butter, or the butter won't get wrapped up in dough and will just melt away. Do you see the point? Rectangle is always approximate, but the more rectangular you can make it, the happier you will be.

Spread your rectangle with the magic spicy butter. OH NO. Do not eat any more of the butter or you will have to start again. ⟶

Instead, observe your rectangle of dough. Imagine it divided into thirds horizontally, like in Fig. 1.

Fold up the bottom third. Fold the top third down over that, as shown in Fig. 2.

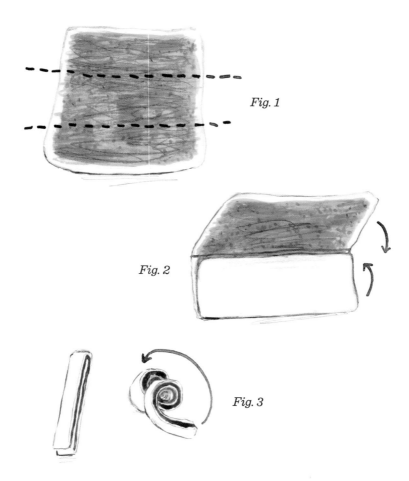

Fig. 1

Fig. 2

Fig. 3

Slice this third-of-a-rectangle, now full of layers of butter, into thirteen pieces. This is a baker's dozen, so that you will be able to say 'I have made a dozen buns' but also have eaten one in the kitchen to check.

Sharp knife. Some people use dental floss here. I do not get it. Sharp knife all the way.

Take the first of your thirteen strips of rectangle, and very gently str-e-e-tch it out nice and long. (Don't snap it, but.)

Wrap one end around two fingers of your left hand. Keep wrapping until you have about 4cm of dough left. Take your fingers out, and tuck the remaining 4cm of dough into the space where your fingers were, as shown in Fig. 3.

Tuck the loose ends underneath, and set on a baking tray lined with baking paper.

Repeat another dozen times, knowing full well that you will improve as you go on. Bun thirteen will be gorgeous.

Let them prove for an hour, and go away. Do the washing up, make a coffee, whatever. An hour is so much less time than you think (unless you're waiting for someone to ring you, when it's eternity).

Pre-heat the oven to 220°C. Bake the lovely buns for 8 minutes, and make the glaze while they're baking.

The glaze is madly easy: bring the ingredients – water, sugar, cardamom – together in a little saucepan, and simmer until the sugar has dissolved and the glaze has reduced by half.

Remove buns from oven. Remove buns from baking sheet, but not from baking paper. Set baking paper, plus buns, on cooling rack.

Pour glaze liberally over buns while they are still hot. Georgie brushes hers on with a pastry brush, but I like the messiness, and the spun-sugar lace that sets at the bottom as they cool.

Eat warm for best results; eat later for very nearly best results, plus lovely caramelly sugar lace. I love buns very much.

Iron Soup

We have no furniture to speak of, and I think I've forgotten how to cook.

We appear to only be eating takeaways, baking and eggs – which is pretty wonderful, as far as it goes, but I am beginning to worry about anaemia and scurvy and rickets. I can't remember the last time we ate anything substantial that didn't come in a little plastic tub. I wish for kitchen chairs, a dining table, and iron –something nourishing and wholesome. Something sensible; and something with a punch it hasn't just lucked into through liberal applications of salt and butter. I want a dining table, and everything that the dining table implies. I want dinners and dinner parties and people. I pace the space where the table will be. How can I cook without a table? How can I get anything done without a table and chairs?

'We need a table,' I say to Jo, when she comes home from rehearsals. 'We need a table, we need a table, we need a table.'

'So we'll get a table,' she says, mildly, so just like that we get the table; and I'm thinking *chairs, chairs, we need chairs*, and all the dining chairs are either horrible or a thousand pounds and then, one dreary day, Annie spots six perfect white pine chairs stacked up in Deptford Market, huddled between the house-clearance cookers and old exercise books and work-out videos.

It's raining hard by the time I get there, and I look so bedraggled – and, possibly, my shirt is so visibly transparent – that the stallholder gives me the lot for a fiver each. Annie Tetrises all six wet chairs plus me into her car, and drops us home.

And so then there's a table and chairs and no more space; and I go into the kitchen and decide that I'm going to have to cook something now. And besides I am hungry. And besides I want iron.

A lifetime ago, I was so good at cooking for iron that they called me the Kitchen Witch. They called me this on the Day Unit of the hospital, where they give the more chill kind of chemo, and sometimes stem cell infusions and blood transfusions. That kind of thing. It's where you go if you're waiting for results that are probably not going to be great; and where you go if you're not sure what exactly is wrong. It is the last place I saw Jim as himself: the last place I saw him walk; the last place I heard him talk in his own voice. The last moment of our old life. $\longrightarrow$

→ He was often anaemic, which made iron the central focus of our lives for a little while: beef as red as a pomegranate, leafy greens as dark as blood, and soup to hold back the dark, to make you strong, to keep you safe. It's lentils (iron) and leafy greens (iron), with tomatoes for lycopene, and vitamin C to help absorb the iron. It's rich-bitter olive oil, and hot sauce, and smoked salt, and saffron yoghurt for a splash of gold amongst the crimson.

They used to think iron would keep back bad magic: a horseshoe over the door to keep witches from your home, a railing round a graveyard to keep the dead from walking. I am already afraid of the dead walking, and so I remember this soup I used to make, and make it for us both.

And it's still as good as it ever was, before anyone had died, and before this house was ever ours.

For 2

1 small onion

1 tbsp extra virgin olive oil

2 tsp Sriracha or other hot sauce (*gochujang and/or fermented black beans also good*)

1 x 400g tin of chopped tomatoes

2 tomato-tins of water

1 vegetable stock cube or stock pot

300g puy lentils

3 big handfuls of any leafy greens (*probably kale, maybe cavolo nero, not spinach*)

Smoked sea salt

Black pepper (*optional*)

2 eggs

1 tbsp butter

Saffron yoghurt, to serve: 2 tbsp yoghurt, pinch of saffron, pinch of salt and stir (*optional*)

Gently chop the onion. I say gently because maybe you are feeling fragile, but look, that's the only bit of chopping. Chop the onion and sauté it in the olive oil – by which I mean, take your saucepan, add the oil, put it over a medium heat and add the onion. Cook it for 15 minutes, or until soft and translucent.

Inhale lovely onion smell. Add the hot sauce, tomatoes and the two tomato-tins of water. Stir in a vegetable stock cube.

Yes, of course you could use 800ml vegetable stock instead, but I am just almost never the kind of person with vegetable stock in the fridge. Marigold powder is perfect. Stock cubes are perfect. The stock pot is the most genius culinary invention since sliced bread. Maybe one day we'll be stock people, the sort who always use homemade stock, but a) what a waste of homemade stock when you could just drink it and b) imagine.

Rinse the lentils in a sieve – one of my favourite kitchen jobs. I find the weight of wet lentils in the sieve to be unbelievably satisfying. It's just weighted right; it makes me feel like they're real, and maybe I am too. Lentils act as a kind of reality check, somehow? Anyway, try it. Try it, before you tip the lentils into the soup and cover the pan. Turn the heat right down and go away for half an hour.

Shred the greens, yanking them from their fibrous stalks and tearing them to bits.

Taste the lentils: add a little smoked salt, maybe some pepper.

Toss in the greens and cook for 2 minutes. In those 2 minutes, fry the eggs in the butter: high heat, lid on.

Divide the soup between two bowls; slide an egg on top of each one. Saffron yoghurt, if you made it, bright as a penny. To the table: to the new chairs and the new table and the sound of the rain.

Cardamom Cinnamon Chicken Rice

It takes me longer than it should have done to discover the corner shop.

Jim, in our old life, was larger *than* life: everyone knew him, and I drifted in his shadow, and Jim's shadow loomed large over everything we did. When I went to places without him, it was like I had become invisible; when we went to places together, everyone knew him. They gave him his favourite table in every pub, and every meal ended with limoncello and things stricken at random from the bill. The woman in the greasy spoon knew his order by heart (sausage baguette, brown sauce, no butter). The men in the supermarket beneath our house would call out to him in the street when they got the meat in for curry goat. The man at Gaby's would give him Styrofoam cups of hummus, whatever he ordered: hummus and baklava and extra salt beef. The corner-shop guy started stocking weird ciders he liked, just for him. Jim was simply very difficult to ignore; and more difficult to forget.

'Tell him to give 'em hell,' said the corner-shop guy, to me, when I told him Jim was in a sort-of coma. I was buying the things Jim always bought, which was perhaps why he remembered who I was, and asked where Jim was. He never had remembered me before. 'Tell him to give 'em hell.'

'I'll tell him,' I said. But I didn't know how to tell the corner-shop guy that I didn't think Jim was really listening; and that I thought hell was the last thing we needed; and I didn't know who we were supposed to give it to. It only really mattered that the corner-shop guy had wanted to say something to Jim; and I knew that Jim (or the person Jim used to be) would have been pleased.

Jim loved to be *somebody*, and he was a corner-shop *somebody* without ever really trying; and this, I suppose, is why it takes me nearly three weeks to brave ours. So far I've been walking all the way to the big supermarket halfway up the street every time we need a pint of milk. There is something deeply comforting in the bland anonymity of it: identical things on identical shelves up and down the country, and nobody to wonder if I used to live in someone else's shadow.

And then it's raining again, and I'm running out of time to get the dinner bits, and I think: *well, fuck it, got to brave it sometime.*

The corner-shop door is ajar, and it smells like spices and doughnuts and someone else's dinner, and inside is – well, inside is the world.

There are wonton wrappers and parathas and an extensive range of oven pizzas and little tubs of exotic American ice cream (mini marshmallows! cereal bites!). There are stuffed vine leaves, and rat traps, and twenty-three kinds of pasta. There are racks and racks of Arabic fizzy drinks, the kind I haven't seen since school. Pickled lime leaves and six kinds of lime pickle. Mrs Naga Hot Pickle. Mr Basil orange drink. So many pickles; and vast jars of pimento-stuffed olives, like a party in the eighties. Sacks of spices – real sacks – and organic micro-herbs and cling-filmed trays of oxtail. A vast range of halal meats. Coriander in huge bunches. The good butter. Pop Tarts. Coco Pops in the big box. Dumplings, frozen and fresh. Even goat, I note, with a little stab. Jim would love this, Jim would love the way it's all here, Jim would already be in conversation.

Every label is in a different language, a different alphabet, a different script. Everything is everywhere. A world in a corner shop; eternity in an hour. I pick up milk, and chocolate oat milk, and soft fat little pitta breads. I can't resist black cardamom pods, and a scoop of sour cherries dried to puffy, crinkly sharpness. In the halal meat section I find a packet of chicken thighs, and there it is: dinner. $\longrightarrow$

Is this Ottolenghi? Was this once Ottolenghi? I think so; it feels like a Yotam thing, a Middle Eastern thing; like something a little bit Emirati, Omani, Israeli. It feels like the kind of recipe I cooked once from a book, a thousand years ago, and made it over and over again, twisting it and tweaking it for maximum efficiency.

Listen to this: caramel, char, chicken skin, blistering under the grill; cardamom, cinnamon, cumin; golden, saffron-scented rice, sticking a little in a kind of faux-*tahdig* to the bottom of the pan for a sticky, crispy secret; red onions tangling for almost an hour in the skillet, with butter and oil; redolent, fragrant, windows steamed up. One single pan. Onions, low and slow. No, slower. Sour cherries, softened in chicken stock, tender and yielding like the chicken itself, the meat falling away from the bone. Think of the onions and the spices, warm and tender. Think of the washing up, or lack thereof. And that, maybe, is what makes this mine and not Ottolenghi's (if it was his in the first place): I'm a domestic cook, an I-know-I-have-to-clean-the-kitchen cook, a can-I-buy-this-in-the-corner-shop cook. Think of this as a bastardised weeknight version of the real story.

I tip it into two bowls, balance a chicken thigh on each steaming, saffron-scented heap, and call Jo through: *bring squash,* I tell her, *bring squash and spoons.*

For 4 (maybe with leftover chicken, maybe not)

Big pinch of saffron + 2 tsp milk (*optional; saffron is so expensive that having it as a non-optional ingredient is quite stressful*)

2 big red onions

2 tbsp olive oil

10 black cardamom pods (*if you can't get black, green is fine*)

1 cinnamon stick

2 tsp cumin seeds

8 smallish chicken thighs (*skin on, bone in*)

500ml hot chicken stock (*I use a cube, obviously*)

300g basmati rice, washed

30g dried sour cherries

2 tsp sesame oil

2 tbsp chopped flat-leaf parsley

2 tbsp chopped coriander

4 tsp sesame seeds

If you're using the saffron – more expensive than gold (and I like that, that flowers are, in the end, worth more than metal) – soak it in the milk and set aside.

Slice the onions into half-moons, and then into half-rings.

Add a tablespoon of the olive oil to your biggest oven-proof heavy-bottomed skillet, and heat over a low flame. When it feels warm (hover your hand over to test – and if you're too scared to do that because the oil is sputtering, it's too hot), add the cardamom pods, cinnamon stick and cumin seeds. Toast until you can smell them: warm and inviting and familiar. My grandmother's house smells like cumin and Imperial Leather and soil, and I miss it very much.

Toss the onions into the skillet and stir them through the spices. Cook for a long time. Longer. We're talking at least 30 minutes just on onions, 40 even, maybe closer to an hour if you've got an hour. Anyone who tells you to cook onions quicker than that is wasting your time, and making you eat bad onions. Stir them occasionally to stop them sticking, but they've got oil, and should be fine. Just keep an eye on them.

When the onions are ready – a bit caramelised, a bit sticky – add the remaining olive oil and then the chicken thighs, skin side down. Let the skin get crisp and golden, then flip them over and brown the other side. This is an annoying bit, but necessary: lift the chicken out of the pan, and set aside; it just can't be done any other way without getting dry rice stuck to the crispy skin. I am sorry.

If using saffron, stir the saffron-infused milk into the stock.

Add the rice to the skillet and stir thoroughly. Add the cherries and stir again. Make little hollows in the rice for the chicken thighs (it's probably eight of them?) and sit them in, skin side up. Pour the stock directly over the rice, around the chicken, then cover tightly and cook over the lowest heat for about 20 minutes.

Taste the rice. Is it tender? If so, a quick grill, and you're there. If not, leave for 5 more minutes and try again.

Brush the tops of the chicken thighs with sesame oil, and bash the skillet under a hot grill for 4–5 minutes, or until the chicken skin blisters and chars. Scatter with the parsley, coriander and sesame seeds; serve directly from the skillet.

February

Turkish Eggs

There is a particular kind of nudity that can only be experienced at the Lido in February: the nudity that occurs to you the moment you drop your towel. The punctuating of the nudity with a small bit of Lycra doesn't make much difference, and plus there is the getting changed.

Well, no: you don't actually drop your towel, you hang it on the hook, because the ground is cold and puddled – bare feet on icy concrete – and you're going to want the dry, tough warmth of it so, so badly in thirty minutes' time. The Lido is heated, in that it's warmer than the air around it. Which, when the air around it is ten, or six, or two degrees, seems to mean very little.

The Lido, in February, steams like a stockpot. It's best in the rain, because it feels so unlikely; the rising scent of chlorine meets the oncoming clean of the storm, the surprise of it, the shock of being near-naked in the open air.

Above the frame of the Lido – the changing rooms, the gym, the café – is the broad sky, the bare twists of the trees, the birds. Mostly crows; sometimes a magpie, solitary and salutable. Gulls, a long way from home. Chlorine, hot chocolate, some artisan street-food stall, and the hum of traffic, and the moment when you can't clutch your towel around you anymore, can't think about it anymore, and in you go.

I am swimming because for a long time I couldn't swim, by which I don't mean that I couldn't *swim* but that the selfishness of swimming – unreachable, uncontactable, anonymous in the chlorine-blue – felt monstrous to me. The idea then that I might have regularly locked my phone in my locker – the idea that it might ring and I not answer – the idea that I might for a moment be hard to find – the idea that my movements weren't circling, desperately and tightly, around the compass point of his hospital bed: well, it felt impossible to me then, and then so many impossible things happened, and here we are. It is, I suppose, one of the perks of Jim's death that I am no longer on call, all the time, for his dying. I am no longer *poised*. I dive; the water shatters; steam rises. I swim because he died, and because I can.

And afterwards I step out and grab my flimsy little towel (*thank you, thank you, thank you, towel*) and go for breakfast without telling anybody where I'm going.

At the door to the café I hesitate in spite of myself, because even now I am incapable of going anywhere without a certain set of calculations. The angles of accessibility, and in particular Jim-accessibility, are so drilled in that I do them without thinking and without utility: if the ramp is so wide, at *such* an angle, then that kerb is going to be a problem; and also is that ramp *really* going to take the weight of a large man in a larger wheelchair; and if I do get the chair up the ramp, then we're going to need *those* people in *that* corner to move so we aren't blocking the— You see how it goes. The lack of calculations thrills me; the lack of calculations appals me; the freedom is horrible to me, and still it is freedom; he would never have come here, not in a million years, not for black coffee and Turkish eggs; and instead, cancer or no cancer, we would have been perched outside the greasy spoon two doors down (sausage, brown sauce, no butter), which I don't even *like*, because we never do anything I like, never did, and—

It's hard to finish sentences when the sentences are about Jim.

It's hard to do both sides of this fight.

Turkish eggs, for the uninitiated, are eggs in yoghurt. The yoghurt is garlic-flavoured. There is a chilli butter component. There may also be chickpeas. (There are chickpeas.)

'Eggs in yoghurt?', he would say, if he were here – which he isn't, because he's dead. 'Eggs in fucking yoghurt?!' Then he'd wheel himself away, if it was one of his good days; or wave his hand for me to do it, if it wasn't.

But Jim is dead, and so I order. The eggs are poached, the yoghurt gently infused, the chilli butter drizzled; the whole thing is a dreamy cloud of gold and russet and billowy white, like a sunset or a ballgown. The richness of the yolk. The pillow of the yoghurt. The lemony bite of the pul biber and the soft earthiness of chickpeas. The swirl of the butter, the scarlet scatter of the Aleppo pepper. Smoked salt. I order coffee and sourdough toast; my hair is wet; and my phone is quiet and full of pictures of only happy things: babies, and puppies, and other things just becoming alive.⟶

For 2

2 tbsp butter + more for
  the toast

1 tsp pul biber (*or chilli flakes,
  if you can't get hold of it,
  but you will be able to*)

1 fat garlic clove

150g full-fat yoghurt (*I don't
  trust low-fat anything*)

1 tsp tahini

200g tinned chickpeas

4 eggs

Bread, for toasting

2 tsp sesame seeds

2 tsp smoked sea salt

2 tsp chopped coriander,
  if liked

Start by melting the butter in a saucepan over a medium heat; let it foam, in that gorgeous gold-and-brown nutty way, then stir in the pul biber. Quickly take it off the heat, pour into a little bowl and set aside. (You could use another saucepan for the next bit, but we all know the limitations of my kitchen.)

Mince the garlic very, very finely; and set the saucepan back on the heat, this time to make a bain-marie. You'll need a Pyrex bowl that will sit over the saucepan without coming into direct contact with the base of the pan. Add just enough water to the saucepan that it can come to a simmer without touching the base of the bowl.

Add the yoghurt and garlic to the bowl; let it warm through, stirring all the time, for about 5-ish minutes, until the yoghurt is smooth and warm. Stir through the tahini until incorporated, and then the chickpeas, and keep stirring. Warm, warm, warm. Turn off the heat, but don't move anything else: this is how it will all keep warm while you poach the eggs.

Poach the eggs (page 50).

Make toast; butter toast; decant the warmed yoghurt into two bowls and slide the poached eggs right into the garlicky, sesame-y yoghurt. Drizzle over the chilli butter; scatter with sesame seeds, smoked salt and coriander, if using; serve with hot buttered toast.

A new kind of blessing: *I wish Turkish eggs for you.* I wish Turkish eggs for you; and the possibility of a life full of gold and russet and white, weak February sun on the back of your neck, damp hair drying – and some peace, if peace is what you need.

Sticky Toffee Skillet Guinness Brownie Pudding, for Blood

In the greengrocers on the way home from swimming I see dates – dates and dark chocolate and ground almonds. I slip them into my basket on autopilot before I realise I'm still thinking about iron: iron and blood and stars.

The Kitchen Witch simmers under my skin still, even though she's pretty useless now. There's nobody who I need to nudge out of a blood transfusion; no possibility that by cooking something *just right* I might pull off the mad magic needed to buy us an extra night at home. I loved it; it was like a spell. I loved that I could do something. I loved that in my kitchen I could buy us just a little more time at home, a little more time in our old life.

The price of time was a can of Guinness, a block of dark chocolate, butter and almonds and prunes. It wasn't a cure, but it was something. And was it true? I don't know. I don't know now if it was the cooking, or the love, or the combined force of my desire for him to be home, and his desire to give me whatever I wanted. He really loved me, was the thing. That's the thing I forget sometimes. It might, maybe, be better that way.

I said I never wanted to write about the past again, but it gets in anyway. I didn't want to write about death, and how it shaped me; I didn't want to write about how watching death made me understand, perhaps for the first time, why I had to live. And yet, here we are. I wrote a lot, while Jim was dying. I wrote columns – largely and primarily to keep us financially afloat – and I wrote a lot just for us, or I suppose just for me, as I'm the only one left. Websites fold; blogs lapse. You upgrade your phone, and an inept phone-shop employee wipes all your texts. You forget to renew a membership on an old email server. You move house, and a box gets left on the kerb with the rubbish. It goes bit by bit, and this is not a tragedy: this is the way of grief, and this is good grief.

Things go. Things fade. Sometimes it's better when they don't come back. Sometimes it's better to see things as they are, to tell the story that's in front of you, to tell the truth.

The truth is that I was glad to have lost the texts, and the emails, because you shouldn't be able to scroll up and up through a whole lifetime of conversation. You shouldn't be able to remember what you said to each other every single day of your lives together, because in that way you have to relive it alone. You can't live in the past; you can't hold onto everything, no matter how much you want to.

And just as you can't live in the past, you can't grieve in the past: you have to grieve in the present, and you have to love the dead as they are, not as you wish they were. You have to love people as they are, not as you wish they were, and the dead are no different. You have to love them actively; mourn actively; grieve actively, alive-ly, in everything you do you make them breathe too. You make them live again as they should live again: not as some half-spectre, but as a story, as a story that shaped you, as part of a story that's going on and going on, living and breathing every second you're alive, this great web of connection and love and pain and grief and love all over again, of breathing and living and dying, and so what else could I do? What else can any of us do?

I take the train home; and when I'm home I make this for the living, in memory of the dead; and Jo, coming home from rehearsals, stops dead in her tracks and says, 'Oh my God,' like I've done something magical, which I guess I have: the house smells like a perfect hybrid of Guinness cake, brownies and sticky toffee pudding, and we spoon ice cream on top of the hot skillet and eat it with spoons in our empty living room. $\longrightarrow$

For a 24cm skillet (serves 4 as a dessert, with plenty left over)

100g dried dates

150g prunes

200g Guinness (*I measure this in grams, not millilitres, because it's easier, simpler and more accurate*)

1 tsp vanilla extract (*not essence! never essence!*)

100g darkest-possible chocolate

100g + 50g unsalted butter (*I know; I almost never use unsalted, but this gets...salty*)

4 eggs

100g ground almonds

50g dark soft brown sugar

Big pinch (*like, a TV chef pinch, three fingers*) of flaky sea salt

Ice cream, to serve

- -

Stick the kettle on.

Weigh out your dates and prunes: I have given measurements, but you can adjust the proportions to suit what you have in, if you're the kind of person who has both dates and prunes in. Put them in your largest saucepan and pour over the Guinness. Add the vanilla extract and set the saucepan over the lowest heat you have.

Take a second saucepan and pour in boiling water from the kettle to about 2cm deep: you're going to set a Pyrex bowl over the top, and it absolutely must not touch the water, so you might need to fiddle with this a bit; I always do. Turn on the second-lowest heat you have and put the saucepan over it.

Weigh out, straight into the Pyrex bowl, the chocolate and the 100g of butter, and put the bowl over the saucepan. This is, basically, a bain-marie. (I am often wrong about things with cooking: that's what comes of mostly teaching yourself, and doing it piecemeal. I don't think it matters too much: it's ok to be wrong. It's all right to make mistakes. It took me a long time to learn this lesson, and I still am, but cooking's as good a school as any.)

Stir the butter and chocolate occasionally, and make sure it's not going too quickly: otherwise the chocolate risks going grainy. When the butter and chocolate are melted and combined, you're ready to go. Turn off both burners.

Dig out your hand blender, and whizz the date/prune/Guinness/vanilla mixture to a smooth-ish paste: the important thing is not to have any big lumps of prune. Nobody wants to encounter a lump of prune in their pudding. (This smells like Christmas, and is totally divine, in the most lovely sense of the word.)

Then pour the lovely buttery chocolate into the prune paste, find a balloon whisk and whisk for one hundred strokes. (Really, a hundred. I know. It's important.)

Crack in two of the eggs, then carefully separate the other two, transferring the yolk between the shell-halves until you've shed all the white. Add the yolks to the pan and whisk for another hundred strokes. (I am so sorry about this. Your arms are going to be killer by the time you've finished. You're really going to earn these brownies, is what I'm saying.)

Add your ground almonds and whisk the batter for another hundred strokes. (Oh God, I am so sorry. Your poor arms. The incorporating is REALLY important here and I promise you, it's worth it.)

You could 100% do this in a stand mixer, if you had difficulty whisking; I just can never bear the thought of having to wash up another bloody bowl.

Pre-heat the oven to 180°C.

Now tip the water out of the bain-marie saucepan, then dry it. Weigh out the sugar and pop it over a low heat with the 50g of butter. Stir continuously until it all melts together. This will smell divine – it's a kind of rough caramel. When it's one glorious, melty mixture, tip it into the batter and stir it lightly: you don't want to incorporate it, just to wave it through, like those pictures children make with washing-up liquid and ink.

Pour into a buttered skillet, scatter with sea salt, and put in your hot oven for 35 minutes. (If you have no skillet, feel free to do this in an ordinary 30cm x 20cm tin, as you would for brownies.)

Eat warm, with ice cream, but really this is excellent cold for breakfast and any other meal you care to name.

Poached Eggs are a Scam

In the florists this morning I am looking at the cards by the bouquets, and thinking of how many of them are romantic. Exclusively romantic; by which I mean the kind of cards that imply a kind of romance that restricts itself to one person, and one only; a kind of romance tied only and explicitly to sex, and desire. And I'm looking at the cards, and ordering poached eggs on toast (for our florist doubles as a café), and thinking of how many flowers I have been given in my life by people who love me, and how many fewer I have been given by people I have gone to bed with. It makes sense to me this way round, for the great romances of my life have never been restricted to those latter people at all, although it must be said that being in bed with the people you love – however you love them – is itself a great pleasure: climbing in with the morning coffee to dissect your dreams; falling asleep with the laptop balanced on your shared knees, movie still playing. The sofa-bed duvet over us both until lunchtime; or waking up, the cat between us.

When we were kids, my sisters and I often woke up in the same bed, even though we'd gone to sleep in separate rooms, compelled by some late-night imperative to find each other. When I was in my early twenties and things were bad, my friends slept curled around me like breathing dreamcatchers. They would do it again if I needed them; I would do it for them. These are the great romances of my life, all of them, every one. All different. All magic.

I worry sometimes, and looking at the cards this morning, that we're supposed to save the flowers and the chocolates and the poems and the songs for the One. What a waste! What a shame!

You should write your friends poems; sing them songs down the phone for their birthdays; send flowers for no reason. There's always a reason for flowers. 'Congratulations on your new dining table,' I write on the note accompanying a riot of peonies. 'Well done on your continuing great beauty,' in the card tucked into a bunch of yellow roses; 'BECAUSE WE MISS YOU,' all caps, on a sprawling bouquet of stargazer lilies. There's always a reason, if you want to find one.

I don't remember why my friend Danny came to write me a poem about poached eggs: what the reason was, or whether there was one, but I remember the poem and I remember him, which is the point of everything. Danny – like so many people I love – has left London for the sea, for another city. Which is difficult, of course, but there are always trains. We see him when we can, and I remember the poem every time I eat poached eggs – and more significantly, every time I try to make them. The poem claimed that only cafés could make poached eggs, and this seemed very true to me.

And then – in a blow to Danny – two things happened.

First, the person that I live with started making poached eggs. Just when she felt like it; just when she fancied. No bother. Just a poached egg, easy as.

Second, somebody gave me a poached egg pan for my birthday. He gave it to me because he was tired of listening to me complain about poached eggs, even though he had never asked me to stop complaining about poached eggs, and that is love.

A poached egg pan is a nifty little gadget that has two tiers: one for eggs (each in its own little cup) and one for boiling water, and then you put the lid on and set the pan over a low heat and the eggs are, basically, poached. They are sort of flatter than regular poached eggs, obviously, with a shape that isn't just 'soft yielding egg-bag'. But they do the job, and I believe only cafés can do it without one; and I will never try it without a pan again – so instead of a recipe, I will write: *get the damn pan*. Life is very short and full of horrors. There are so many things for which there is no shortcut; no available cheat code. Why make life harder? Why make it worse? Buy the poaching pan and make as many eggs as you want.

Pistachio Pie

I have never liked Valentine's Day. It isn't that I don't like romance; and it isn't that I liked it before and hate it now. I like romance, and dislike Valentine's Day. Jo says this is because I don't like organised fun: she says I don't truly like birthdays either, don't like anything where the niceness has to run to some preordained timetable. She says I like my joy organic. Maybe she's right, but I'm trying, and so it's Valentine's Day.

'*Galentine's* Day', corrects Annie, earnestly, with her whole golden heart. She is the kind of person who – ignoring the parade of romance in the shops – has made everyone here a card. I have merely made everyone pancakes. (And a pistachio pie.)

Jo and Debo are folded into each other on the sofa; Flora, very pregnant, is settled into the new blue chair; the rest of us are on the floor – me, and Max, Annie, Tessa, Rachel. The carpet in the new house is unexpectedly soft and thick, grey and speckled like a dappled horse, which is good, because we don't have any other chairs. Nancy is curled up on a bag of old costumes, like a cat among the rhinestones and tangled wigs.

From the kitchen, the sweet nutty smell of frangipane and toasted butter drifts down the long corridor. It's dark outside the bay window, and almost raining. And because it's Valentine's Day we're talking about romance. I like romance; I only watch movies where people kiss. I like people to be in love; I like my friends to be in love; and if they don't stop talking about being in love I might scream, or put my hand through the bay window out into the night, or anything to make them stop.

I feel – have felt – very married for a long time: I have loved someone in sickness and in health, until death did us part. I have done my part. I have had my chance; and I have felt no less married, no more single, in his dying or after his death. And that has been the case for a long time, and suddenly it seems impossible that that should be the case, and so instead of screaming or putting my hand through the nice double-glazing of the big bay window, I jump up and go into the kitchen to finish making dessert. I find the golden icing sugar, slice raspberries into neat heart-shaped halves, and wonder what the fuck I am so upset about.

'You know,' Deb says, stepping noiselessly to my side (thick carpet), 'I think you could just try falling in love, if you wanted.' $\longrightarrow$

→ 'I don't need any help,' I tell her. I sift the icing sugar into a bowl, partly (pointlessly) to get rid of any lumps, and partly to show her that I'm fine. 'Anyway, I am in love.' I gesture along the hall to the sitting room: to Annie and Nancy and Max; to Jo. I gesture to Debo herself.

If it were Jo – if it were Annie or Nancy – they would take the sieve from me, but Deb just leans on the counter, and watches me.

'More in love,' she says. Then, a correction: 'Different in love.'

I take the pistachio pie out of the oven, and we both admire it for a minute. It is a perfect pie, pistachio and raspberry pie: the kind of thing that little pistachio nuts dream of becoming. This is pistachio heaven. It has a butter shortbread base, made using brown sugar; and the top is a pistachio frangipane studded with raspberries. The shortbread is crisp (because you bake it by itself first); the frangipane is tender and yielding and somehow simultaneously dense and light; and dotted here and there you've got the raspberries gently collapsing into little sticky pools of crimson-coloured goodness. I am explaining this to Deb because I don't really want to think about what she's saying.

I take the icing sugar that I've already sifted once and sift it again over the top of the frangipane. Deb doesn't say anything about the double sifting, which is – itself – proof of love. Different love.

'You could try it,' Deb says, again. 'It seems to be making you miserable, to rule it out. To rule anything out, really.'

I start arranging the raspberries around the circumference of the pie.

'I didn't say anything,' I say.

'I know,' Deb says.

She puts her hand on my shoulder, warm and safe and real.

'You don't need to say *everything* all the time.'

And I think, and I don't say anything, and then I get the little gold-rimmed plates out of the cupboard and the little gold forks from the drawer, and give them to her.

'Thank you,' she says.

'Thank you,' I say, and we go back along the hall together, and everything is butter-soft, pistachio-bright, and better.

For 8

Clotted cream, to serve
(*optional*)

For the shortbread base

140g plain flour

50g light soft brown sugar

130g butter

For the frangipane filling

125g raspberries

125g pistachios

1 heaped tbsp plain flour

85g golden caster (*or light
soft brown*) sugar

Zest of ½ lemon

80g butter

1 tsp vanilla extract

1 egg

- -

This pie is a cinch to make, which it shouldn't be; and if you've
got a food processor it is basically a two-dish problem, including
the tin you make it in. The tin I make it in is a 23cm flan tin with
fluted sides and a removable base, which makes the getting-out
part of it much easier. The other secret is butter. (Isn't it always?)

If you have a food processor, put all the shortbread ingredients
into it and blitz until they form a dough (like, 2 minutes) and there
are no streaks of butter visible.

If you don't have a food processor, you can use a stand mixer
(paddle attachment, medium speed, maybe 3 minutes), or make
your shortbread the old-fashioned way, by hand: rub the flour
and sugar into the butter until it forms crumbs, and then form
the dough from those crumbs. Either is fine, although I'd advise
putting the sugar through a sieve first to get rid of any lumps.
(*Why does soft brown sugar do that? How do I make it stop?*)

Butter the flan tin thoroughly (including the sides!) and, using
your fingers, press the shortbread into the tin. You want to make
it into a tart case, essentially, so press it flatter in the middle
and up the sides of the dish. Prick it all over with a fork.

If you can be bothered and/or have time, FREEZE IT for
20 minutes. (I frequently skip this step – like, frequently-
frequently – but it does make a difference to the delicate
flakiness of the shortbread. Sorry. I wish it didn't.) ⟶

Pre-heat the oven to 180°C, remembering (obviously) to take out any of the tins that routinely live in the oven.

Put the shortbread base into the oven and bake for about 15 minutes.

While it's baking, you're going to make the frangipane.

Rinse the raspberries now, before you start, so they have a chance to dry off without getting bruised (leave them in the sieve or whatever you rinsed them in).

Grind the pistachios to a fine powder. Ideally, you'd do this in the same food processor in which you made the shortbread, without washing it up. I know. How neat is that? Unhappily I no longer have a food processor, so I do this bit in a little mini-food-processor thing that you attach to a hand blender. You could use a coffee grinder or similar, though the best nut-powder I have ever made was with the milling blade of a NutriBullet, now – alas – also lost to me. Grind the nuts to powder, is what I'm saying.

If you're using a food processor, stick everything else in (zesting in the lemon) and blitz until it forms a paste.

If not, stir the nuts together with the flour and sugar (by the way, you can completely get away with light soft brown here, if you don't want to buy two kinds of sugar; it just muddies the frangipane a bit). Zest in the lemon, reserving the juice just in case (you probably won't need it, but since baking changes so much with humidity and altitude and a million other things, it's worth hanging onto. Plus it's always worth hanging onto a lemon). Beat in the butter and vanilla, and finally the egg. (If it isn't binding together, add a squeeze of lemon juice here.)

Take your shortbread out of the oven, and leave it to cool. (This is another step I frequently skip if pressed for time. You can totally tell when the cooling has been skipped – the shortbread will be wetter, from the steam, and less flaky – but, you know, we live in an imperfect world and people are very lucky you're making them dessert.)

Spoon the frangipane (however you made it) onto the shortbread and stud with raspberries. You can make a pattern, whatever, or don't. If you're planning to serve it for a dinner party or as a sort of pudding centrepiece, reserve a few raspberries for the top. (Take a picture at this point, when the green is very, very green and the pink is very, very pink.)

Bake for about 45 minutes – you want a skewer to come out almost, but not completely, clean. (This is so you get a nice neat slice, but still have some of that gorgeous squidginess to the middle.)

Scatter with any reserved raspberries (and maybe any leftover pistachio dust from when you blitzed the nuts.) Serve by itself, or with a spoonful of clotted cream like a king; be adored.

This is best the day it's made, but will keep in the fridge for a day or two. The shortbread gets squidgy – but that's not such a bad thing, really, in the grand scheme of it all.

Chaat Butter Greens

I'm walking over the heath on the way back from the shops with a bag full of cavolo nero and butter and a little thing of chaat masala, and I'm on the phone to my friend Georgie, and Georgie says the world might be ending.

This is a twist. This is supposed to be the year when the world, my world, starts again; the year we have our new house, with the soft carpet and all the space; the year the tsunami of grief recedes to an ordinary tide; the year I am starting to wonder whether we could live here, and even be happy, in this ocean. This is not the year the world is supposed to end, because my world has already ended.

'Something *already* happened to us,' I say to Georgie. 'No more things can happen now!'

'I think life is just things keeping on happening,' Georgie says, and I think about this and decide she's right, and then I'm coming down the hill and up the other hill, and down the hill to our house. I keep Georgie on the phone while I unpack the shopping, and keep her on the phone while I cook, and while she cooks. We often do this, since Georgie left London; wander round shops together, cook together, eat together, her voice in my headphones and mine in hers.

I think, really, everybody should have a friend they call while they are cooking.

Cooking is, for me, the exact and elusive middle ground between solitary and sociable; the impossible centre of the Venn diagram where I like best to live. I used to think I was an introvert (because I liked being alone); then I thought I must secretly be an extrovert (because I liked talking to people); and now I think it's not an especially useful designation. I am probably more easily overwhelmed than many people (I like the bit of the party where everyone except us goes home), but also less easily overwhelmed than others (I like having parties in the first place). Everything is a balance; everything is a spectrum. There was a little while there when I felt strongly that everything would be simpler if I could only find the right words, the right labels, and now I don't think that at all. I think everything is complicated, and people are complicated, and you don't have to decide on one thing and stick to it – but that also if you are the kind of person who gravitates to the kitchen at parties, we are probably the *same* kind of person, and I hope to see you there soon.

The reason kitchens at parties are so good, especially if you have a job to do, is because you can be both by yourself and with people: the middle bit of the Venn diagram. You can talk or not talk, as you please. You can be the host of this party-within-the-party – but also a silent worker bee. You can have the kind of conversations where nobody needs to feel obliged to be there, because you clearly have a job to be getting on with, and they at any point can lean hard into the social obligation of returning to the real thing next door. Everyone in the kitchen at parties wants to be there, which makes them the place to be. But then I would say that. I always think the kitchen is the place to be, particularly if you get really into talking to people on speakerphone.

I have always spent a lot of time talking to people on speakerphone in the kitchen. I have made bread over Skype; had coffee with my mother four thousand miles apart; sat on the balcony steps with the phone tucked between my shoulder and my ear, shelling peas. Together, apart; apart, together. I like talking on the phone while I'm cooking. My favourite person to call when I'm cooking is Georgie, who lives in the countryside; we talk on the phone a lot, sometimes twice a day, maybe even more. We used to get lunch together at Dishoom, that Indian chain restaurant with vast marble counters and wicker chairs and bottomless chai. It's harder now she's in the Cotswolds, surrounded by rolling hills and green and sandy stone; but this is good, too. *Not better, not worse, just different*, as our friend the Crab once said about life after a break-up. *Not better, not worse, just different.*

We call, sometimes, for coffee in the morning, and again for cooking in the evening. 'What's the plan?' she asks me, at nine a.m., and I tell her what I'm going to cook. Then I ask her. We work on the phone, too: virtual colleagues, reading out each other's work, checking our facts, checking techniques. 'Talk me through it,' I say, at five p.m., and she does; and then I talk her through what I'm doing, and we cook together, the sound of her knife in the Cotswolds chopping in rhythm with mine in the city.

The thing about aligning your mealtimes with someone else's by phone is that you start to know the kind of things they eat when they are alone. You start to know what they would actually choose to eat, and what they love; and it is always interesting and often surprising. $\longrightarrow$

The surprising thing about Georgie – a person I have known for half a decade – is that Georgie eats vegetables. No, not just eats: Georgie loves vegetables, really truly loves them the way normal people love carbohydrates. Georgie would rather (I know because I asked her) have a bit of broccoli than a Twix. Georgie would rather eat a carrot than salt and vinegar crisps. Georgie would genuinely rather eat a turnip than a slice of buttered toast, and this is *insane* to me, but here's the thing: she really knows her way around a vegetable.

And so when she told me that her favourite breakfast – really, her actual favourite – was greens with an egg, I was sceptical, but also extremely willing to trust her. I trust her enough, on this mid-February afternoon, and on the subject of apocalypses, to fill the freezer; I trust her enough to make greens for breakfast, or an easy lunch.

For 1

100g cavolo nero (*or kale*)

1 tbsp salted peanuts

2 x 15g pats of butter + more
    for the toast

Bread, for toasting

½ lime

1 tbsp chaat masala
    (*you can get this spice mix
    from Waitrose, or online*)

2 eggs

Sriracha sauce, to serve
    (*optional*)

- -

Start by washing and drying your cavolo nero, then strip it from the stems. You can do this by hand, just pulling it away, and then tear the leaves into bite-sized pieces.

Heat a big frying pan over a medium heat. This frying pan should have a lid, ideally, for the greens to be perfect. In with the peanuts – just dry-fried, for 3 minutes in the hot frying pan, and then tipped onto a board and chopped roughly. Perfect.

Melt one pat of the butter in the frying pan, and turn the heat up to high. Toss in the cavolo nero, cover; shake, so that the butter clings to the warty little leaves, and leave for 4 minutes. The colour will suddenly get very vivid; and then – perfect bit – the leaves will start to char. This is where the flavour comes from.

(Stick the toast in.)

Lid off. Squeeze the juice of your lime half over the greens. Shake in your chaat masala; lid back on, and shake again to coat. Find a plate; butter your toast; toss your greens over your toast.

In the same frying pan, melt the second pat of butter. Crack each egg into a glass, and then tip into the pan: this helps keep the yolks together, if you're prone to splitting them, as I am. Quickly spoon the melted butter over the egg whites, pushing the white of each egg towards its yolk, then cover the pan for 3 minutes.

Slide the eggs onto the greens and scatter over the peanuts; drizzle with Sriracha sauce, if liked.

Welsh Eggs

There is this place we go.

I don't want to tell you too much about it, because it's mine. Not mine like money mine; not mine like I bought it or built it or live in it. But mine like I love it. Mine like I miss it when we're not there; mine like I think about it, mine like I dream about it sometimes. Mine like home. (There are so many homes in this book, and every year I find more. This is the thing about surviving: there's so much more to life than you thought there was going to be. *Every day something new happens*, like Hera Lindsay Bird says in the poem.)

There are no good stories about phones, Nancy says, and there are no phones here: no signal, no reliable internet. It's like going out of time.

We take the train there, low and slow, the three of us: Jo and me, and the man we call the Crab.

Jo found the Crab one bad night in Newcastle, and then I found Jo, and then here we were, by the sea. We have very little in common, collectively; we have never lived near each other, never gone over for dinner. It is one of those friendships, for all three of us, that has never needed any effort, and never made any sense: and yet it makes sense for us to be together. I can't make it any clearer than that. Some people just make sense together, and we did. We do. Like falling in love, I suppose, is supposed to be.

It's late February, and the world is meant to be ending soon, so we've come to the sea, in case it turns out to be true.

The Crab lives in Newcastle, and we live in London, and all our summits are held here: mutually inconvenient, mutually beloved. It's in Wales, this place, on the edge of a cliff. The cliff is falling into the sea, and you can see the sea from everywhere you are in this house, and everything in this house moves slowly and with purpose. Days pass like decades. We take many naps. We fit jigsaws together in almost-silence, dividing the picture into swatches of colour: her hands on the blues, his on the greys, mine on the whites. Each hour is an epoch of its own, delineated only and sketchily by cups of tea and the changing blues of sea and sky. The kettle takes a century to boil. We call this Wales Time.

And I am thinking about eggs. Scrambled eggs, done on Wales Time: slower than you would believe possible, lower than you would believe possible, creamier and better than any scrambled eggs you've ever had.

You don't add cream, or need a double boiler. You don't add milk. You have only eggs and a bit of butter, an ordinary pan. It's easiest with a silicone spatula, but I shouldn't think it would matter without: it's only that the silicone means you waste less, and this isn't a house for waste. Everything here is here because it's useful and good; and so you, too, are useful and good here.

There are storms across the sea, and the bay is shrouded in cloud, and all the trains are delayed and cancelled, and it's hard to care, because at the other end of the trains is the end of the world, and here is everything we need. Couldn't we just stay here, the three of us? Couldn't we just stay here and nothing ever change? And yet even here, the clock moves; even here, a moment drifts into the next; even here, the eggs thicken – slow, slow, but inevitable.

The butter glides across the pan, drifting like the tide into foam. You beat the eggs so gently that the fork doesn't touch the Pyrex and intrude into the quiet. You pour the eggs into the pan, and wait, and sometime stir, and wait. They thicken like curds, one slowly over the other. It is a miracle, I suppose, another miracle, like a pie that gave me a life, like the kind of miracle that would bring me to this place on the edge of a cliff. *Every day something new happens, and I think / so this is the way things are now.* What a life. What a miracle. What eggs. ⟶

For 3

15g butter   Buttered toast

6 eggs

- -

You don't need a recipe, really, you know it all: time, stillness. (*Thou foster-child of silence and slow time*, as Keats should have written about eggs.)

Melt the butter over the lowest-possible heat; crack the eggs into a jug and beat them lightly with a fork. Don't incorporate them all the way; let there be yolk, let there be white.

Tip them into the butter and stir just a little. Let set for 20 seconds or so, then push the egg from the sides of the pan into the centre with a silicone spatula. It's sort of a slow, rolling motion; just try it. You're forming curds, not scraps. Keep the heat as low as possible; don't hurry it. Don't stir it constantly. Curds, curls, slow movements. You're fine.

You have to do the eggs so slowly that you don't think they are going to cook, over such a low heat that you can't believe anything is ever going to come together. You stir slowly, too, and not much; you bring the edges in to the centre and the centre out to the edges, folding slowly, folding carefully, every so often. It thickens like curds, over perhaps 20 minutes. A miracle.

Watch the eggs all the time; and when you think *these aren't quite done*, take them off the heat; take plates; take toast. Slide eggs onto plates (they will have cooked to perfect doneness while you found plates and did the last bits of buttering). Eat, and watch the sea.

March

Storm at Sea Scones

It's early March, and somewhere out there the world is ending. Our friends cancel dinner plans for the following Friday, and we're a little relieved: we can't see when we'll be home, how we'll get home.

The storms have stopped the trains; but then, where would the train take us? In London everything is shutting down, or has shut down. If you hold your phone above your head the signal flickers into life long enough to watch a jerky fragment of a government briefing: *stay indoors, stay home, look but don't touch*. Half Boccaccio, half Stephen King, all absurd. Don't touch your friends. Don't touch your lovers. They might have it in their hands or on their breath or on their bodies. Whatever *it* is. If you touch someone's hand, you are touching everyone and everything they touched, and vice versa, like a human chain. We are all dependent on each other; we are all attached, and connected, whether we knew it before or not. I find this sort of comforting, even as it's supposed to frighten me. I find it sort of comforting, although there's nobody to touch but Jo.

It's Jo and me now, Jo and me and the sea, and we've done all the jigsaws, read all our paperback books, and there's still a storm out at sea. Writing isn't helping, and so I do what I always do when things are bad: I go to the kitchen and wonder what I can make. I lean on the countertop, watch the grey sea raging against itself. The low shapes of birds, high above the sea, but level with the kitchen sink. The silhouette and bright flash of the buoy that marks the channel. The hull of the wrecked fishing boat, high on the shore for as long as I've known it, lashed with spray, and then – when I look again – suddenly gone, an absence. I rummage in the fridge, where there is almost nothing left. There's no super-market here, so we bring our food with us, tucked in alongside our swimming things and chunky jumpers. What do we have? What can I bake?

I know this kind of feeling; this feeling of waiting for the hospital to call, for the government to change, for the other shoe to drop. I am used to waiting for apocalypses, but I don't want to do it again, and so instead I shred the end of the Cheddar into a cup patterned with clowns and JOSEPHINE spelled out in alphabet blocks.

I find flour, from the time before the time before; a little butter; a feeble triangle of crusting Brie. The milk is going sour. There is only one option, really: the thing I always bake just before we take a long train journey, before we leave here or go there. They are leaving scones, or travelling scones: the sharpening milk, four kinds of ageing cheese, flour and paprika and just a little butter. New Zealand cheese scones in triangles instead of rounds. *Not better, not worse, just different.* I bake them in spite of the fact that the trains are cancelled, in spite of the fact that another friend has cancelled a plan, in spite of the flickering government briefings.

Our New Zealand friend Hazel used to bring these scones round to us when things were bad, to my house or to the hospital or wherever we were when we needed feeding, and I would microwave them or just eat them cold in the park. Jim ate them in hospital with cold bolognese when he couldn't eat any more hospital swede; I ate them when I couldn't go home, when things were too precarious, too frightening. It was a small niceness in a very bad time, and making them now I think of Hazel, herself far from home, and how Jim had loved them, and how he had loved Hazel, and how we had loved him, and how far we are drifting away from that time, whether we like it or not, like the hull of a wrecked boat swept out to sea.

And I think, too, as I am grating the cheese and rubbing it into the butter, and the butter into the flour, that even here time is passing: that in a day or two the storm will wear itself out and we will take a train back to uncertain London, and the possible apocalypse – and we will do it, as we always do it, with a train picnic, and tea in a Thermos, and Jim's old Christmas-cake tin full of chocolate-chip cookies, and I will have made more perfect cheese scones. $\longrightarrow$

Makes about 7 scones, for 2 or more hungry people

220g plain flour

3 tsp baking powder

3 tsp smoked paprika
  (*you can substitute regular
  paprika, or 1 tsp chilli powder,
  or just skip it*)

1 tsp celery salt

30g butter, grated

125g cheese, grated
  (*look, ok, if you were to, say,
  push this up to 150g or even
  175g, nothing bad would
  happen – the scones will be
  extra cheesy – but you can't
  recommend people do that
  in a book in case they start
  counting calories*)

100ml milk (*slightly sour milk
  is fine here*)

Pre-heat the oven to 200°C.

You now have two options.

One: if you have a food processor, tip everything except 25g of the cheese into the food processor. Blitz.

Two: I did this by hand for years and it was also very easy, so don't let it put you off. In a large bowl, weigh out the flour, baking powder, paprika and celery salt and stir together. Cut the butter into chunks, then use your fingertips to rub it into the dry ingredients and form fine crumbs, like making a crumble. Add all except 25g of the cheese and stir again. Add the milk and mix with a butter knife until it forms a dough: maybe you need more milk, maybe you need less milk. Go slow and see. You might have to get your hands involved, which is also fine. Don't do it all with your hands, because too much handling will make it kind of tough. But you are almost certainly fine.

However you did it: bring the dough together (maybe more flour?) and lift it out onto a baking sheet. You probably don't need to oil or grease the baking sheet, even – they should come right off! Lining it is fine, if you are not feeling like scrubbing off baked-on cheese.

Press the dough into a rectangle about 5cm deep, and press the remaining 25g of cheese into the surface. Slice the cheesy rectangle into triangle pieces of roughly equal size. This is... look, I'm not a mathematician, there is absolutely a way to cut a rectangle into n right-angled triangles, but I just lop bits off and squidge them into shape. This makes about seven scones: six proper-sized ones to serve in a basket or whatever, and one runty one to break bits off to see if it's cooked right and also to eat in the kitchen. Call it a baker's half-dozen.

Put the triangles onto the baking sheet. Bake for about 12 minutes, until the dough is high and the cheese is crispy.

Break your tester one in half: it will be a little doughy, but obviously bread-ish. You good to go? You're good to go.

Pergolesi Pork Belly & Parsnip Purée

When we get home there is nothing to say. The storms and the sea feel a long way away, but so too does everything else: our house is an island, and the streets are empty, and the busy road beyond the bay window is still. There are no people, and outside the kitchen door the wind pushes through the fire-escape steps and howls like the tide.

But the sky is blue and high, and we have been travelling a long time, and there are small green shoots in the abandoned pots on our patio, and green stems pushing up between the unloved squares of concrete. Spring is coming, if not already here; and we are here, back in a city on the edge of something, against both our better judgements, but at least we are together, and at least there are green things. I don't know what any of the green things are. We have been away for so long, and they were so new when we left, that I had forgotten about the new bookshelves we built, and the long pine dining table we bought for guests who might never come.

And so, I suppose, in a kind of celebration of all we had done and lived up to that point – and in spite of the guests who might never come – I make this. I play Pergolesi very loudly on the little blue kitchen speaker – *too sad*, said my grandmother once, *too sad for most people, but not too sad for us* – and roast pork belly, low and slow, crispy like bacon and tender like butter. The pork belly was in the freezer; I had filled the freezer very well, when we moved in, for some kind of endtimes, some kind of apocalypse, for – it strikes me as very funny – exactly this kind of situation. I had been squirrelling away milk and butter, meat and fish and bags of sautéed greens with all the water squeezed out.

I rub the pork belly with honey and gochujang, this fermented Korean chilli paste I love, and know as I'm doing it that they're going to shut the city down, and my butcher's, my Korean supermarket, my Indian supermarket, my fishmonger's, my greengrocer's, will all be too far away. Once I went to see Pergolesi's *Stabat Mater*, by myself, in a church in central London, and as I slide the pork into the oven and turn my attention to the carrots and the parsnips, I think that the church will also be closed now, and that central London might be lost to me too.

The new pine table is empty, the garden full of unknowns. And all I can do is stand in the kitchen, and listen to the *Stabat Mater* (*too sad, too sad for most people*) and make what I can from it.

For 4

500g pork belly strips

4 tsp sesame seeds

For the marinade

50g gochujang

50g honey

10ml sesame oil

4 garlic cloves, grated

For the parsnip purée

500g parsnips, peeled
and chopped into
smallish chunks

500ml chicken stock
(*easy to substitute with
vegetable, obviously*)

75ml double cream

30g butter

Nutmeg – 1 tsp ground, or a
few fresh gratings, to taste

Juice of ¹/₂ lemon

- -

Whisk together the ingredients for the marinade and set the pork
belly in it. Leave it for at least an hour, maybe 24 hours. Who
knows? What is time anymore?

Marinate the pork, then roast it. Roast it for 15 minutes at 220°C;
and then, slowly, for 45 minutes at 150°C.

While the pork is roasting, make the parsnip purée. Easy-peasy,
this one. Parsnips in the saucepan, chopped and peeled, and the
cold stock poured over. (Quite honestly, I use cold water and a
stock cube – it's not worth using your good homemade stuff here.)
Bring to a simmer, stick a lid on it, and cook until the parsnips are
so tender you can press them apart with a spoon: 20 minutes?

Using a slotted spoon, lift the soft parsnips into the bowl of a food
processor – I have recently acquired one, a sorry-your-boyfriend-
died present from my nice dad – and add the cream, butter,
nutmeg and lemon. Add, too, a tablespoon of the parsnip liquor.
Blitz to a fine purée, adding more liquor if it seems too thick. It's a
purée, not mash; it's a silky little condiment, not a big hearty boy.

Scatter the pork belly with sesame seeds and serve on top of a
heap of the parsnip purée (or mash, or a mess of wilted greens).

Crisis Cardamom Coffee
Banana Bread

I cook in a crisis.

I am good in a crisis; most of the time I am afraid of everything, but in a crisis I feel at home, like a sailor too used to being at sea to walk comfortably on land.

Sometimes I feel like those cornflour solutions that they show you in school: slipping through your fingers, soft and useless, when things are good, but tough and solid when met with force. I am afraid of everything, but when the things I am afraid of happen, it's like freedom. If everything is already at stake, then nothing I do will make it worse – so let's go. I don't think I'm alone in this: I think lots of anxious people, when they are backed into a corner, become more capable and strong than they ever thought possible. Sometimes I think this is because we have spent so much time imagining the corner that when we get there, it's sort of like home.

I did not imagine a crisis like this one – a complete crisis, one with everyone in, a whole world at sea – but it's familiar to me, nonetheless. I know about mysterious diseases; I know about infection control and intensive care. I know about trauma, and waiting, and hoping. All crises, maybe, are the same at their bones: an intake of breath, a pause held too long, a space where the normal world should be and isn't. Which means I know what to do: it means I know what to do now, as I have always known what to do in a crisis. Maybe I will always know, if knowing always means being in the kitchen.

The kitchen: the comforting rhythms of knife and pestle, the hiss of the gas and the warm electric whirr of the oven, spices and butter. Everyone is cooking now: it seems, this spring, that everyone is making banana bread: easy and precious, thousands of miles apart and all united.

I don't know what's going to stick, from this weird too-hot March when the world seems so uncertain. It takes time – years and years, decades even – to see the shape that trauma has made you into. Trauma changes people, the way wind hollows dunes: some parts it takes away, some parts it merely twists and curves into something else. Something, sometimes, more beautiful. $\longrightarrow$

→ I can't imagine ever not thinking, now, when I touch a person, of everyone they themselves have touched; can't imagine not thinking, on the bus, of everyone who held on as I myself am holding on. I cannot imagine not thinking of people as a kind of internet, a kind of web, a map: one thing leading inevitably, inextricably to another. I don't know if this is a bad thing, but I think it will endure nonetheless. I hope it does, and I hope banana bread does, too. I hope, specifically, this banana bread does.

Cardamom and coffee are so perfect together, and this is where I think they are best: sweet, musty banana; a dense high loaf with a cracked top, baked, cooled, sliced, toasted, buttered. Brown Earl Grey butter; full-fat Greek yoghurt; whipped cream; crème fraîche, speckled lightly with chopped rosemary, a pinch of smoked salt. Strawberries, raspberries; blueberries, if there happen to be some in that fleeting moment between ripeness and pappiness. Plain, good, salted butter. Is banana bread breakfast? I don't want to live in a world where it isn't. The world is hard enough as it is; the world is weird enough, upside-down enough, troubled enough as it is. Thick slice of banana bread for breakfast. Cake for breakfast. Why not?

Makes 1 loaf

120g butter

500g brown bananas
(*it's 5 normal-sized ones*)

2 big eggs

1 tbsp vanilla extract
(*don't worry about using
very expensive stuff; they've
run tests and you can't tell
in baked goods*)

200g + 25g dark soft
brown sugar

250g plain flour

2 tbsp espresso powder

2 tsp baking powder

2 tsp ground cinnamon

1 tsp ground nutmeg

12 cardamom pods

100g dark chocolate, roughly
chopped (*optional*)

This is incredibly easy, and you can tell because everyone in the world started making it at once. Banana bread, basically, is dry ingredients (all) into wet ingredients (also all). So.

Butter a 450g (1lb) loaf tin and line it with baking paper or one of those incredibly handy paper loaf-tin liners that are already in the shape of the tin. Pre-heat the oven to 180°C, and make sure you've got a rack in there in the middle – somewhere where the top of the loaf won't catch on the element.

In order to save on washing up, I melt the butter in the bowl of my stand mixer, set over a saucepan of simmering water (you could also do this in the microwave or just a saucepan). Drop the peeled bananas into the bowl of the stand mixer, and beat butter and bananas together until smooth-ish. Add the eggs and vanilla, and beat again until basically incorporated.

Put the 200g of sugar, the flour, espresso powder, baking powder, cinnamon and nutmeg into a big bowl. Use a pestle and mortar (or the end of a rolling pin in a sturdy bowl) to bash the cardamom pods, then shake all the little seeds free; grind the seeds finely and add them to the dry ingredients. Stir.

Sift all the dry ingredients through a sieve into the stand mixer bowl and beat together to form a smooth batter. You can, if you want, stir in some chocolate shards here.

Pour the batter into the prepared tin and scatter over the 25g of sugar. This is going to go crispy and brilliant. The batter will fill the tin. Do not worry. It is supposed to do this. This is how you get perfect, tall banana bread.

Bake for 25–35 minutes: you're looking for it to be coming away from the sides of the tin, and also to smell absolutely incredible.

Hearts & Hummus

I once read something that explained that trauma was like dropping an anvil through the floor of a house, and the hole never being mended.

After trauma, the baseline for sadness is that much lower; you can always fall all the way down again. The smallest things can go deeper than they ever would before. You drop a penny and it falls past where the floor used to be, and all the way down through the hole the trauma made, and into somewhere else.

Which was interesting, of course, because down there in the dark – under the floor I'd lived with all my life – *was* somewhere else. There was somewhere new in me I'd never been. Down there in the dark was possibility, a whole extra floor that could be lived in, lived on, lived with, and that in doing so it makes every other floor of my house that little bit higher. My house is so much bigger than it used to be.

Death turned out not to be an end, but a shift; it hurt not because I had lost something but because I had gained something, and while the something was *pain* it was still a something. It was still new. It was still a whole other floor to fill with people. It felt like guilt. It felt like freedom.

I think about the house I lost when Jim died; the Tiny Flat, frozen in time, held in amber in the book I wrote and the pictures we took. I think about myself in the kitchen, trying to keep him alive: my whole world focussed on iron counts and potassium counts, on red cells and white cells, marrow and bone, livers and hearts. I used to cook these hearts for him, diced and marinated, rich and savoury. I never ate offal until those years, really.

I thought it would be bitter and dirty, and in some ways it is, but in a good way: a good rich way, that tastes like terracotta under the sun, like wet footprints drying off; like smoke, like earth, like life. I love these hearts: the red smell of cumin, smoky with black cardamom, tender with vinegar and slick with olive oil, charred in a pan. I eat them over hummus, or stuffed into a pitta, or tangled with sticky leeks, an egg the size and shape of the end of the world soft-boiled and smashed on top. There's sun on the balcony steps and I sit with the plate on my lap, late March drifting slowly into spring. It's good, out here. ⟶▷

For 4

500g lamb hearts, cleaned and chopped into bite-sized chunks (*the butcher will do this, thank God – and if you haven't got a butcher, don't eat hearts*)

Hummus and pitta breads, to serve

For the marinade

2 tbsp black cardamom pods

1 tbsp cumin seeds

2 tsp coriander seeds

1 whole ancho chilli

100ml red wine vinegar

100ml extra virgin olive oil

- -

This is really all about the marinade. Start by toasting the spices in a dry frying pan until they smell amazing. Cumin is a good one to watch, because the colour of the seeds goes from brown to a kind of tobacco.

Pound the seeds together using a pestle and mortar, then hold it up to your face and breathe. Breathe deeply. It smells real and alive and nothing like a hospital, and that is one reason to love it. You learn, when you have been in and around hospitals, to cherish things that smell like real life: and this is real life.

Toast the chilli for a moment, too, and pound with the pestle and mortar. Ancho chilli smells like chocolate and coffee, and is one of those spices that makes even people who don't cook feel amazed. It is the kind of spice that reminds you of what it must have been like in the olden days, when spices came from ships, stolen from afar; and when worlds and wars were won and lost just for this brand new air.

Tear the toasted chilli into strips and pound it with the other spices. Tip all the spices into a bowl and add the vinegar and oil. Add the lamb hearts and mix well, then cover and marinate overnight in the fridge.

You can either make skewers of these, and do them on a barbecue (God, I miss having people for a barbecue; I miss the weather for a barbecue) or in a skillet, frying each piece until cooked through, a little pinkish in the centre and brown and crispy on the outside. Spoon some hummus onto a plate and top with the hearts; pitta in place of cutlery.

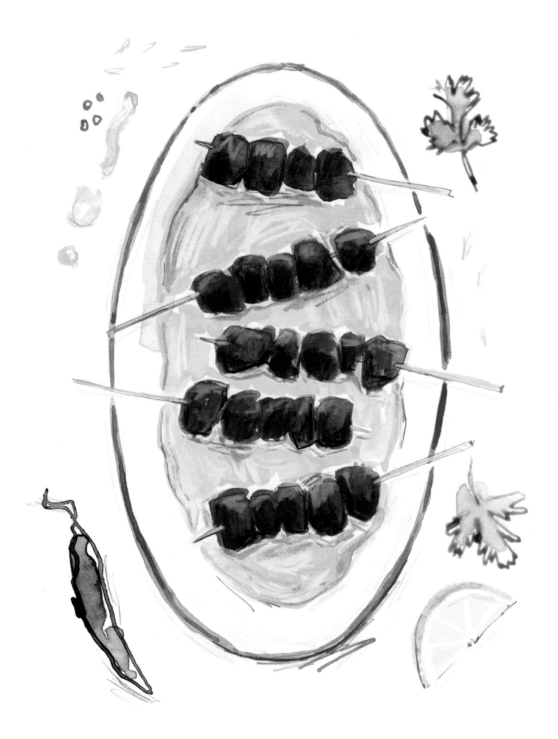

Brown Butter Friands

'Say this goes on for, what, two more weeks? Three more weeks?'

We are trying to figure out how long an apocalypse might last. Nancy is on speakerphone; I am trying to think of something to do with a jug of egg whites that need using up today at the latest.

'Three weeks,' I say. 'Let's err on the side of caution and say three weeks. At least.'

I am pulling things almost at random out of the cupboard: half a jar of pistachios leftover from a frangipane tart, baking powder, golden icing sugar.

'Do you think I could use chocolate in these?' I know she won't know, but I'd like to change the subject.

'I don't care,' Nancy says.

'I think I could use dark chocolate, maybe, but it wouldn't be as nice as blueberries.'

'I don't care.'

'I think maybe I have raspberries at the back of the vegetable drawer if I pick out the slightly manky ones, raspberries would be actually perfect here—'

'So I think you should text him,' Nancy says.

'Nancy,' I say, warningly. 'Oh, fuck—' I knock over the icing sugar with my elbow, and a cloud rises.

'If this goes on for three weeks, you can just text; you don't have to meet him or anything; you don't have to even talk to him on the phone—'

I am sweeping up icing sugar, and don't say anything.

'Theo is very nice,' she says. 'He won't hurt your feelings.'

'My feelings are fine,' I say. I take a hunk of butter out of the fridge and toss it into the saucepan to brown.

'You have his number,' she says. 'You have his number, and I know you don't want me to interfere or tell you anything about him, but he really is very nice and won't hurt you.'

'Nobody is going to hurt me,' I say. Brown butter, nutty and foaming and gold. I tip pistachios into the blender and pulse, to drown out Nancy.

'Nope,' she says. 'But you should text him. Just for the three weeks, or whatever. Think of it as practice.'

Tip out the pistachios; tip in the egg whites; blitz until foamy. I have made friends so many times I don't even need a recipe ⟶

anymore. They are like little celebratory cakes – like fluffy, high financiers – although I don't know what I think we're celebrating. This man Theo having my number. My having his. Nancy's tentative matchmaking. Three more weeks of the apocalypse. (At least.) March. Tuesday. Nothing at all.

'Practice,' I say. Pistachios and egg whites and icing sugar and brown butter, blitzed until foamy. No need for a recipe now. Practice makes perfect.

There are no good stories about phones, and I look at mine. Nancy's voice comes out of it, distorted from the speaker.

'You don't have to fall in love with him, or anything,' Nancy says, and it hangs there in the air between her phone and mine: *famous last words*.

Makes 18 little friends, or 12 big ones

110g butter	150g icing sugar
25g + 75g unsalted, shelled pistachios	*(golden or otherwise)*
	$1/2$ tsp baking powder
25g ground almonds	4 egg whites
2 tsp vanilla extract	About 200g raspberries

Let's start by browning the butter. I almost always start by browning butter, because it's one of those things that takes perhaps 3 more minutes, at most, than simply melting it – and those 3 minutes are worth every second. It makes the house smell amazing; it makes everything taste amazing, deeper, richer, cleverer.

You brown butter by melting the butter, and keeping on melting it, over a lowish heat. Let it foam, let it catch, let it literally brown. It will smell nutty – in French it's called *beurre noisette* ('hazelnut butter') – and kind of silky. Don't let it blacken, but don't worry if it catches. It takes maybe 5 minutes. Let it cool slightly before using.

Pre-heat the oven to 180°C, and dig out some kind of small 12-hole cake tin: I use a silicone cannelé mould, which is perfect, but you could use a fairy-cake tin or a madeleine tin or anything like that. Use your butter wrapper to grease the holes well.

While the butter is browning, weigh out the pistachios: 25g you should chop into shards, for decoration and texture. The rest we're going to grind in a food processor. (Honestly, if you haven't got a food processor, don't bother with the pistachios, just use more ground almonds instead – it's a bit less good but not enough of a difference to make it worth pounding them by hand with a pestle and mortar.) Grind the 75g of pistachios in the food processor to as close to flour as you can get, then add the ground almonds, vanilla, icing sugar, baking powder, egg whites and browned butter. Blitz (or whisk by hand) until foamy, then pour into the prepared tin.

If you're using a silicone cannelé mould, the mixture will be enough to fill each mould about three-quarters of the way up. Stud each little cake with two or three raspberries, and a big pinch of pistachio shards.

Bake for 25–35 minutes, until a skewer inserted in the centre comes out clean (stray jammy raspberries aside). Serve warm, but they keep like a dream for at least a couple of days, and only get chewier and damper in an airtight tin.

April

Paris Aubergine

April, *not* in Paris.

Out there somewhere is the Seine, cherry blossom, all that, and I'm sitting on the balcony steps again, with my back to the kitchen. I'm sulking, and thinking about Paris in the spring, which is a cliché, but *my* cliché. A poor thing, but mine own.

I don't go to Paris *every* spring, not being a dowager doyenne in the twenties (dripping with emeralds, caked in panstick, the story of my grief rehearsed and pat). I thought I would, when I lived there a long time ago, but life happened: I was too afraid to travel, for a while there, and then we couldn't go too far from the hospital (and I couldn't go alone, and leave him there), and then I thought I'd go this year, but life – as Georgie says – *keeps on happening.* Still, Paris; Paris in April, April in Paris.

My Paris, that is: I know nothing of the Louvre or the Eiffel Tower, but I'm extremely good on bakeries of the 10th arrondissement and of small suburbs on RER E. I know exactly what I want you to bring me back from Monoprix (disco cutlery, Brillat-Savarin, own-brand cornichons). I know what butter I like. I remember where we found a piano on the street and Teddy played it. I remember Orangina in a park in the shade. This is how I like to see places: I like to make them my home, for a little while. I sleep on Zelda and Teddy's sofa. I settle in at cafés. I like to work, when I travel. I like to write and cook. I like supermarkets and working and people, and pretending – at least to myself – that I live there.

I do this everywhere. I went to Transylvania and stood in the 24-hour minimart counting kinds of crisp, and drinking coffee while walking briskly through the cemetery, which is all I really do at home. I went to Rome for a week and saw the greengrocer three times, the butcher five times, and the butcher's mother four times – and the last one of those, she put both her hands on my face and blessed me. (I think she blessed me, but I don't speak Italian.) In Berlin I left my friends to look at saucepans in a department store and exercise books in a stationers, and sat with my laptop in a café near the station looking out at the snow. In Dar-es-Salaam I saw a little black cat crossing a basketball court at the YMCA, everything tinged – at least in memory – a sort of soft and rosy orange; in Mombasa I ate chicken rice from a big tin tray, reading *Bleak House* – the only book in my bag – on repeat. I don't know anything about these cities except what I ate and what I read, and small things I saw.

When I'm in Paris with Zelda I walk through the markets; we buy an aubergine, coriander, a lime. We meet people. I miss meeting people. I miss the possibility of going to places, and it's only been a few weeks. I miss possibility.

You could meet someone if you wanted, I imagine Nancy saying, and my phone is heavy with possibility in my pocket. I bat imaginary Nancy away; and imaginary Paris too.

This – the dinner Zelda and I always make – has, I suppose, a kind of Vietnamese vibe. It is honestly the best thing one can do to an aubergine. You roast it, then toss it with a fish-sauce-y, shallot-y, coriander-y dressing and serve it over rice, and it's so unbelievably simple but also very good, and good for you. I could eat so much of this. I do eat so much of this. It isn't elaborate, but it feels it. I think of it as Parisian aubergine, but that's only because I learned how to make it in Zelda's tiny Paris kitchen, high up in their old white building in the 10th. Their kitchen window is tall and thin, with a balcony the depth of a single plant pot, and the balcony has a plant pot just big enough to hold the world's tiniest lemon tree, still bearing lemons. There are copper pans, in their kitchen, that Zelda is polishing very slowly (she sends me pictures), and spices everywhere, and little paintings, and some cats; and a whole lot of sky.

Still, though. There is sky here, too. There is a whole lot of sky above the fire-escape steps, and while our backyard is chilly concrete, four doors down there's a cherry tree in radiant pink ⟶

→ bloom. The self-seeded grass is verdant green, and the sky –
although not so high and wide as from the fifth floor in Paris –
is blue and white and endless, and there is an aubergine in
the vegetable crisper of the fridge, and I always have a lime,
and coriander.

I'm home, and the sky is blue, and perhaps it's time to learn
to make home into other places, the way I make other places into
a home. April in London; the balcony in late, bright spring.

For 2

1 big aubergine	Small pinch of chilli flakes
1 tbsp olive oil	2 shallots
Salt and pepper	Bunch of coriander
6 tbsp lime juice	Rice, to serve (*Coconut Rice,*
3 tbsp fish sauce	*often; page 93*)
Big pinch of brown sugar	

- -

Pre-heat the oven to 200°C.

Slice the aubergine into thin rounds, slide it onto a baking sheet
and dress with olive oil, salt and pepper. Just drizzle it with the
oil; don't worry. You're good. You got this. Roast for 8 minutes,
then flip the slices over and roast for 8 minutes more – soft and
yielding and possibly a little charred.

Get some rice on, however you make it (me: 2 cups stock, 1 cup
rice, lid on, low heat, 16 minutes) and get stuck into the dressing.

In a bowl, whisk together the lime juice, fish sauce, sugar and
chilli flakes.

Chop the shallots and coriander very, very finely.

Grab the aubergine from the oven and, as soon as it's cool enough
to handle, chop it into chunks with scissors. Drop it into the
dressing, then shake over the coriander and the shallots.

Rice into bowls; with a slotted spoon, lift the warm dressed
aubergine onto its bed of rice. So clean, so perfect.

Coconut Pow

'You,' Jo says, 'should give this a name.'

We are both sitting on the outside steps, with a folded old curtain underneath us. The wind is lifting the leaves from the willow a few doors down with a faint *shusha-shusha* kind of noise – like the sea, if the sea wasn't so far away – and it is still so unseasonably warm for spring.

I think, irresistibly, of the April when Jim had died. It was too hot then, too, and I bought a gold bikini he would have hated, and lived off champagne and rotisserie chicken and went dancing for the first time in years, all out of sync with the world, the way the spring was out of sync with the old seasons, the way this year is out of sync with all other years, the way all years are out of sync somehow or other.

'It's a Vietnamese rice bowl,' I say. 'Sort of. Ish. Not really.'

'A proper name.' $\longrightarrow$

Something having a proper name, in our house, means it's on the regular rota: not just 'that thing we had that time', but something dignified and complete. Or at least, an idea that's dignified and complete: I almost never make something exactly the same twice, if I'm cooking for us, but the concept of the thing stays the same. The bones of it. The bones of this are rice with vegetables, and sometimes protein. Always coconut rice; almost always salted mango; often pink pickles. Vegetables. Protein.

I hadn't expected Jo to like this, let alone love it enough to name it. Broadly speaking, in our house, I skew East and she skews West. Pasta bakes are for her; gravy, butter, cheese, potato. I skew to lime and coriander, sesame and soy.

But sometimes I make things because I like them, which is the perk of being the cook, and something I have had to learn to do. The first week we live together Jo invents the Self-Esteem Finger: you hold up one finger, to indicate a desire that has no reference or recourse to anyone else, and you say 'self-esteem!' Then you express the desire. We have to do this because I have been a carer for so long – subservient, essentially, in a way no other adult relationship demands – that I have forgotten how to want things, or rather how to be allowed to want things. I have wanted things for so long, and she is determined I should have them. I don't know what to do with a love like this except make the things she loves; and sometimes – 'self-esteem!' – the things I love, to prove to her it's working.

This is one of those. I miss being able to order South-East Asian food – there's nowhere open near us – and it is already hot enough, this April, to want it – hot enough to want lime, mango, coconut. I want South-East Asian flavours, and so I make this – which hits the spot, if by South-East Asia you mean a concrete slab in South East London.

I make coconut rice, and I pickle rhubarb and ginger and red onion in fish sauce and sesame oil. This time I salt mango. For a treat I fry prawns briefly until they blush pink and fat. I slice avocado; I sliver broccoli and asparagus for a hit of health, and toss them in sesame oil too. I shred coriander and mint.

'Coconut pow,' Jo said, scraping her bowl clean.

'Coconut what?' I said.

'Coconut pow!' she said. 'Pow from the lime! Pow from the fish sauce! Pow, pow, pow!'

'Like in a comic,' I said.

'Like in a comic,' she said.
'Ok,' I said.
'Good,' she said.
'Do you want more?' I said, and she did.

This isn't a recipe, but a collection of recipes; an idea, and a title, and a series of variant meals we eat two or three times a week. The amounts here are basically **enough for 2.**

I put the **coconut rice** on to simmer first: **one tin of coconut milk**, one tin of stock (use the coconut milk tin as a measurement; I add **one stock cube, usually chicken, and an empty-coconut-milk-tin of boiling water**), and **one empty-coconut-milk-tin of jasmine rice**. Pinch of salt. Rinse the rice in a sieve until the water runs clear. Rice, coconut milk, stock in the pan. Stir it; turn the heat down to low; cover it; 18 minutes. I find it overwhelmingly soothing.

I make the **salted mango**: **200g vivid orange flesh**, cut into thin slivers (everywhere sticky with sweet bright juice), plus **two teaspoons of smoked salt, the juice of two big limes, a handful of coriander (chopped), a handful of mint (chopped)**. I could eat this every minute. I slide it into the fridge to chill. I want it cold and bright and sharp.

And what else? I stand at the fridge and think.

I grab the jar of **quick pink pickles** (page 95), *Blue Peter* style – *here's one I made earlier.* If there were no pickled onions, I'd go for sushi ginger, just for the delicate salmon of the colouring. I love pink now; I never used to.

Sometimes we have flakes of hot-smoked actual salmon, bought like that from the shop, and flaked gently with a knife. Sometimes leftover chicken, or tofu, if I can be bothered to press it; mostly whatever is in the fridge or freezer, fried and made hot and crisp.

But today I find a little packet, **150g, of peeled and de-veined prawns**, grey and blue, and fry them in a **generous bit of butter** and **three crushed fat garlic cloves** over a low heat until they too blush pink and into life. I like them uncooked better here: it's too easy to overcook the others while you warm them through, and an overcooked prawn – curling itself into tight little puckers – ⭢

→ is a tragedy and a waste. If you're going to eat seafood – or maybe, actually, any animal products at all – it has to be worth it. It has to be good quality; and you have to treat it right. Don't overcook your prawns.

Then I think about vegetables. Often I have this coconut rice with blistered cavolo nero (page 58), sometimes with frozen edamame or peas or broad beans (depending on the freezer situation). Maybe there's some **roast aubergine** (page 88) left over from yesterday – in which case I'd leave off some of the pickles. Maybe there's an avocado I can slice for extra texture, or some asparagus. It's all to taste, and it's all the whim of the fridge.

But today there's Tenderstem broccoli, and I know what I can do with that. What if Tenderstem broccoli...was even thinner? What if Tenderstem broccoli was in fact, a quarter of the size, cut into tangly ribbons, like a badly organised craft drawer? What if I dressed it with sesame oil and tahini, whipped smooth and thinned with lime juice, and scattered with toasted sesame seeds for crunch?

I take **250g Tenderstem broccoli** and slice it lengthwise, then lengthwise again. Sometimes I have to pull two stems apart; I want the thinnest bits I can. I toss it into a pan of boiling water and cook for 3 minutes. While it's cooking, I whisk together the dressing: **a tablespoon of tahini** and **a tablespoon of mirin**; **two teaspoons of rice vinegar** and **two teaspoons of sesame oil** and **two teaspoons of lime juice**. I drain the broccoli and put it back into the hot saucepan to briefly steam dry. I don't want any more moisture that isn't adding flavour. I toss the broccoli with the dressing.

I spoon the coconut rice, soft and sticky, into wide flattish pasta bowls. I divide the prawns between the two bowls, and arrange them around the side, pink on white. I take the salted mango out of the fridge, and arrange that beside it (orange, pink, white); then the broccoli. Leftover aubergine on mine, but not for Jo, who doesn't like it; some cold edamame I found in the fridge. I slice **avocado** for both of us for extra green.

I scatter with **toasted sesame seeds**, some black, some white. I dress the bowl with coriander flowers from the bolting plant on the balcony. And serve. Coconut pow.

Rhubarb & Radish Quick Pink Pickles Redux

I have finessed these pickles down to a fine art: I always have a jar in the fridge, making them as fast as I eat them. The theme is pink: onion, rhubarb, radish. Pretty in pink. It's a tangle of punchy, tender onions; bitter, paper-thin discs of creamy radish; sour-sweet half-moons of pale pink rhubarb; a gingery, sesame-y liquor with salt, brown sugar, rice vinegar and the fermented funk of fish sauce, softening, sweetening and sharpening into one vivid bite of sensation and flavour. Picture that dolloped onto soft coconut rice (page 93); or swirled through hummus, speckled with feta cheese; or packed into a soft hot pitta with a smashed soy-marinated egg (page 160) and salted sticky mango (page 93). Plus, pickle juice makes an excellent dressing – and apparently is somehow good for post-exercise hydration.

Perhaps to justify some future drinking of pickle juice, I drag my yoga mat into the yard while the pickles are pickling. I leave my phone upstairs, in case someone texts me. *If I don't look at my phone*, I think, *he will text me.* Then I feel fifteen, and stupid, and banish the thought by contorting myself into a folded, one-footed, pigeon. I survey the concrete. Time to make this a garden, I think.

Makes 1 medium jar

6 radishes	1 tbsp sesame oil
1 small red onion	1 tbsp rice vinegar
1 stalk of rhubarb	1 tbsp brown sugar
1 tbsp grated ginger	1 tsp salt
4 garlic cloves, grated	1 tbsp fish sauce
Juice of 2 limes	

Slice the radishes and onion paper thin, and the rhubarb as thin as you can manage. Add the ginger and garlic, and pack into the jar.

Whisk everything else together and pour over the vegetables (and fruit). Refrigerate, leave for at least 2 hours, and use within 3 days.

Airing Cupboard Bread

I think a lot of things are magic, including myself; I tell tarot and wish for things, consider myself cursed and cursing, blessed and blessing. I believe, in my secret heart, that I make things happen by wishing for them too much or too little; that evil can be warded off with a number of charms – some orthodox, some not so orthodox. I salute magpies, carry stones with a hole at their heart, believe in sacrifice; and I believe in bread, an old magic – one of the oldest kinds there is, next to blood.

And I believe in the magic of this bread, specifically, because I cannot fathom how it happens. Stir together flour and water, stir in starter or yeast and salt; forget. Forget it for an evening, a night, a day. Shape, score, bake. Transformation, abracadabra! Voilà! Bread like from a bakery. High crumb, crisp crust, a good all-purpose loaf.

I usually find breadmaking a weekend task – a project, if you will – but not this one. This one answers to me; my hands are clean, no kneading is required. It sleeps when I sleep, like a well-behaved baby. And like a baby, too, the bread is warm and heavy in the hands in the cloth: alive and impossible, sturdy and delicate, whole as itself, the most magic thing there is.

I am thinking – with this bread – of a time before the world shut down.

In the memory I hold my new godson on my hip, his cheek against mine. He likes me, this baby; he smells like milk and yeast and heft. He has such fat legs, and I kiss his knees on impulse. His older sister hits my knees, in return, with her book ('Read, Miss Ella!'), and his eldest sister, my first godchild, our Nora, looks at me as if I might be becoming lost to her under this pile of babies, and says, with a perfect and calculated pain that makes me love her more: 'Miss Ella, are you *ever* sad your boyfriend died?'

The ever kills me: so casual, so calculated. She has always called me Miss Ella, although I think it's fading now she's bigger. 'Miss Ella, are you ever sad your boyfriend died? Because I'm sad that he died.'

She loved Jim, but she was so little when he was alive that I think he must be fading in her mind too; her brother and sister never met him. A Sylvanian Families party set with a Cinderella postcard, just before he got too sick to think of things like that;

and before that, maybe, a pair of too-big red boots, and the snap of a two-arm crocodile crawling across the floor of the flat in Banner Street. He was too tall to get down on the floor, but he always got down on the floor to be a crocodile. I wonder if she remembers. I wonder what is left of him, to her. I wonder at the way she wanted me to listen to her; and the way she knew then that to speak of grief is to command attention; and I wonder at how like him it is – charming and manipulative and transparent. I hope Nora remembers him; I hope something of him stays. Maybe it will; maybe it won't, but I hope it anyway.

'Do you miss him?' I say.

'Read!' says her sister. I read the first two pages of *The Gruffalo's Child*, which I happen to know by heart.

'Uh-huh,' Nora says. 'Are you sad?'

'I'm sad sometimes,' I tell her. 'I'm sad sometimes, and it's ok to be sad, but I like being happy more.'

I never made bread when Jim was alive, not really, and that I make bread now is a change, as I have changed. I have changed into someone who makes bread, and someone who has lost, and someone who is happy.

'Huh,' Nora says.

'Do you want to talk about him?' I say to her, in between lines of *The Gruffalo's Child*. The baby is playing with my hair.

'No,' she says. 'But I wanted to tell you that if you wanted to have another boyfriend you should wait until you're ready, and then that would be ok.'

'What made you think of that?'

'Dunno,' she says, and I tell her that I have no imminent plans to have another boyfriend. Then we go off and do something else – drink raspberry-blue slushies, eat cheese and ham toasties, talk about writing, talk about love – and then it's the end of the world and then it's now.

It's now, and I make bread, so that Jo and I can have it for toast tomorrow morning. Lazy Saturday out on the fire escape with fresh French boule and the best butter the corner shop can sell us. Jo is the most impressed by bread of anyone I've ever met, and maybe that's why I make it now: a charm for her, a mark of home.

The neighbour cat startles a flock of green parakeets from the weeping willow; the sun creeps a little higher in the sky; my phone buzzes in my pocket, and I dust the flour off my hands to pick it up $\longrightarrow$

in more of a hurry than I'd like to admit. I turn it face down on the kitchen surface so I don't reply too quickly or too keenly. Practice.

Somewhere across town, my godchildren are changing without me there to see it; somewhere, outside in the yard, things are starting to be something else; and in here, overnight, the bread is becoming. This is the real magic, that everything changes, and everything is always becoming something else.

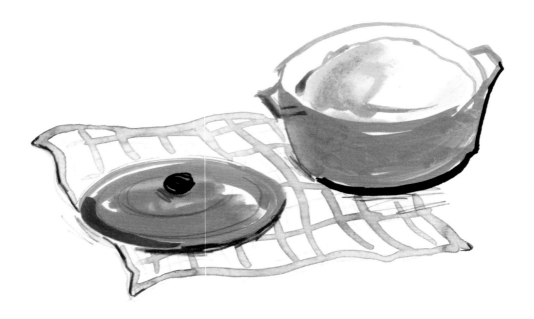

Makes 1 loaf

430g strong white bread flour	2 tsp salt
¼ tsp instant yeast	390ml water

- -

There's a pattern to these recipes. This is the easiest bread I know and it tastes like it's from a French bakery, which is nice when going to France is a crime and my local bakeries are shut.

Stir everything together in a big bowl, cover with a clean tea towel and stick it somewhere warm, like in the airing cupboard. (Airing cupboards are so nice, and even nicer when they are full of bread.) Go about your life for, like, 12–18 hours. I mean it! That's it! You stir it up, then forget about it for basically a whole day! Lucky you!

Be very smug the next day; your bread has been doing things by itself. It will be high and risen and just outrageously cool and alive. It's alive! It's doing things without you!

Now you knock it back. You fold it in on itself, and then again, then let it sit for 15 minutes to get used to everything.

Next you line a big bowl with a tea towel, and you dredge the tea towel in flour. (The original recipe used cornmeal, but it's not the kind of thing I have in, so I just use flour.) DO NOT USE A TERRYCLOTH TEA TOWEL, OR FLUFF WILL STICK TO THE DOUGH.

Fold the dough again, drop it into the floury tea towel, and leave it for another 2 hours. There's a lot of leaving this dough to do its own thing, which gives a nice rhythm to time. We have been short on time-rhythms, this year, which is maybe why we're all so mad.

An hour before you wish to bake the bread – an hour after the tea-towel business – put a large, lidded cast-iron casserole in the oven, and turn the oven up to the highest it will go. You're making a kind of mini-oven.

Carefully (the cast iron will be red-hot), take off the lid and plop the bread inside: just shake it out of the tea towel, seam side up. Score the top with a sharp knife. In it goes. Red-hot lid back on, then back in the oven. Bake for 30 minutes, then lean in and very carefully grab that lid off; 15 minutes more.

LET IT COOL AS FAR AS YOU CAN BEAR – but listen, you're only human, and this thing will look so perfect that you won't know what to do with yourself. I once came back into the sitting room to find Jo had eaten half a loaf, still hot from the oven, and it was hard to begrudge her anything. It's always hard to begrudge Jo anything, but especially not when the bread is this good, and this tempting.

Outside Cat's Anchovy Toast
with Lacy Eggs

There is a cat that has started coming to visit us. She scares the parakeets out of the trees, lounges on the thinnest of fences.

She has fur like feathers, all black and white, and she comes all the way up our steps and through our open kitchen door. I call her Mitski, like the singer, because she seems happy when we play Mitski on the little blue speaker. One day I hear our downstairs neighbour call her Angus, but she doesn't belong to him either. She belongs to somebody, or – like most cats – entirely to herself.

Cats, like books, come and go, and it's a mistake to be too precious about them.

When I look at this cat I think of this thing my friend Freddy said, this text he sent the other day: *well, don't get attached.* He was talking about men, but men and cats: it's all the same. *Don't get attached. Don't fall in love, or anything.*

One day I shut the kitchen door with Mitski on the wrong side – the inside – by accident, and she gives me imploring eyes before I've even had the chance to open it again. An outside cat; a cat who knows where she wants to be.

When I was small, somebody read me a book about Outside Cats and Inside Cats: an Outside Cat who gets trapped in a house and longs so much to be back where he belongs. 'I can *see* out,' said the Outside Cat, in the story. 'So why can't I *get* out?' Why can't I *get* out, I used to think in my early twenties, in conference centres and backstages and exam halls, on the Tube, on a plane: *why can't I get out?*

And then months in sealed hospital wards, which I left only after dark. There were double sets of doors onto the ward – a sanitiser station between them – and another set on the airlock to the side room where we spent so long; at first watching snow drift past the window, and then, later, blossom. The airless quality of the ward was like being below deck on a ship. Why can't we *get* out?

And now we're indoors again, and I can't bear cooking, so I just make toast with yesterday's bread and storecupboard things: eggs, anchovies, chilli flakes. Coriander and parsley from the pots I've wedged onto the windowsill. They are growing better than I hoped, and I'm thinking again about what I need to make a garden, as I sit down on the steps with my blue-and-white plate of golden-yolked eggs and chunky little anchovies and butter-soaked toast.

Mitski the outside cat comes and presses herself against my legs, hoping for anchovies, I think, or maybe eggs. Maybe it's the buttered toast she's after. She twines herself around my ankles like a monochrome ribbon. I can't help it: I love her. I would miss her if she were gone. I would miss all this.

This is, truly, an exercise in both simplicity and eggs: fried in a good, deep spoonful of golden, green-scented olive oil, until the edges go golden-brown themselves, about 3 minutes over a hot flame. You spoon the hot fat over the eggs as they cook, basting them. The whites bubble and spit and are transformed into amber-coloured lace, their bases crisp and their tops tender; the yolks are orange as a sunset – the most beautiful thing in the whole entire world. It is an entire world, and if we can't get out like that we might as well get out like this: a garden, a cat, an egg.

Do you need a recipe? Two perfect eggs; a tablespoon of extra virgin olive oil; two slices of sourdough toast. A tin of anchovies, three laid over the top of the butter and under the eggs. A tiny handful of chopped coriander and flat-leaf parsley, shredded down to nothing. Best butter, sweet as cream; smoked salt. A sprinkle of chilli flakes. Assemble. Eat.

Chargrilled Spring Onions
with Feta & Lemon

We once watched a bad movie about a tomato festival. It was a
long time ago, before anybody we knew had died, and we were
in a heap on the sofa like teenagers. Nancy had her head on my
shoulder, and I was leaning on Jim, and we had drunk two bottles
of wine. We were only just not teenagers, but we felt older then.

The plot of the movie was incomprehensible, soundtracked
by a medley of 1980s pop hits, and in the middle of the movie was
this tomato festival. The heroine sang 'Walking on Sunshine' as
she ran through the tomatoes, and we laughed so much I thought
I would never be able to breathe again. We laughed so much that
I still find myself thinking of this film – this invented tomato
festival – all the time. Everything was covered in tomato; they
had armfuls of tomatoes, huge bountiful heaps of them, and
they were flinging them at the heroine, and she was singing and
running through the streets, scooping up her own armfuls of
tomatoes from the crates that lined the streets, and the hero was
chasing her with tomatoes, and we were crying with laughter.

I have missed, I suppose, that kind of abundance.

And so maybe that goes some way to explaining why I have
carried home all this earth, and these tiny little tomato plants,
and these tiny baby leeks the size of a matchstick, and all these
tender little seedlings wrapped in straw in brown-paper packages
tied up with string. Gardening is a leap of faith that the year will
do what it's always done, and that you'll be here when it does.
It's a vote for survival. And that is why I am digging through this
heap of earth, folding it in spadefuls into tubs and sacks and
troughs, because if I'm digging I am – *again, always, practice* –
not looking at my phone.

It is the wrong time for all of this, in so many ways. It is the
wrong time to be starting a garden when I don't know anything
about gardens, and when everyone I know who knows about
gardens is far away. It is the wrong time to meet anyone when you
can't meet anyone. It's the wrong time, probably, to do anything
at all. But here we are, and so I press the tiny little tomato plants
down into the earth; and then I plant the next set of containers
with sprawly baby courgettes; and in the boxes on the steps I prick

out places for beetroot and carrots; and then, last of all, I do the leeks, mounding up the earth around the tiny baby greens, kind of like they were calçots instead of leeks.

Calçots are like sexy spring onions, and there are calçot festivals in Catalonia, I think – like the tomato festival, but less messy – where they throw the calçots onto a grill to char, and then suck the tender slippery insides from the smoky green wrappers and bite the white bulbs clean through. And I'm thinking about festivals, and calçots, and how you could toss calçots with ricotta and mint and little curls of lemon zest – and how maybe I will next summer, when the shops are open again, when these leeks I'm planting now are grown, and how maybe next summer there will be festivals again, abundance and intimacy, and how maybe by next summer, maybe, just maybe...but no, because that line of thinking leads me into freefall, and so I turn my hands back to the solid earth, and then, after a little while, I go inside and make this.

It's not calçots, and it's not ricotta, but there's spring onions griddled in the same way – salty, slick with green olive oil – and a handful of Turkish white cheese that comes in a tin from the corner shop, and mint from the plant on the balcony that seems to thrive no matter what I do.

My phone buzzes on the kitchen surface as I come in. A message. Two messages. Theo, twice; *he*, apparently, has no qualms about playing it cool.

I want to know everything about your garden.

And then, ten seconds later: *I want to know everything about everything.*

And I am trying very hard to keep this in proportion, so I eat my spring onions, twirling them around my fork, and feel the sun on my face, and pretend that the garden and the onions and the sunshine are the only reason everything suddenly feels brighter, and messier, and more stupid.

Easy, this one; the kind of thing you can make at the end of the world; the kind of thing you can make when you're trying not to notice you're falling in love; the kind of thing you can make when you're in the middle of making something else, like a garden. $\longrightarrow$

Precision isn't really necessary here, so let's say, for an exciting side for 4, or a bowlful for 1

Bunch of spring onions

1 unwaxed lemon

2 tbsp extra virgin olive oil

1 tbsp smoked sea salt

1 tbsp mint leaves (*basil also nice, coriander and parsley great; do not use dried mint*)

2 tbsp (30g) crumbled white cheese (*feta, probably, but ricotta also great here; try burrata for decadence*)

1 tsp chilli flakes

- -

Wash your spring onions, and if necessary – if they aren't particularly spindly – slice them in half lengthwise. You want them narrow and tangly.

Zest the lemon. (Honestly, don't even try with the zesting side of a box grater; it's only there to make you unhappy. It makes you unhappy in the grating and the washing up, and if it gets your thumb, the eating also. Just use the smallest grating one that isn't a nightmare.)

Take a griddle pan, the cast-iron kind with the ridges on it, and stick it over a medium-high heat. TURN THE EXTRACTOR FAN ON.

In a large bowl, toss the spring onions with the zest, olive oil and salt; then throw them into the smoking griddle pan. Cook for 3–4 minutes, turning every so often, or until charred and blackened.

While they are cooking, chop the mint finely: you should use a big knife, and kind of see-saw it through the leaves. The knife should be like it's on a pivot, with your hand holding it down at the handle end, as you rock it up and down through the mint. Do you see what I mean? It's smoother than you normally think of as chopping, maybe? But give it a whirl anyway.

Return the spring onions to the bowl and toss with the cheese, mint and chilli. Serve immediately as a side, or just, possibly, as a feast for one from the bowl with a fork.

May

Lewisham Cheesebread

It hasn't rained for weeks, and so I go out with a watering can in the early morning. We don't have a hose, or an outside tap, and everything is thirsty. I go up and down the steps, filling two cans at a time: a can for each sprawling baby courgette, a can for the tomatoes, a can for the leeks, a can for the beetroots, a can for the carrots. The herbs on the balcony need it, too, except the mint. The mint is thriving by itself, and the Greek basil is happy too. Everything on the balcony smells like Greek islands: like wet sap and hot metal and that strange, almost-bodyish scent of mint, thyme and basil crushed underfoot or between the fingers.

Everything, actually, is thriving. Everything is green and alive and visibly growing day by day; every day there is a new change. The courgette plants are putting out more of these wide flat leaves, and the tomato vines are twisting around their stakes, and everything is still very tiny, but growing fast. This is how plants grow in Dubai, where I spent part of my childhood. A bougainvillea, when watered, creeps along a wire as you watch: you'll almost see it move, if you sit still enough and long enough.

The autumn before Jim died I had to go back to my parents' house in Dubai for a long time, because I had had – in dated, but very real terms – a nervous breakdown. I couldn't remember how to dress myself reliably; I couldn't remember how to sleep for more than an hour at a time; and Nancy found me, bleeding and barefoot, in the café of the National Portrait Gallery. It was bad. And so I had gone home to my mother, and the wild green of the garden jungle, and an invasive peacock eating my mother's aubergine plants. I did a lot of stretching, a lot of swimming. Jo and I started talking every day, which we had never done before: her broken heart, my breaking heart. I ate all the things I had eaten as a sad teenager: soft oatmeal-raisin cookies from Spinney's, coconut rice, and Lebanese cheesebread. *Manakish*, it's called really – *manaqish*, or *manoishe*, or *mana'ish* or *fatayir* – and other names besides: a soft, yielding, unhollow pitta of a bread, spread with salty-soft melted white cheese and scattered with za'atar. But we called it Lebanese cheesebread, because everyone knows that Lebanon has the best baked goods in the world. You can't get the cheese here, not properly. You can't make it how it is there. But you can make something.

The sun, now, is level with the tops of the terraced roofs to the east, and there are no clouds. I kneel down and breathe in the smell of just-wet earth under the spreading courgette leaves, and wonder if I'll see them grow if I stay here long enough. I think about my parents, far away, and the city I love there that I'll maybe never see again. My home, for a while. I miss home. I miss my parents. I miss my people. But I've been grieving now for years, and grief sets 'missing' as your default state. I'm always missing someone; and I've learned to live along the line of something being lost. I've learned to cultivate happiness in absence, and to love an empty space where something used to be in the quiet hope that it won't be wasted: something always turns up to be loved, a fox, a star, a courgette. A cat. A home. A person.

Anyway, I made this, door wide open to let in the sun and to see my garden blooming: pitta-style flatbread dough, cooked soft in a frying pan to avoid switching on the oven; a mixture of mozzarella and grated halloumi, to make something like the proper akkawi cheese; za'atar, toasting the spices and pounding them so that the cumin, the sesame, the sumac all rise up and mingle with the scent of green and growing things, and the brewing coffee, and you might be anywhere, anywhere at all, but you're in Lewisham, London, and it's May. ⟶

Makes 6 cheese flatbreads

250g self-raising flour

1 tsp salt

2 tbsp za'atar

250g thick full-fat Greek
yoghurt

1 tbsp olive oil + 1 tbsp for
frying + 1 tbsp, possibly, extra

1 x 125g ball of mozzarella

1 x 200g block of halloumi

1 tbsp sesame oil

2 tbsp sesame seeds, or cumin
seeds or Dukkah (*page 162*)

- - - - - - - - - - - - - - -- - -- -- - -- -- - -- - - - - - - - - - -

Easy as you like: stir together the flour, salt (pinch it to dust first,
if using flaked) and 1 tablespoon of the za'atar. Use a fork to mix
in the yoghurt and 1 tablespoon of oil, then bring together to form
a dough. Knead until smooth: you can do this in a stand mixer
with the dough hook fitted, 2 minutes; or with your hands,
4-ish minutes. You might find you need a little more oil; you
might need a little more flour. Yoghurt is so variable that you're
just going to have to trust your hands here: you're after a supple,
smooth dough, flecked with green from the za'atar. There should
be no flour visible anywhere in the dough, and no stickiness –
either on your hands or the worktop.

Leave the dough to rest for 30 minutes while you grate the
mozzarella and halloumi into a bowl. Stir through the other
tablespoon of za'atar.

(You can, and I sometimes do, make the za'atar yourself; but that
seemed to me to be a complicated step too complicated far. Keep
it simple, and if not – one sunny Saturday – you can Google it.)

Divide the dough into six portions. Roll each portion into a ball
with your hands; then, with a rolling pin, roll each ball into a disc
of dough about the thickness of a pound coin.

So, look, two options here: one is slightly quicker, and one is
slightly better.

Quicker option: we layer the rolled-out discs of dough on a plate,
with baking paper between each one to stop them sticking, and
then we fry them just as they are. This makes completely fine
flatbreads. This is the way I do it if I am in a hurry.

Better option: as inspired by parathas and all kinds of other flaky bread products the world over, we take one disc of dough at a time, brush it with olive oil and roll it up into a sausage, with the olive oil on the inside. We then coil each sausage into a snail shape. When they're all done, we rest the dough for another 20 minutes. Then – again, one at a time – we take those coils of dough and roll them out into discs again. What we're doing is creating little pockets of fat in the dough, so it will go flaky and puff up in the frying pan, like a paratha or a croissant.

Whichever way you went – easy or fancy – take a large non-stick frying pan and set it over a medium-high heat. If you have a house like mine, with a smoke alarm that likes to throw her weight around, fling open the window and turn on the extractor fan. I don't know why, but these are sometimes oddly smoky. (Possibly the olive oil? But it doesn't happen with anything else, so I don't know.) If you are in a civilised household, where you want to serve all six flatbreads at once, turn your oven to low and set a baking sheet in there, so you can keep the cooked ones warm and lovely while you do the rest. If you are a house of hoodlums, as we are, gather plates and people and flip the flatbreads straight onto plates as you finish each one. (These also freeze fairly well: simply assemble them raw, including cheese and za'atar, fold, wrap in baking paper, and then fry from frozen.)

Heat a little olive oil in the frying pan and toss in your first flatbread. Cook for 4 minutes, then turn it over with a spatula. Sprinkle with roughly one-sixth of the cheese mixture and fold the flatbread shut. Cook for 3 minutes, then turn again and cook for a minute. You might want to press it closed with the spatula, so that a tiny bit of molten cheese hisses out, hits the hot pan and becomes lacy and delicious, and then you can eat that in the kitchen on your own. You might want to do that.

Hoik the cheesebread out of the pan – either onto the baking sheet and into the warm oven, or onto a plate. Repeat, repeat, repeat.

Just before serving, brush with sesame oil and scatter with sesame seeds. (You could also scatter over some cumin seeds, and/or a little crunchy dukkah, if you have it.)

Salt & Vinegar Crisp Omelette

The cucumber plants arrayed along the kitchen windowsill
are taller every morning than they were the night before, and
their green stems twine around their stakes (pencils, gaffa-
taped together). They are so tall that they are starting, a little,
to block out the sunlight through the window. There is a kind
of living green-y underwater feeling when you stand at the sink;
a strangeness to it.

I'm sitting on the kitchen floor, with the door open, organising
the cupboards.

Tea towels *here*. Chopping boards *there*. Spices in the big
slide-y drawer, and flours and sugars and pastas and pulses in
the shining Kilner jars I've been amassing since my late teens.

My phone, beside me on the floor, lights up. *I want to know
your taste in pepper mills and salad forks so intimately that
I could replace your whole kitchen from a John Lewis catalogue
if I had to*, he says.

I look at the things I am folding and sorting and think: *so this
is my taste*. This is my taste; this is my life; this is my story, for
everything here has a story. The tin in which I made my first ever
roast chicken, which was also the first ever thing I bought for
my own kitchen, and the tin in which I do everything: brownies,
lasagne, sausages. My one enormous, ancient tablespoon. My
pistachio-coloured KitchenAid, my pride and joy. And other
things, too, where the story is one of absence.

A cast-iron casserole that was once my anniversary present
from Jim, missing the matching griddle pan and skillet that were
mine to him. One of a pair of plastic chopping boards from my
hyper-sterilised former kitchen, still marked with an RM for
Raw Meat. (The other, long gone.) Two cheap supermarket
paring knives I bought the day after we moved in here, to replace
the knives I'd always used.

And yet, in those spaces, something new – slowly, and from
these bits of flotsam, something new. There's space now to fill
the windowsill with cucumber plants, the drawer with disco
cutlery from Monoprix in Paris; to choose for myself the things
and colours and sensations and tastes that make me happy, not
anyone else. $\longrightarrow$

→   Never in my life have I lived like this. Not when I was a child, not when I lived in Paris, not when I lived with Jim: an adult with space and time and even money to choose, within reason, what I wanted. And this is why, maybe, the cupboard below the cutlery drawer called to me, when we first moved in. I wanted a Treat Cupboard. I wanted KitKats and crisps and shortbread. As children we had never lived in that kind of house: we had Fairtrade date bars, homemade salt-free pizza, an orchard full of apples and pears; and other kids – I knew them! – had Dairylea Dunkers and Müller Corners and drawers full of crisps, every day full of crisps, where they could go and help themselves and know there would be more. This kind of abundance set my mind on fire. Didn't they just eat them all day long? Didn't they just do nothing but eat crisps?

It turned out no: it turned out once I could have everything I wanted, I didn't want everything all of the time. And it was better. Everything got better, once I had a cupboard full of crisps.

One of the things that got better was midnight snacking. Not crisps alone, but crisps as condiment: crisps in a sandwich, crisps in a toastie, crisps (go with me here) in an omelette. When you think about it, crisps are only a form of thinly sliced potato; and potato omelette is very Spanish. Also, when you think about it, salt and vinegar crisps and cheese go perfectly together: the bite of Cheddar and the bite of the crisp, the double-salt punch, the softness and the sharpness. And cheese omelette – done right, so it's fluffy on the outside, and soft and yielding and melty in the middle – is one of life's great joys. So why not? Anyway, Ferran Adrià also puts crisps in an omelette, and he's one of the great big-boy chefs of all time. It works, I promise you. It works, especially late at night, if you're alone, and you don't have to worry – maybe for the first time in a while, maybe for the first time ever – about what anyone else wants. What do you want?

I break eggs, and make a list of desires in my head. I grind pepper. Pick up my phone.

FYI, no pepper mill, I write. *Pestle and mortar because the pepper mill broke. Look.*

I send a picture of the pestle and mortar, granite and smooth. It was Jim's: one of the last things that was ours, and is now mine. I do everything in it: cardamom for banana bread, coffee beans for the morning; pesto, salsa verde, cumin seeds for everything. *Here is a story. Here's a life.*

For 2

6 eggs

70g salt and vinegar crisps

1$^1/_2$ tbsp butter

40g Cheddar, grated

-- -- -- -- -- -- -- -- -- -- -- -- -- -- -- -- -- -- -- --

Crack the eggs into a bowl, and whisk until very frothy. Making a good omelette is one of those things they famously test you on at chef school, because it's harder than it looks, but the secret starts here: get it really frothy. Use a balloon whisk rather than a fork.

When whisked, add the crisps. Let it sit for a minute to get good and eggy.

Non-stick pan over a medium heat. Butter in. Eggs in. Cook for 90 seconds; then scatter over the grated cheese, and fold in half. Cook for 40 seconds more – no longer – so that the centre is still cheesy and oozy and golden, and the crisps are chewy and tender and perfect.

Revelations Club Crispy Cauliflower with Green Cauliflower Sauce

Some days you are just going about your ordinary day, doing your work diligently, sending emails, walking the dog, et cetera, living your completely normal ordinary life; and then you happen to catch a glimpse of yourself in the window of a parked car, and you realise that you are having the best hair day of your life to date.

This never happens to anyone on any day when they have anything planned. It is one of the immutable laws of the universe, unchanging and eternal: your hair will always look at its best in the late afternoon of a day when your only evening plans consist of washing your hair. I don't know why this happens. I don't know why perfect hair days never happen when you're going to a big meeting or giving a talk or going on a date or going out for dinner.

Perfect hair days do happen, apparently, in a minor apocalypse.

In the real world, of course, there is only one thing to do when this happens, and it is immediately to go and make some plans. I don't care what you plan to do. But you must do something. Life is too short to waste perfect hair by being on the sofa, watching *Friends* and wondering whether you'd have been happier if you got a cat. There are a million other days to do that. Today, you have to make a plan. You have to take advantage of the way that having truly excellent hair can, however briefly, make you feel: like God, or like the Queen. Like a person who might take a selfie and send it to a stranger; or, if you're a person with social anxiety, like a person who could call someone on the phone and demand they ask you to dinner.

This is how I ended up eating this cauliflower for the first time.

I had met my friend Rachel in a queue at the Edinburgh Festival, and a week after that she came to lunch and stayed for eight hours – we ate chicken with our hands the whole time, and a week after that I went to her wedding. Because sometimes you just know. And sometimes people just understand, and Rachel is a very understanding sort of person.

So I rang up Rachel, and explained about the hair, and asked her to dinner. She was already having dinner with someone else, a nice girl named Immy who taught art, so she asked me to dinner with them instead, and I was having such a good hair day I didn't feel terrible about it. That's what a really good hair day does for a person: makes you not mind gatecrashing dinner just to show off.

We talked about revelations, I remember: a better way to change the duvet. A better way to walk home. We formed a club for having revelations in, and made a WhatsApp group just for that purpose. Sometimes things just occur to you, and change your life. Sometimes there's been something easier there all along, something simpler, something better. Sometimes you realise there's a new way to be.

This cauliflower, which we ate then, was just such a revelation. Fancy cauliflower, barbecued in spiced butter, drizzled with a yoghurt-tahini sauce, and scattered with rose petals – tender and crisp and yielding. Fancy cauliflower, for a fancy hair day, when I was God or the Queen or a person who could call someone out of the blue and ask to go out for dinner. I had never felt like this about cauliflower before.

And here's the thing: sometimes you deserve fancy cauliflower, even if you haven't got fancy hair. You can't always be brave and ask your friends to ask you to dinner. You can't always go out. You sometimes can't take trains, for lots of reasons: too mad, too sad, a minor apocalypse. And you can't have perfect hair every day.

But you can – if you so choose – make perfect cauliflower. And you can – if you so choose – live the kind of life where you're $\longrightarrow$

→ open to things being better. You can join the Revelations Club, and realise that you're happy. You can join the Revelations Club, and realise you're in love. You can join the Revelations Club, and realise that your hair was perfect all along.

And you can take a selfie, and send it to a person: somebody who used to be a stranger, and is now – strangest of all things – something else.

Serves 4 as a substantial side, or 2 who are mainly committed to eating cauliflower

1 whole cauliflower, with the nicest leaves you can get (*about 500g, I think, but don't worry*)

1 (large) lemon

1 fat garlic clove

50g flat-leaf parsley/ coriander leaves (*half and half is fine, but so is any other combination you have*)

1½ tbsp cumin seeds

2 tsp whole black peppercorns

50g butter, slightly softened

3 tsp sumac

2 tsp dark soft brown sugar

2 tbsp olive oil

1 tsp red wine vinegar

1 anchovy

1 tbsp full-fat yoghurt

½ tbsp tahini

1 tbsp cold water

Dried rose petals (*optional – but you can get them in Waitrose, and why not?*)

- - - - - - - - - - - -- - - - - - - - - - - - - - - - - -

This is a very Ottolenghi-length ingredients list, but please do not be afraid. It's not even difficult. To get over the ingredients list, we're going to start by sticking the kettle on.

While the kettle is boiling, split the cauliflower into florets of varying size: some very small, and some a bit bigger. While you've got the knife and chopping board out, halve the lemon and coarsely chop your garlic and herbs.

Rinse the cauliflower florets well, and the leaves too. Put the florets and leaves into a large saucepan with a big pinch of salt (be generous!) and cover with boiling water from the kettle. Set a timer for 7 minutes.

Meanwhile, pre-heat the oven to 220°C.

In a large, dry non-stick frying pan, toast the cumin seeds and peppercorns over a medium heat for about 2 minutes. Tip into a pestle and mortar, then pound to coarse powder. (You could, of course, use pre-ground, but oh my God, the smell of toasted cumin is the best thing in the whole world.)

In a bowl, beat together the butter, cumin-pepper powder, sumac, sugar and the juice of half the lemon.

When the timer goes off, drain the cauliflower. Put all the florets and half of the leaves onto a baking tray; the other half of the leaves can go onto the chopping board.

Rub the spiced butter thickly over the cauliflower and leaves on the baking tray, then put it straight into the hot oven. Set a timer for 15 minutes.

Roughly chop the rest of the cauliflower leaves, then sweep them, along with the garlic and herbs, into either a large bowl or the bowl of a food processor. Add the olive oil, red wine vinegar, anchovy and the juice of the other lemon half. Blitz, using either a hand blender or the food processor, until you have a green sauce that's as smooth as you can get it. Spoon into a pretty bowl.

Remove cauliflower from oven and shake it about a bit; return cauliflower to oven. Set a timer for 15 minutes.

In another pretty (small) bowl, stir together the yoghurt, tahini and cold water.

You're now done with cooking, pretty much. Do the washing up. Stack the dishwasher. Return the kitchen to harmony.

Take the now blackened, crispy, sticky cauliflower from the oven. Arrange artfully on platter. Dot with some of the green sauce and yoghurt-tahini sauce, then scatter with rose petals. Serve with the rest of the sauces for dipping. Truly, you are a hero for our times. An Instagram hero. And your hair looks great.

Three-Ingredient Brownies

Nancy says: *It's legal to walk now, isn't it?*

Neither of us are sure. I need to walk; need to see Beezle the dog; need, above all, to see Nancy face to face and without a screen between us. Of all the ways to categorise friendships – all the rankings and not-rankings – I never thought before about categorising them by the tangible differences in the ways we talk.

It never seemed *relevant*: some people I texted every day, some people I rang on my way home, some people I saw for impromptu dinners eight times a year but never talked to in between. Some people I saw every day, and others I saw for coffee when they happened to be in town. You get the picture. It's nothing to do with closeness, or intimacy: it's just the way the file format works.

I talk to Georgie every day, for hours, FaceTime propped up against the toaster. Debo and Annie and Jo and I talk every Monday, for what we're calling Soup Club without ever really eating soup. And yet I have no idea what Rosa and I would talk about on the phone, but we've known each other for a decade, and she's the mother of my godchildren. What would I say to Fred if he rang me? *I'm going to be late to the pub*, or assume someone else has died.

And I have never really talked to Nancy on the phone, either: never needed to. Why would we speak on the phone? What would we have to say to each other that couldn't wait for the morning walk?

There are no good stories about phones, and yet I'm in one.

I need to walk; need to split a brownie and drink a coffee and tell her, face to face, how stupid this all is. How stupid I am; how stupid he, Theo, is; how this has all got just a little out of hand for people who don't even remember meeting. How I need *don't get attached* and *don't fall in love, or anything* tattooed on my forehead and painted on the bathroom mirror.

I need my best friend; and I need sugar.

If it's legal to walk, it must be legal to eat a brownie while you walk.

If it isn't, I write, *I – for one – am willing to go to jail for snacks.*

I follow it up with the little policeman emoji, and the chocolate one. Then I write:

Normal way, normal time?

Nancy agrees; and I go to the cupboard and start digging. These are Nancy brownies, late-night brownies.

A memory: Nancy, smoking, pyjama-d legs over the back of her couch. There are orcas on the pyjamas, and the orcas are holding little hearts. 'Make me brownies,' she says. Her eyes are almost closed. 'Make me brownies? Can you make me brownies with what we have in the house?'

'I don't know,' I say. 'What do you have in your house?'

'Dunno,' she says, and inhales lazily. The table before her contains the remains of our takeaway: two empty pots that once contained broth; two empty plastic containers that once contained beansprouts, rare beef and green herbs; two spoons. We have watched four episodes of telly, drunk two bottles of wine.

'Dunno then,' I say. I get up and start opening cupboards. I don't really cook in this kitchen, and yet I know it like my own; ⟶

there's no cupboard I wouldn't rummage through, no drawer I couldn't guess the contents of. I could draw you a picture, right now and a year away, of the likely contents of the fridge. This is a kitchen where I eat Cheerios from the packet while I'm thinking; make myself tea in my favourite mug (orange, here, with Nancy Mitford on it); find, late at night, the things to make brownies, because she wants them and I love her, and this is us at our best. In daylight we walk, we work, we talk – but when we see each other in the evenings it's always just the two of us and the telly: a throwback to the days when she stayed with me for long nights when Jim was dying; a throwback to the days when I lived in her house several nights a week, kept pyjamas under the pillow of her spare room (my room). Things change; everything changes; but the thread that holds us together is something untarnishable, something golden. I will always make her brownies.

I find a box of golden-yolked eggs, too good really for what I'm about to do; I find a bag of self-raising flour; I find (bingo) a full jar of Nutella. There's a jar of instant coffee, and sea salt on the side – and while both of those are optional, I'm glad they're there.

'I can make you brownies,' I say, and I do: crisp-topped with fudgy centres, unbelievably fast, unbelievably easy. Eggs, when whisked, do amazing things. Nutella is only fat and chocolate. Espresso powder for depth, smoky sea salt for the faraway ocean. They are too good to be true, and too easy to be real.

Right now, I find the Nutella; the last two eggs; the espresso powder. I chuck the brownies into the oven and find my trainers. The world is waiting: let's go.

Makes 12 brownies

2 eggs

1 large jar of Nutella
  (*you'll need 300g + 50g*)

75g self-raising flour

1 tbsp espresso powder
  (*optional*)

1 tbsp smoked sea salt
  (*optional*)

- -

Pre-heat the oven to 180°C. Line a small baking tray with baking paper, or, possibly, just grease with butter and hope for the best. We're working with what we've got here.

In a food processor, beat the eggs until properly frothy, then add 300g of the Nutella (a rubber spatula is invaluable here).

Shake in the flour, and the espresso powder if you're using it. Beat until lumpless and smooth, and pour into the small baking tray. Bang the tray the counter to help it settle evenly.

Dollop the remaining 50g of Nutella on top, and swirl through, with the wrong end of a spoon. Scatter with smoked salt, if you have some, and bake for half an hour.

Take the brownies out of the oven. Pretend you might let them cool; don't.

Burn your fingers snatching at them, because some things are too good for waiting. For some things you've already waited long enough.

June

Apricot Almond Salad, Lamb Steaks

And suddenly there are roses and rosemary and spinach and strawberries and sunflowers and thyme and tomatoes and ivy and kale and carrots and coriander in the garden and cucumbers on the kitchen windowsill – everything blooming, if not yet in full fruit. Cucumber flowers are yellow and shaped like stars; courgette flowers are deeper yellow, and long and delicate. There are violas appearing, self-seeded, among everything else. The tomato flowers need plucking off, my grandfather says, but I can't bear to. I want more of everything: *more and more and then more of it*. I can't bear for any of it to be less than it is right now.

This is it, the abundance we spoke of.

This is the garden I hoped for, and Jo and I drink prosecco on the steps and the days go on forever. Jo's shoulder, freckled and golden, is against mine, her hair freshly dip-dyed pink in the kitchen sink by yours truly. I have secured some fresh apricots and a bundle of green herbs; managed to acquire a pair of tidy little lamb steaks. The apricots I have poached in a glass of the prosecco. I'll use the syrup in cardamom vodka tonics or rippled through Greek yoghurt with smoked salt. The steaks are sitting in the little blue and white enamel dish, soaking in my best olive oil, with lemon zest and pink pepper. I can smell the lemon on my hands, the mint in the air. Nothing to go in the oven, and nothing from the garden yet – save mint – but it's coming. It's all coming.

They say we might be allowed out again soon, but I don't trust it. That feels like hope, and I'm scared of hope. Better to trust in this, and the goodness of this: the smell of sunscreen and chicken-shop chips on the balcony, nail varnish the colour of a sunset, tender apricots with just-seared steak, pink hair, a gold bikini. Good cool earth, and the watering can. All these yellow blooms; all these pink roses.

Mitski the cat pushes herself through the railings and back again; her fur has that transient warmth from lying in a sunbeam. She is so vain, this cat; she preens and poses, rolls lazily towards us, across the old curtain we're sitting on. Mitski tilts her chin towards me. I take her picture; send it.

If I got a kitten, would you come over and meet him?

Just to meet the kitten, I write.

Oh, obviously, he writes.

Then: *We could do next weekend.*

Then: *I probably won't have the kitten by then.*

Then: *But still.*

Then: *Or I could come to you.*

Then: *What if his name was Weetabix?*

I flip my phone face down, eat a handful of chips, fuss Mitski's feathery belly. This feels like hope, and I'm afraid of it. *There are no good stories about phones,* but there's been nowhere else to make a story this year: I'm good at stories, and good at phones. Writing is easy. Talking is easy, too. And yet I'm afraid of what might happen next; afraid that in person I'll wake up and realise I'm still married to someone else, married to a ghost. Worse, I'm afraid of what might happen if I wake up and don't think that at all. Ghosts and words are my home, and both live in my phone.

Sometimes I have felt part-ghost myself, these last five years. Doctors saw right through me, as if I wasn't there at all. Everyone, it sometimes felt, saw right through me to look at him: $\longrightarrow$

⟶ Jim, the Tall Man, the hero of the story, the great romantic lead in everything I ever wrote. And I wrote. I wrote to make myself visible, as if writing was the only thing that gave me edges. I wrote to be real. What would happen if I stopped?

This feels like hope, and something more than hope, and I'm afraid. And yet – with the railings at my back, and Mitski lying comfortably on my bare feet, and the garden all buds bursting into bloom and soon to fruit, two glasses of prosecco in, the undeniable reality of poached apricots, and seared lamb, and sirens on the main road and sunshine and the solid sureness of Jo pouring us both a third glass of prosecco – there seems to be only one thing to say, and so I say it.

Let's do it, I write.

And then: *And look at kittens.*

And then I turn off my phone, and turn my attention to Jo, half-asleep in a pink bikini, and to the apricots, now cool, and to the lamb steaks, marinating in their little blue-and-white dish. (Don't be too precious about the marinade here: it's wine and lemon and olive oil, grassy and green, and herbs. This is what I had, and this is what I used: bright mint, sharp chives, the low hum of thyme – like bees and brooks and damp grass. Don't be too precious, in fact, about anything.)

For 4

4 x 100g lamb leg steaks

1 tbsp each of mint and thyme leaves + more to serve

1 tbsp chopped chives + more to serve

1 unwaxed lemon

4 garlic cloves

1 tbsp pink peppercorns, crushed

2 tbsp white wine or prosecco

2 tbsp extra virgin olive oil

For the salad

About 8 apricots (*unripe fine*)

250ml white wine or prosecco

100ml water

2 tbsp honey

Stalks from the thyme and mint

1 tsp black peppercorns

200g peas (*or broad beans*)

400g cooked grains: think freekeh, or pearl barley

100g feta cheese, crumbled

2 tbsp whole salted almonds, roughly chopped

Take a dish big enough to fit the lamb comfortably, but not much bigger. Finely chop the herbs into the dish with scissors. Zest in the lemon and grate in the garlic using the second-smallest rung of a box grater – or use a Microplane if you have one (ours has lost the handle and is sort of unpleasant to use, so I have given up on it for a bit). Stir in the pink peppercorns, wine and olive oil. Squeeze in the juice of the lemon. Drop in the steaks, turning them so they are well coated. Cover and marinate in the fridge for half an hour, a few hours. Whatever.

Next, apricots. Quarter them, yanking out the stones if you can. If the apricots are not very ripe, they won't come out easily. Don't worry about it.

In your widest saucepan – you want the apricots to sit in a single layer – mix the wine, water and honey. Add the stalks from the thyme and mint (waste not, want not) and the black peppercorns. Bring to a simmer over a low heat, stirring until the honey dissolves. Slip in the apricots and simmer for 5–6 minutes: you want them tender, but holding their shape. DO NOT LET THEM DISINTEGRATE. DO NOT WALK AWAY. Lift them out of the syrup with a slotted spoon and leave to cool.

Take out the lamb, then tip the marinade into a non-stick frying pan and set over a medium heat – this will act as your cooking oil. Basically, you sear the steaks on each side, but the exact time will depend on how you like your meat, and the thickness of the steaks. (If you are fussy about meat, or scared of it, INVEST IN A MEAT THERMOMETER, IT WILL CHANGE YOUR LIFE.) I do my lamb steaks for about 4 minutes a side, so they're crusty brown on the outside and pink in the middle. Let them rest for 5 minutes (no, really, do this or you'll end up with meat juice all over the plates and it will not look pretty) while you finish the salad.

Cook the peas. Toss together the grains and peas, then toss through the apricots. Divide between the plates and scatter over the feta and the almonds.

Roughly chop the extra mint, thyme and chives. A lamb steak on each plate; herbs over each. (Edible flowers also very good here – violas, and so on, but not necessary.) Serve. More prosecco. Summer just beginning.

Rhubarb & Custard Cake

The first person to come to our house again, after the pause, is also the first person who ever came to this house. I like the symmetry. Douglas, all home-cut hair and beautiful shirt, drives over one early June afternoon with a car full of recording stuff, so that he and Jo can make weird sound-theatre in the garden. He admires the sprawling green of it all, the splashy little roses – and while they're making their radio show, I make this cake. Jo makes our house a place where people make things, and I won't be left out.

It's too hot to turn the oven on, but it's been too long since I got to make anybody a cake, and so I bake in a bikini with an old shirt of Jim's over it for decency. It feels incongruous – but then, what doesn't? And what's the point of the world turning upside down if you can't turn with it? You do what you have to do; you take joy where you can find it.

Diana Henry wrote a recipe for a raspberry cake with yoghurt in the batter; and this started off like that, and got out of hand. Besides, hers is an elegant thing: a yellow-crumbed loaf cake with a delicate drizzle of water icing, a thing you could serve to a duchess. This is...not that.

I make it partly for the cook's perks: licking the beaters clean. You wouldn't have thought that yoghurt was the secret to making birthday-cake batter that tastes like birthday-cake batter, but I think it is: butter and sugar creamed until fluffy, and yoghurt and flour and eggs folded in. But I make it, too, for what it is when it's done: a tender pale crumb, and, suspended within it, bright sharp strands of rhubarb and jammy pools of denatured, yielding raspberries. A sweep of canary-yellow icing with a familiar hint of floury custard, like the pages of old books; and a citric acid tang of boiled sucky sweets; and dotted here and there with freeze-dried raspberries and, ludicrously, popping candy. Just joy. And life is so short that there's no time for anything else.

Grief comes upon you so quickly and unexpectedly that you want to take your delights where you can, you see, and this is one of the simplest ways I know: an afternoon spent in the kitchen, licking the batter-beaters with a kind of absorbed and inward look; and the early evening spent cross-legged on the old teal curtain in amongst the growing jungle, breaking cake with the people you love. ⟶

Makes 1 x 22cm round cake

125g butter (*you'll use the other half of the pack for the buttercream; leave the wrapper out to grease the tin*)

225g golden caster sugar

100g rhubarb
(*about 2 stalks*)

300g plain flour

100g raspberries

2 tsp baking powder

2 eggs

1 tsp vanilla extract

115g natural yoghurt

Freeze-dried raspberries (*you can get these from Waitrose*)

Popping candy (*ditto*)

For the buttercream icing

125g butter

200g golden icing sugar

50g custard powder

2 tsp citric acid (*sometimes called lemon salt in Turkish grocery shops*)

1 tsp rhubarb extract (*you can get this from Waitrose too*)

1 tbsp milk (*if needed*)

- -

As soon as you decide to make the cake, get the butter out of the fridge: it's harder to beat cold butter, especially for buttercream.

For the cake, weigh out the caster sugar into the bowl of your stand mixer, or your Main Bowl. Wash your rhubarb (don't peel it; you'll lose all the pink), then chop it into centimetres and put it in a dish. Add two teaspoons of the pre-weighed sugar and stir, then set aside (this softens the bite of the rhubarb).

Weigh out your flour into a separate bowl. Wash your raspberries and put into another dish. Add 2 teaspoons of the pre-weighed flour, stir and set aside (this stops the raspberries from sinking to the bottom of the cake as it bakes). Add the baking powder to the flour and stir well.

Pre-heat the oven to 180°C, and grease and line a 22cm round springform cake tin. The more neatly you line it, the tidier your cake will be. If I'm making it just for us, I shove in some baking paper and flatten it down to the shape of the tin, letting it creep up the sides; if I'm making it for a party, I neatly cut out the shapes of rectangular side and circular base. This is probably very obvious, but hey, maybe you don't bake often either. Maybe you didn't bake often before now.

In the bowl of your mixer (or your Main Bowl, whatever), add 125g of butter to the sugar, and cream together until light and fluffy: you want the butter to be more pale than yellow, which shows that the air has got into the mixture. Break in the eggs one at a time, beating each one in well before adding the next, then add the vanilla. Now gently stir in the yoghurt (slow down your beaters on your mixer, if you can). Sift in the flour and gently fold it in. Turn the mixer off; fold in the rhubarb and any syrup that has collected in the dish.

Dollop a third of the batter into the prepared tin; scatter over half of the raspberries. Another third of the batter, the other half of the raspberries, and the final third of the batter (don't worry if you can't cover every raspberry). Bang the tin on the side lightly, to help it settle, then bake for about 50 minutes, or until the cake is golden and a skewer comes out clean...or clean-ish. It will not be clean if you pierce a raspberry.

Meanwhile, wash up the mixer (or Main Bowl), and the many other bowls and dishes you have accumulated.

For the buttercream icing, beat together the now-softened butter, icing sugar, custard powder and citric acid. (I have never found a way to make buttercream that doesn't leave a fine dusting of icing sugar over everything, so you'll just have to get on with it. Sorry. It's worth it.) If you're using a stand mixer, it tends to go to crumbs first and you'll be tempted to add milk or something. DON'T. NOT YET. After the crumbs, it comes together. Now add your rhubarb extract, and *then* a splash of milk to loosen if needed. You'll know if you need it because it will not be swirling around like dropped silk, but will be kind of clumping about in the mixer like cookie dough. This icing is a very lovely sunset kind of colour.

Let the cake cool completely. I mean this: if you put buttercream on a warm cake, pools of butterfat will rise to the surface. Ice the cake fairly lazily, with a regular table knife. (Rough and ready is in, so don't worry too much.) Use more buttercream than you feel like you ought to. The best way, I think, is to put huge dollops of buttercream on top, and then sort of use the knife to smudge the dollops in a spiral direction until the whole top of the cake is covered. If in doubt, more buttercream. Scatter with freeze-dried raspberries and popping candy. Feel very smug.

Pancetta & Leek Freekeh Pilaf

For a long time, when I was incredibly sad, I used to go and hang out in the Waitrose Cook's Ingredients aisle. It has the exact same vibe as the haberdashery department of large department stores, and also of old and empty churches: a sense of comfortable wealth and infinite possibilities. It is possible to believe in God, in the John Lewis fabric department. It is possible to believe that anything is possible with your hands on Morris-print 'Purple Damson' cotton voile. It is possible to believe, in the airy porch of an ancient church, that you might make something worthwhile with the fabrics you've not yet cut and buttons you've not yet bought; and it is possible to believe, in the Waitrose Cook's Ingredients aisle, in God, in ghosts, and the afterlife. I miss the Waitrose Cook's Ingredients aisle, and all the other places I used to go to commune with the dead. Central London feels risky to me, still. I never liked the Tube anyway: I spent a long time trying to unlearn that fear, and now it's back. It will go again; I know it will. But I feel no urge to hurry the fear away. It's been useful before. It may be useful again. My trauma and I, we're learning to be allies.

The part of death that seems to me the most incomprehensible – and also maybe the worst? – is the part where the dead person can't learn anything new. You can't tell the dead anything; or at least I can't; or at least I can't expect anything back when I do. I used to call him from Waitrose, and pretend to leave messages on his disconnected phone. *Call me back. I need to talk to you. There's something I need to tell you.*

I used to tell him about the new John Ajvide Lindqvist novel; about the new Assassin's Creed game; about the new range of ingredients in Waitrose. We used to go to Waitrose for my birthday when we were very poor, and we would stand in front of the Cook's Ingredients range and choose maybe three or four precious things: a little tube of saffron strands, a squat tub of barberries, a jar of preserved lemons pickled in their brine. Then we'd get the bus home and talk about them, or I'd talk and he'd listen, and sometimes he'd say something insightful and sometimes say something stupid. You're not supposed to remember the stupid things dead people said while they lived – but I do. I remember all the stupid things, and all the cruel things, and all the awful things, and I'm glad about it all. He was real, and he lived, and we loved him exactly as he was, for exactly who he was, and you can't really regret anything that lets you say things like that.

I'm glad, too, that he isn't here to see what I did with the jar of zhoug I bought myself from the Waitrose Cook's Ingredients range. Zhoug is a kind of Yemeni herb-chilli paste, which is very delicious and not – actually – very complicated to make. I do, sometimes (page 158) – but making it, here and for this, would defy the whole point. This is easy cooking, get-on-with-it-cooking. Open a jar. Go on. There is also only one pan to wash up, if you can believe it.

It's somehow fresh and hearty and light all at the same time: don't ask me how. It's a little bit Italian, but also very Middle Eastern; it's a bit spicy and a bit smoky and very green. You could leave out the pancetta without any problem at all, but I put it in because, you know, why not? You're fancy like that and so am I. It's so easy, too: nearly everything comes from jars and packets. The fresh herbs are great, but you've got them in the zhoug anyway – you can skip them, if you can't be bothered.

My ghost would have absolutely hated this dinner. Barely any meat? Nothing roasted at all? Whole grains? But now I get to cook things he would have hated with ingredients he would have loved and he can't do anything about it. I say aloud in the kitchen, 'You don't get a say! You are dead!', and a ghost stirs the curtains crossly. This is how you keep someone alive; this is how you live with a ghost. You argue. You talk. You live, fully and properly, and you make things you'd never have made for them because life goes on and that's all there is to it. You make them for their friends; and live – not how they would have done, but in honour of them, with their best actions guiding your own. You do your best; you make dinner; you live. —▷

For 4

2 big leeks

1 x 77g packet of smoked
diced pancetta

1 tbsp butter

2 handfuls of kale

Handful of coriander leaves
(*optional*)

Handful of flat-leaf parsley
leaves (*optional*)

1 x 250g packet of pre-cooked
freekeh

1 x 95g jar of zhoug

$^1/_2$ lemon

Salt and black pepper, to taste

Arabic flatbread, to serve
(*optional*)

- -

Top and tail the leeks. Slice them into quarters lengthwise, and
then into thirds. Rinse them thoroughly (dirt clings to leeks).

Set a large frying pan over a medium heat and fry the pancetta
until crisp. I almost never use oil with pancetta (a non-stick pan,
plus the fat it yields up) but keep an eye on it – a tiny splash won't
hurt, if the pancetta looks like it needs it.

Add the butter and let it melt and foam: you're going to slightly
brown it, for complexity of flavour. Give it a minute, then turn
the heat down low and add the leeks. Let them soften: this will
take about 10–15 minutes. Don't hurry it – this whole recipe is so
simple that you can give them time. (There's always time.)

Chop together the kale, coriander and parsley (if using).

Shake the freekeh into the pan and stir through the zhoug.
Squeeze in the juice from the lemon half.

Fold in the kale and herbs, and cook for no more than 2 minutes
(otherwise you lose the fresh, lovely green).

Taste; add a bit of salt and pepper if you think it needs it. It
probably won't.

Serve with Arabic bread, if you can get it, or ordinary bread if you
can't; or neither, if you're not the kind of house where bread goes
with absolutely everything.

Impromptu Green Tart

I can't remember who figures out first that Georgie could – if she chose – get in her car, and be with us for lunchtime. She lives so far away; has been so far from us for months.

Is it me? Is it Jo? It's probably Georgie herself: hypothetical, not wanting to presume.

Well, it's technically possible, I imagine her saying, tentatively. *It is technically correct that I could eat lunch with you in your garden and then drive home.*

And two hours later there she is. Georgie drives a purple convertible, like Barbie, and when we see the convertible at the top of the road, I clutch Jo's hand and realise I'm crying. I don't know why, exactly, except that we woke up this morning and something new happened in the day that we didn't plan before. Trauma is so boring. All trauma is boring, even the things that seem exciting in a book: madness, death, the end of the world. It's boring to write about; it's boring to live through, because you're stuck in the same place, going through the same things in your mind, over and over and over again. You know exactly what's going to happen, because you had to live it in the first place. And nothing new happens. Nothing new, and nothing that you didn't plan.

And yet, here is Georgie, and her purple car. She backs it delicately into our driveway, avoiding as much of the jungle as possible, and nothing and nobody has ever seemed more beautiful than this interruption to our routine. She hands over a vast can of olive oil – Greek and spicy green – and a peace lily, pretty and sprawling. I am so pleased to see her.

I love to feed people; I love to impromptu feed people. I love to have a freezer full of things, and to have to think on my feet to make dinner stretch. I love for our house to feel like home for many people, and I love to have many homes; and these are always the first things that go when things get tough. Sometimes I forget how much it means to me, and sometimes it's taken from me; but still it always goes, and yet – it is also true it always comes back.

Jo and I sit on the steps, and Georgie sits on the bench at the foot of the steps, and we drink cans of Coke, scarlet and cool in the sun, as if this were a holiday. Jo and I have been drinking a lot of Coke; and eating mostly chicken-shop chips and tuna melts; and pretending – with help from the tuna melts and cans of Coke –

that we were by the pool, on some all-inclusive package break.

But for Georgie – queen of vegetables, accomplished cook, the first lunch guest in too long – I make a green tart instead.

I've always been a doodler. I can't keep my hands still, and I can't think without a pen in my hand; if there's no paper, I'll sketch on the backs of receipts or old napkins, and my laptop is covered with pencil scribbles. Little moons, little bubbles, little stars. I doodle like a teenager, with names in hearts, *IDST* scrawled underneath it, for *If Destroyed Still True*, a tiny forever. On the phone I doodle planets, tiny fragments of the conversation filtering through this inky galaxy. Often I don't know, when I look through old notebooks, what I was thinking. In an old notebook, among a cluster of stars, I find a single word in capitals, carefully embellished: *PLAY*, it says. *PLAY.*

It's easy if you let it be easy, says Jo. Let it be easy; play. It's all a game. Don't overthink it; don't worry about it. Let it be easy, and let it be lovely, and so let's make this – this tart that's like a doodle in pastry and pretty things: green tomatoes and green asparagus, curling under burrata or mozzarella or feta, or whatever you have; crispy greens, crispy broccoli, tiny little pastry flowers and leaves. Any green vegetables, although I'll tell you what I use; a vinaigrette dressing and splashes of white, crisp little edges and tender centres, herbs, olive oil; patterns and doodles and scribbles. Let's make a poem in pastry, and make things more beautiful than they need to be, a hundred times more lovely than they need to be.

Let's play, because we're together again, and we have to enjoy it while we can. ⟶

For 4

1 sheet of puff pastry	4 green tomatoes
50g mascarpone	1 tbsp olive oil
1 egg, lightly beaten	1 tbsp balsamic vinegar
2 tbsp pesto	1 tbsp salt
200g asparagus	1 x 150g burrata
200g Tenderstem broccoli	

These are the best versions of the ingredients, but you know what? It's pretty forgiving. Puff pastry base, soft cheese on top, pesto on top of that, vegetables. More cheese on top for decadence. You can tweak this; I know you can.

Unroll the pastry onto a baking tray, then cut it into a square. Use the offcuts for pretty things: cut-out moons, and stars, and flowers. Whatever cutters you have: I have a crab, and a heart pierced through with a blade, like a tarot card, and so many butterflies. Stamp them out and leave them to one side.

Pre-heat the oven to 180°C.

Spread the pastry with mascarpone, leaving a 2cm border around the edge for decoration later. Press the edges with a fork and brush with beaten egg. Spread the mascarpone with pesto, leaving a 2cm border of mascarpone around the edge.

With a potato peeler, sliver the asparagus and Tenderstem broccoli, then set aside in a big bowl.

Slice the tomatoes, reserving any delicious juices and seeds. Lay the tomatoes atop the pesto and mascarpone, fanning each one out in a line, like fallen dominoes.

Shake the tomato juices, olive oil, vinegar and salt together in a screw-top jar; toss with the slivered green vegetables. Heap onto the tart, spreading them out evenly.

Arrange the hearts and moons, the stars and flowers, and the little crab, around the edges. Bake for 20 minutes, until the pastry is glossy and golden, then top – as you serve – with a whole burrata, ready to spill, like a heart, at the touch of a knife.

Peanut Butter Brownies

Late sun, late June. Georgie, leaning on the bonnet of her car, and me sat down among the green things. I am telling her about everything that is too hard to say on the phone – which is to say, I am telling her about my heart.

'The thing is, you've always been in love,' Georgie says, honestly. 'You're always in love.'

'I know,' I say, unhappily.

'But this is different,' Georgie says. 'I know.' And for a moment we reach out and touch hands. Georgie was there in the worst days, before anyone died; Georgie was there in the neuro ward, in the places I don't talk about, the things I don't know how to write down except in vague and scary allusions. Georgie came and played Trivial Pursuit with the dying. She knows.

'But what can I *do* about it?' I say, to Georgie; and Jo, who is coming down the steps behind me, puts her arms around my shoulders and says, drily: 'Don't you think it's a little bit late for that?'

'It *is* a little bit late for that,' Georgie says. 'And what *can* you do about any of it, anyway?'

'What can *anybody* do?' I say. I mean to sound arch, but instead I sound – even to myself – a little desperate.

Georgie shrugs, and Jo shrugs, and because I hate to be left out I shrug too. And we look at each other, wide-eyed, shrug arms *up*, like *????* – and it is so exactly the only feeling left to any of us, that suddenly we're all laughing, Georgie leaning on her purple car, and me leaning on Jo, and Jo leaning on the cast-iron railings of our balcony steps, and we're laughing and laughing because, really, *what can anybody do?*

It's always a little bit late to do anything about anything, and all you can do is hang on, and lean on each other, and shrug like the shrug emoji, and laugh until you cry.

That, of course, and bake. It's too hot to bake, but I'm too afraid not to, and so it's back in the bikini kitchen.

I am making these brownies to make someone fall in love with me. I am making these brownies to give myself a reason that someone might fall in love with me. I am making these brownies because the alternative – no writing, no ghosts, *and* no cooking? – is too terrifying to contemplate. I am making these brownies because I don't know how to love people without cooking for them.

It's not that I'm trying to buy people's love with baked goods. It's not even that I'm trying to bribe people into loving me with cooking in general. It's simply that for me they have sometimes amounted to the same thing: food and love. Is that a terrible thing to confess? I like to have something tangible: I saw what you wanted, and I gave it to you. I saw what you loved, and heard what you said, and made it real. I like to make things real.

Georgie taught me how to make these brownies; and I knew that they were what we needed, or what we wanted: peanut butter, smoked salt, dark chocolate. They weren't like Nutella brownies – easy, quick, comfortable – or like skillet brownies – dinner party heavy in the skillet, and dense with iron and stories. These were something new; something real. Something a little bit trickier, but also lighter. Something frivolous and important.

So I listened to Georgie; I made them; I made them again; I tweaked them just a little, but not too much; I made more, and more; and I gave most of them to the people of my heart, and wrote Sharpie hearts on the Tupperware boxes that I left on their doorsteps; and they rang me; and I rang them.

And then I put my phone away, and the remaining brownies on a plate, and wait for the person who is falling in love with me to knock at my door. A person who loves – so he says, and I pay attention – peanut butter and smoked salt and dark chocolate.

And then – some time later – I ring Georgie to tell her all about it.

And all that's love, as far as I can tell. $\longrightarrow$

Makes 24 little brownies

1 x 397g tin of condensed milk	150g golden caster sugar
125g peanut butter	4 eggs
125ml double cream	50g unsweetened cocoa
50g salted peanuts	powder
100g + 200g dark chocolate	70g plain flour
250g butter	½ tsp baking powder
150g light soft brown sugar	2 tsp smoked sea salt

- - - - - - - - - - - -- -- - - -- - -- - - - - - - -- - -

First, the fancy bits: the peanut caramel, the toasted peanuts and the chopped chocolate.

In a heavy-bottomed saucepan, over a low heat, mix the condensed milk, the peanut butter and double cream. This is the peanut caramel, and all we're doing is swirling them together with a spoon until they form a smooth sauce. Line a plastic tub – a takeaway container is perfect – with foil, then pour the peanut caramel into it. Chill until needed.

Next, toast the peanuts in a dry frying pan over a medium heat for about 3 minutes, until you start to smell them catching. Tip out onto a chopping board and cut roughly into bits. Chop the 100g chocolate into shards, too. Set aside for now.

Pre-heat the oven to 160°C. Line a 23cm square cake tin with baking paper: you want to do this with two sheets of baking paper, overlaid so that each side of the tin has a sort of handle of paper hanging over the edge. It's like a paper sling. The brownies will be very fragile when they are warm, and will need this extra support.

In a Pyrex bowl set over a saucepan of simmering water – the bowl not touching the water – melt the 200g chocolate and the butter together, stirring constantly. Add both sugars to the lovely mixture, and keep stirring and cooking until they dissolve. Turn off the heat; lift the bowl off the saucepan and onto the side. Whisk in the eggs, one at a time; sift in the cocoa, flour and baking powder; stir in the toasted peanuts and chopped chocolate, then pour the lot into the prepared tin.

Take your peanut caramel and, using a teaspoon, evenly space dollops of it across the brownie batter. Then, using a skewer (or the wrong end of the teaspoon), gently drag the pointy end through the dollops, to make a sort of teardrop effect, like this:

You'll have more caramel sauce than you need for the recipe, but luckily it is incredible stirred into hot chocolate, drizzled over ice cream or simply eaten with a spoon.

Scatter the brownie mixture liberally with smoked salt and bake for 30 minutes, or maybe, maybe 35 minutes. Brownies go from underbaked (better) to overbaked (ruined) in a heartbeat; be careful. Let cool in the tin.

Serve now, serve later, serve secretly in Tupperwares left on your loved ones' doorsteps at the end of the world. Let someone fall in love with you.

July

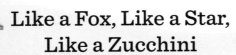

Like a Fox, Like a Star, Like a Zucchini
(Three Ways with Courgettes)

July, and I don't remember the last time we ate indoors. We eat on the balcony, on our folded old curtain, overlooking the garden. And it is undeniably a garden.

There's no elegant hedging, no lawn, no fruit trees. No trees at all. But there is green everywhere, and everything in fruit, and Mitski the cat, and foxes.

I love the foxes: a glossy butch of a vixen, a sleek dog-fox with brush held high. South London foxes are superior in quality to East London foxes. They feel more alive, somehow; less like scavengers, and more like beings independent of ourselves. Which isn't to say they don't scavenge. They do. They scavenge, and they dig. My particular favourite – the dog-fox who comes most often to our garden – dug up a dozen baby courgettes the day after I planted them; I saw him from my window, standing triumphant over the damp earth. I am not sure he saw me, but I like to think so. We have stars here; stars and foxes and courgettes.

The joy and the horror of courgettes or zucchini (lovely word) is that they are very easy to grow. And keep growing. And keep growing and growing and growing. Ours are in black canvas bags against the garden wall, and every day there are more of them.

On our fourth courgette of the season, each as big as a baby's arm, Jo says: 'Just how many more of these things are you planning to grow? Just so I know?'

'Some,' I say. We look at the courgettes: the courgette on the plates, and the courgettes in the garden, under the courgette flowers, where more courgettes are even now threatening to emerge. 'Some.'

'Hmm,' she says. 'Hmm.'

I decide to become much more inventive.

I don't think I am a particularly inspired vegetable cook; I have – or have had, up until this summer – merely a small repertoire of tried-and-tested green sides. I like to tick the box marked Health. I like to be sure we're eating five a day, like children. I buy broccoli and frozen peas. I buy cherry tomatoes and cucumber. Occasionally I buy a lettuce. A bag of salad.

Frozen spinach. You know? The vegetables you buy when you have to eat a vegetable. Vegetables, as widely and cheaply available in city supermarkets, are mostly just ok. There is an argument to be made, I think, that most fresh food from supermarkets is just ok. It's fine. It is a perfectly fine source of the calories we need to survive, and there is nothing wrong with survival. For a long time, I thought survival was the main thing.

But this book is a rebellion against going through things; it's about stopping and looking at things; about making everything really good all the time. There's this weird perception out there that if everything is a treat, nothing is, and it's so deeply puritan it knocks me out.

I want everything, all the time. I want it all to be the best possible version of itself; I want everything to taste of itself but better; I want *more and more, and then more of it*. I want to live. Which means, of course, that there has to be something worth living for.

And that, right now, is this. It's my people, the ones who can walk to our house, and the ones on the other side of town, and the ones on the other side of the world: my godchildren, my sisters, my friends, my family; this new person who wants to know me, maybe lots of new people who want to know me, maybe a world full of them; my best friends and my Jo. Mitski the next-door cat. A gold bikini. Iced water. Cold Coke. Babybels. Big books. And most of all, this: this garden, this ten-slabs-by-ten-slabs square of concrete just off an arterial road; and eating in it, an old teal curtain spread out across the peeling iron of the fire-escape steps, beads of condensation pricked out like constellations across the cold bottle of wine, a pitta bread – hot and tactile – jammed with pea shoots and rocket and butter beans; and boiled beetroot basted with balsamic; and charred courgette, squashy with oil, dredged in salt and tangy citric acid.

I grew the beetroot, and the pea sprouts. You already know about the courgettes. There are three more on the courgette plant as I write; I can see them through the window. Their flowers are the exact sunshine shade of a yellow linen skirt I once owned as a teenager in France. I'm kind of worried about the soil beneath the flowers and the broad leaves: I think it needs more organic matter to hold the water longer. I worry about soil now. I think a lot about growing things, and the way we grow things; I think about water tables and sun direction and soil biodiversity; and I think about →

things that are alive, and being alive, and being alive like a fox and like a courgette and like a star – one thing among many, one thing in the order of things.

It helps, I find, with keeping a sense of perspective.

And so I sit back on my heels, and think about courgettes.

Each courgette recipe here makes enough, roughly, as a component for 4 lunches for me; or a side for 4 people

Courgette in Ribbons

Courgette, sliced into long ribbons with a potato peeler, and tossed in a bowl with lemon juice and olive oil, and huge fistfuls of torn basil, and sea salt; and then – here's the masterstroke – a vast quantity of Parmesan, powdered to nothing in a food processor, shaken over the top. There should be, like, a cloud of Parmesan. This is a Parmesan party, and we're all invited.

The quantities for this are sort of variable. How green is your oil? How enormous is your courgette? What salt are you using, and what sort is your lemon? But the idea is worth telling you about, anyway. This is not the most original of recipes, but it is absolutely failsafe, and deeply fancy.

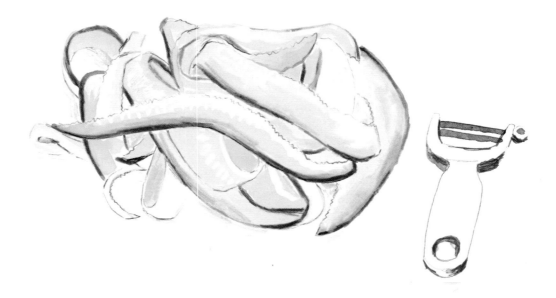

Courgettes, Roasted

Every vegetable tastes better like this: that is just a fact.

I have done it with courgettes because I have a million courgettes; but also I do this with courgettes because they can be, if you treat them carelessly, rather tasteless. Courgettes want to soak up a flavour; they want to be whatever you want them to be.

In this case, what they are soaking up is salt, olive oil, and citric acid. Don't panic. You can buy citric acid online, or in a Turkish supermarket under the name of 'lemon salt'. With some vegetables, you're fine to use lemon juice – and if you can't get citric acid, you could use it here, too – but with courgettes, you want them as dry as possible, so they go as crispy-sticky-tender as possible. That's why we use the citric acid, to eliminate the water element of the lemon; and plus, I like using citric acid in things. I like how much of a mad scientist I feel. I like that it doesn't go bad; I like that it keeps forever, a hit of acid to keep you ticking over.

Basically every vegetable, given oil and salt and acid, will be delicious roasted in a stupidly hot oven: they become intensely snackable, the edges crisp, yielding to sticky-chewy where they stuck to the baking tray, yielding again to tender in the centre. I love anything burnt; I love the blisters on the skin, the black edges, the way the flesh soaks up the gold of the oil. I find them almost addictively good.

500g courgettes	2 tsp citric acid
2 tbsp olive oil	1 tbsp flaky sea salt

Chop the courgettes unevenly, into rough and exciting chunks: some diagonal, some slices, some quarters. This is for texture.

Pre-heat the oven to 200°C. Scatter the courgettes on a large baking tray. Drizzle with the olive oil, scatter over the citric acid and salt. Shake, bake, and roast for 25 minutes or until completely irresistibly jammy and charred.

Courgettes with Chimichurri

This is, I suppose, like the sophisticated, slower version of the roast courgettes on the previous page. You're using the same tricks – smoke, salt, acid, oil – but making it *fancy*: making it something you could serve to guests cheerfully; something you could spend a little time, on a Saturday afternoon in high summer, chopping and tasting and preparing. There's something lovely about treating vegetables the way you might, once, have treated meat: as the star of the show, with care, with dazzle.

Chimichurri is an Argentinian sauce, kind of like a salsa verde but different: chopped red chilli, red wine vinegar, parsley, garlic and olive oil. Slick and sharp, it's usually paired with something smoky and griddled (steak, say – or in this case, courgette).

It seemed to me a natural pairing. I was thinking about *zucchine alla scapece* – which is cold courgettes, marinated in oil, white vinegar and mint; and I was also thinking about chimichurri, and the answer seemed very clear. Thick slices of courgette seared in a hot griddle pan, then tossed and marinated in a (kind of) chimichurri. I say 'kind of' because I have never been to Argentina, I am not Argentinian, and I am 100% certain this is not how they do it there. This is sort of like the chimichurri I have eaten in Argentinian restaurants, and based on reading a lot of recipes for chimichurri, and thinking about it a lot, but there's almost certainly nothing authentic about it. I keep thinking about authenticity: about how there's so little that's authentic about anything, in this book, because I am not a very authentic cook. I am a scavenger, a city-shaped try-hard who buys things and then Googles to find ways to use them up; the kind of person who buys cookbooks on a whim about places I've never been, just to see what they're like, and then forgets to follow half of the steps in the recipes. I would love to be the kind of diligent cook who can make a thing exactly as instructed, but I'm not: I'm an idiot. A happy idiot, who sometimes puts mint in her chimichurri courgettes, and you know what? I don't regret it at all.

I do make my chimichurri by hand, though, and not in a food processor, because the texture is so different. You don't want a smooth paste, here, but beautiful, jewel-like flecks of gold and green and red, suspended in the green-gold oil, the tiny pearls of vinegar.

500g courgettes

For the chimichurri

2 garlic cloves

A couple of pinches of
  flaky sea salt

2 tbsp chilli flakes

20ml olive oil

10ml red wine vinegar

Small bunch of coriander

Small bunch of flat-leaf
  parsley

Few sprigs of mint

Slice the courgettes into thick rounds, splash with olive oil and toss into a griddle pan over a high heat. Let them cook for 3 minutes on each side. They should blacken in pleasing little stripes, and when they are stripy on both sides – and tender to a fork – you can turn the heat off, yank them out and ignore them.

Ignore them. This recipe is all about the chimichurri – and yet it is, I'm afraid, only an approximation of a recipe. I can give you quantities, but you're going to have to get in there and taste. Do I like it? Do I want more oil, more vinegar, more salt, more chilli? You have to add each thing little by little: one garlic clove, one pinch of chilli, a splash of vinegar. I can't tell you how you like this, I can only tell you how to know what you like – and the only way to know is to try it, and to do it.

Take your pestle and mortar, and pound your garlic to a paste. Add a tiny pinch of salt, to help grind it down. Add half your chilli flakes, and pound them, too. Add a little oil and a little vinegar. Add a few leaves of coriander, a few of parsley, a few of mint, and another pinch of salt to help grind them down into a condiment. It will come, I promise. Keep adding; keep pounding.

At this point you can start tasting. Would you, personally, like a splash more sourness? A little kick? If you don't know, just try it. It doesn't matter. See what you like, and whether you like it more like this, or like that. Just try it. Keep trying. I believe in you.

Dress the warm courgettes in the chimichurri: eat now, eat later. Both are great.

Sab-*ish*

I find lunch very difficult. In winter, at least, it can be beans from a tin or spaghetti hoops with little sausages; but in summer I find myself tempted to go for a handful of Hula Hoops and call it quits. Which makes me, every time and eternally, miserable by four p.m.

And so, this. Sabich. Sab-*ish*.

Sabich is a kind of Iraqi-Israeli breakfast sandwich, which this isn't; it has fried aubergine in, which this doesn't; it has a rich theological context and cultural history, which this is also – sadly – lacking. And yet this is enough *like* a sabich, to an idiot, that it both scratches the same itch and couldn't stand alone without this explanation. I made it because there was no sabich option on Deliveroo. I made it because I live on the wrong side of London for Jewish cooking; I made it because I was thinking about pickled mango and sesame and egg yolk. Not quite a sabich, but *because* of sabich. Rather cutely, then: sab-*ish*.

The concept, basically, is a pitta full of stuff: an elevated pitta full of stuff, mostly vegetables, and also an egg. *Sabāh* means 'morning', and maybe this is why it's called sabich, 'for breakfast', but I don't care: it's a better lunch than breakfast, because I don't have the constitution for pickles before noon.

It is a perfect lunch because it is difficult (though not impossible) to feel guilty about eating so many vegetables; and also because it's largely an assembly job. I assume that at some point (probably by the time you're reading this) people will work in offices again, and leave the house, and stuff – and this is also good for that, because it is *essentially* a sandwich. Like, you can wrap it in foil, and it's fine. Better actually, maybe. Better, because sabich proper is traditionally eaten on the Sabbath, when you're not supposed to undertake any tasks. It started – possibly – as an Iraqi Shabbat breakfast of cold fried aubergine, hard-boiled eggs and new potatoes; and somewhere between Iraq then, and Israel now (maybe Tel Aviv in the sixties, but it's contentious), it became something like this sandwich. $\longrightarrow$

⟶   Not this sandwich, obviously. Like everything else I make,
this is chaos. Many cultures, many influences, because that's
what happens when you teach yourself to cook. If I were a chef,
I'd probably feel differently – but, as it is, I'm just doing the most
delicious thing I can with what's in the fridge, in the cupboard,
in the garden. I'm just cooking for me and Jo, and our friends
who come to settle themselves delicately on the old curtain
between the tomato-vine jungle. Nancy stretches herself out
like a cat on the teal curtain; Douglas drops his bike against the
railings, barely even bothering to loop the chain; Debo chases her
new puppy away from my courgettes, although honestly Jo at least
would be pleased if he chewed up every last one. I prop open the
door – has it been closed for a single daylight hour since March?
– and find the lunch things: soft pitta, jammy sauce, green sauce,
dark and sticky marinated eggs with golden, liquid yolks. Quick
pink pickles that live in the back of the fridge. Charred courgettes,
sharp with acid and sea-bright with salt.

The key thing this sandwich, that sabich and the Shabbat
breakfast have in common is that they are all assembly jobs: all
DIY bits you prep in advance and leave in the fridge to assemble
as needed. It looks like a lot of work, and sort of is, but also if you
make these things, you can make this sandwich and also a bunch
of other meals with each component without actually having to
have leftovers (a thing I despise; don't ask). There are *options*
here, you know? The idea is that you make all these things on, like,
a Sunday; and then all week you can easily assemble delicious
little not-quite-Iraqi-Israeli-inspired sandwiches in various
combinations of exciting.

The thing is, lunch has to be delicious and exciting, because
otherwise, why bother? It's hard enough to eat lunch as it is.
Anyway, it has to be great; because nothing is sadder than a
regrettable lunch, because you *tried* and it was boring, and you
could have just had three Reese's Peanut Butter Cups and a
lump of cheese. You could have had thirty to forty olives eaten
straight from the jar, you know? You could have stood at the open
fridge for fifteen minutes on your phone, consuming objects, and
achieved the same satisfaction. And that is partly why I was so
weird about lunch for so long and why this sandwich is so great.
It's so great because it's *worth it*.

It is – and I do not say this lightly – better than three Reese's
Peanut Butter Cups and a lump of cheese. It is better than thirty

to forty olives eaten straight from the jar. It is a lunch that makes you feel thrilled about having eaten lunch.

I chop vegetables, arrange jars and plates, put everything on a tray, and go back down to the jungle-patio. We assemble our sandwiches, spilling cheerfully out of pittas onto the blue and white plates, and everything smells like sunscreen and tomato vines, and the cat is back again, and Jo has gone full lizard, drinking up the sun as if it will make everything better, which it will.

Assemble some, all, of the following. Eggs, in some form, are mandatory. (Yes, you're doing it right.)

For 2

2 tbsp Rhubarb & Radish Quick Pink Pickles Redux (*page 95*)

2 tbsp Courgettes, Roasted (*page 151*)

2 tbsp Blackened Black Garlic Aubergine (*page 165*)

2 tbsp hummus

2 tbsp Beetroot Raita (*page 168*)

2 pitta breads

2 tsp mango chutney, representing a very delicious Israeli-Iraqi condiment called amba (*according to my Israeli-Iraqi sources, this sauce is impossible to make at home – like artisan catsup, when you wanted Heinz – but you can buy it online or, in some form, in Waitrose*)

2 tsp Zhoug (*page 158*)

2 Soy-Marinated Eggs (*page 160*)

2 tsp Dukkah (*page 162*)

¼ cucumber, finely chopped

¼ red onion, finely chopped

Handful of roughly chopped cherry tomatoes

1 tbsp chopped coriander – try mint, try basil, try parsley, something green for lift

Maybe some other stuff you have in your fridge. Scraps of roast chicken (*page 180*). Those readymade crispy tofu bits. Chicken nuggets (*shh*). Fish fingers (*ditto*).

Taramasalata instead of hummus. Baba ganoush. I have a weakness for adding leftover sour cream and chive dip, but I understand this is horrible. Sometimes I just put a splodge of yoghurt; saffron yoghurt left over from Iron Soup (*page 33*); garlic yoghurt left over from Turkish Eggs (*page 42*).

Zhoug

Blame it on an early fondness for Scrabble, but I'm a sucker for anything with a Z. I have also never met a green sauce I didn't love, which makes me a double sucker for this: it's a Yemeni relish, with masses of herbs, chilli and garlic and spices, which is quickly becoming ubiquitous on restaurant menus, and in food magazines and blogs – as is the way when something unbelievably delicious turns up. And by 'turns up', I mean of course when a white person puts it on a menu.

Which is the way of the world, but is also a weird and tricky thing about living in a world like this. You don't want not to be inspired, and you don't want not to learn, and you definitely don't want not to eat. You don't want, either, to be stuck doing only one thing with one ingredient; to be always making a pale imitation of what someone else is doing better. There is such a joy in reading about the world, in eating the world, in taking everything the world has to offer. There is such a joy in using things in your storecupboard in ways nobody could have imagined before the world got small enough to share food across oceans: gochujang on a bacon sandwich, or bacon in a paratha; miso with ketchup, miso egg mayo on an English muffin; zhoug and amba in a scruffy little pitta with leftover roast chicken. This is important, and it's joyous, and finding something new for your stable of staples is a joy too.

And yet, much like discovering the Amazon, or being the first person up Everest, there's this tendency to think you've invented it. But it's hard to invent anything, in a world that's been going for so long. Everything comes with a story already attached; a history you can learn, and absorb, and be glad in as well. Everything has a story; and it is when we ignore those stories entirely – when we don't acknowledge where things come from – that we lose something good.

When I was a kid I was obsessed with family trees, some imaginary and some real. Think of this as the family tree of the things that you make: zhoug speaks to chimichurri speaks to salsa verde, and how all those sauces can speak to a sauce you're about to make in your kitchen, even if it's far away from Argentina or Yemen or Italy. And how this sauce, this zhoug, or zhoug-like thing, makes everything hotter and better; and how you need it in your life, no matter where you are.

Makes 1 medium jar

4 cardamom pods

½ tbsp caraway seeds

2 cloves

½ tbsp cumin seeds

2 tsp salt

3 green chillies

Big bunch of coriander

Little bunch of flat-leaf
  parsley

Lemon (*at least half, but maybe
  more to taste*)

75ml olive oil

Blitz all the dried spices and the salt in the little bowl bit of a food processor until powdery. (If you have no little bowl bit, you can do this with a pestle and mortar; if you have no pestle and mortar, honestly skip this recipe and buy a jar of readymade. Why make life harder than it already is?) Add the chillies, coriander, parsley and a squeeze of lemon and blitz again.

With the motor running, drizzle in the olive oil and blend to emulsify, so it all comes together. Taste. More salt? More lemon? Blitz until smooth.

This is best on the day it's made: I tend to eat it over a few days, keeping it in the fridge, but I'd serve it to guests on Day One.

Ten-Minute Eggs; Soy-Marinated Eggs; Miso Egg Mayo

We all know, by now, how I feel about eggs. Eggs are little miracles in all forms. It's too hard to be grateful for the big things. You end up feeling resentful and bitter. But being grateful for an egg is easy, and if you think I sound sanctimonious and preachy, then it is almost definitely time for you to eat an egg and shut up.

Here are three ways with eggs, plus a peeling tip: each technique builds on the one that came before it, but each one stands alone as useful.

We start with basic jammy-yolked eggs; then unbelievably punchy soy-marinated eggs (and for sab-*ish* this is where we stop); and then – because I love having an extra lunch option – we make the greatest egg mayonnaise in the world. (Or at least, the greatest that doesn't involve making your own mayonnaise.)

To turn it into a sandwich, you will also need good bread, and maybe lettuce, and maybe a few little pink pickles. I also like grated carrot and cabbage, but that's just me.

For 4 eggs

4 eggs

For the marinade

4 tbsp soy sauce

2 tsp miso

2 tsp rice vinegar

2 garlic cloves, grated

For the mayo

2 tsp extra virgin olive oil

1 tsp miso

$1/2$ tsp mayonnaise

1 tsp Dijon mustard

- -

First, we cook the eggs for 10 minutes. This gives you the exact consistency of jammy egg – custardy, sticky yolks – that will peel easily, and slip beautifully into a sandwich or a bowl of ramen. It is as simple as it is delicious: fast-boiling water, eggs in, lid on, heat off, 10 minutes. Lift the eggs into a bowl of cold water and leave for 2 minutes.

Peel the eggs: tap the biggest end hard on the work surface, and find the little air pocket there. Catch hold of the fine membrane bit between the shell and the egg, and peel. (The tip, as promised!) And maybe this is where you stop.

But maybe we then marinate the eggs for a couple of hours in a Ziplock bag. Take the bag; combine the marinade ingredients. Add the peeled eggs, and let sit for as long as you can: an hour, overnight. (This is where you stop, if you're making the sab-*ish* on page 154.)

But then – if you want to go the extra mile, and because I couldn't leave out this excellent extra lunch option – we make the greatest egg mayonnaise in the world. Beat together the mayo ingredients until smooth; beat in the (marinated?) eggs with a fork. Spoon into sandwiches, add salad bits. Eat and be happy.

Dukkah

I spent a lot of time, in my big grief, thinking about Victorian mourning dress. They started off in black, the Victorians; then after some time into half-mourning, into grey; and after that, quarter-mourning, with lavender and mauve. And after that, they went back to normal clothes, or maybe just a black band around the arm.

I didn't want to wear the actual dresses – it's hard to cook in bombazine – but I wanted something, some marker of my inside feelings on my outside body. I wanted to show that something had happened to me; I wanted to show the change. But I had worn black for a long time, and grey too. And I had, in the last days, eaten like that too. Jacket potatoes. Toast. Ready meals. Beige things. That was his dying, to me: a slow draining of colour from the world, and when he died I felt that I could lose no more colour without losing myself completely.

The day after Jim died, I bought a gold sequin bikini; I painted my nails a vivid Tango orange. He had been, I suppose, a colourful kind of character. What else could we do? I dressed my grief in gold and Daisy Dukes and yolk-yellow taffeta, and fed it with flavour and spices and texture and colour. I still do. Some losses, I think, are too loud to be muted in black. Some pain has to be lived with in full and glorious technicolour; or maybe it's that to live a life in full and glorious technicolour there has to be some pain in it. Or maybe it's that you don't know how important colour is until you've tried to live without it.

Whatever it is, it's the reason for all of this. It's the reason to wear a gold sequin bikini; it's the reason to paint your nails Tango orange; and it's the reason to make every meal – every bite – as bright and good as it can be. I think about colour, now, in a way I never did before. I look at a lunch plate, and think: pink pickles, green leaves and green herbs, gold yolk. Colour is important, which doesn't mean it's always easy. That's one reason for these recipes: these recipes for stuff you can make when you do feel like it, when you can get through the grief or the stress or the chaos to do it, and then you can use them when you need them.

Dukkah is this Egyptian-Middle Eastern spice mix: you make it with bashed-up nuts and seeds and fennel and cumin and sesame and stuff. You scatter it on things. You dip bread in it.

You drop a handful of it into – in this case – sab-*ish*, for texture and crunch and deep savoury flavour and (yes) more colour.

Some versions of dukkah aren't as colourful as this, but Yotam Ottolenghi puts paprika in his, and it made it such a perfect vivid orange that I couldn't resist. It makes everything brighter. Every salad, with this dukkah, is a riot.

Makes 1 medium jar (each serving size a couple of teaspoons)

140g whole hazelnuts	4 tbsp sesame seeds
2 tbsp cumin seeds	2 tbsp black peppercorns
2 tbsp fennel seeds	3 tsp smoked paprika
4 tbsp coriander seeds	1 tbsp flaky sea salt

There are three steps to this recipe: roast the nuts, toast the seeds, whizz everything together.

Start with the nuts. Turn the oven to 150°C and shake the hazelnuts onto a baking tray (with a lip, so that they don't roll off). Slide the tray into the oven and roast the nuts for 20 minutes.

While that's doing, take a big frying pan (a cast-iron skillet works really well here) and set it over a medium heat. You don't need any oil here – in fact, it will go very wrong if you use oil. We're going to dry-fry the cumin, fennel, coriander and sesame seeds and the peppercorns for about a minute, maybe a minute and a half. They will smell amazing. Amazing.

Tip the seeds into the little bowl of a food processor. Add the paprika and blitz – just enough to crush the peppercorns and rough the seeds up a bit. This is not a paste, obviously; this is a kind of crumble topping texture. (You can easily and meditatively do this using a pestle and mortar, but I feel like if you own one you are the kind of person who can figure this out by yourself.)

When the nuts are ready, add those too. Blitz very lightly – use the pulse function if your machine has it – because we don't want any kind of paste. Tip into the jar and add the salt. Jar lid on. Shake, shake, shake. Lid off. Inhale. Isn't that a beautiful sunset orange? Doesn't that smell like heaven?

Blackened Black Garlic Aubergine

The weekend after Jim died, I went to a party at my friend Annie's house. She wasn't my friend then – she was an almost total stranger – but she was Jo's friend, and Jo didn't want me to be alone, and I didn't want Jo to miss out. And somehow we ended up at this solution that pleased neither of us, standing in one of those concrete corridors you get in blocks of city flats. Something in this memory is a bright blue (a car? a door? a pillar?) – which tells you how traumatised I still was: my memory is all fragments, from that time, fragments and chaos. Not unhappy chaos, not all of it, not even most of it, but chaos all the same, all colour and shape and touch. It's better now, some years later, but the kaleidoscope memory mostly remains: I remember touch, sensation, colour, as if I'm dreaming all the time; but now I know I have to write things down just as they happen, so I can make sense of it. It's like I'm a kaleidoscope, now, and writing is the only way to steady it at all. It's like, I suppose, looking into a diamond; like looking through a jewel at the world.

But I didn't know about this then – it was so early on – and so I remember only this bright blue colour, and Jo's hands on my shoulders, and her whispering, very seriously, into my ear: *if anyone hurts you, I will kill them*, and I knew she meant it. And so we went in to this party, this compromise of a party, and so I met Annie.

Annie is one of those people who has a heart that is pure gold: a pure, shining, radiant, soft gold heart. Her goodness – her whole goodness, like a sweet apple – is the bane of her life. I think Annie would like to be hard, sharp, spiky and cool, like a stiletto; but Annie is a golden apple who wishes only to be good, and bring goodness to others. She is the most good-hearted person I know, I think, and the evidence for this is that immediately after the party was over, she took me, and Jo, and my kaleidoscope mind, and our friend Debo, to the seaside for the weekend. It was a very strange weekend. The house was haunted, perhaps by ghosts Jo and I had brought with us, and there were locks on all the wrong parts of the doors. One morning Debo and I came downstairs to find all the house doors swinging open; one morning Jo woke up in her little bed under the eaves to find her door locked from the outside, by a bolt. We walked by the sea and drank too much, ⟶

and I tried to write Jim's name in the sand, but the stick broke in my hand, and I tried to do a small private ceremony in place of a funeral, but the wind whipped away the things I had thought of making; and we made ragù, and ate it, and watched *Paddington*, and slept a lot, and drank, and slept, and saw the waves. And then it was better; not fixed, but better – and without Annie and the sea, it would have been harder still.

Which was why, when it got to Annie's birthday several Julys later, it was the kind of thing I put some real effort into. Even in the dark time. Even then.

One of the nicest things about being able to cook is being able to cook people the thing they want, and sometimes before they even know that's what they want. Annie likes food to be dainty; she likes to serve herself; she is like the Prioress in Chaucer when she eats, clean as a cat. She likes little things, pretty things, beautiful things that come in many dishes. We made menus, which Jo wrote out in coloured pencil; I ironed napkins and found the disco cutlery. It shimmers in many colours, the disco cutlery; it reflects the light – a kaleidoscope itself.

I made her quail, which did not turn out so well; and a shaved green salad, which did; and these Ottolenghi-inspired aubergines, which turned out so beautifully I wrote down the recipe immediately, and here it is, for Annie.

Serves 4, as a side

500g baby aubergines (*or a big whole one, cut into chunks*)

60ml olive oil

Flaky sea salt and black pepper

Handful of pomegranate seeds

For the garlic and lemon yoghurt

1 lemon

2 garlic cloves

100g full-fat Greek yoghurt

For the black garlic dressing

1 black garlic bulb, peeled (*you can buy it in most supermarkets now!*)

2 tbsp miso

1 tsp pomegranate molasses

1 tbsp chilli oil

2 squares of dark chocolate

A little lemon juice

Pre-heat the oven to 180°C. Slice each baby aubergine in half, and toss with the olive oil and a good shake of salt and pepper.

Spread out the aubergines on a baking tray and roast for half an hour, which is just enough time to make the garlicky-lemony yoghurt and the black garlic dressing. (More like 45 minutes if you're using whole chopped aubergine – just keep an eye on it.)

For the garlic and lemon yoghurt, zest the lemon and, without cleaning the Microplane (or grater), grate the garlic cloves. Whisk both together with the yoghurt, then put in the fridge to chill.

To make the black garlic dressing, blitz the garlic, miso, pomegranate molasses and chilli oil in a food processor. Grate in the dark chocolate, using the Microplane again (no need to clean it) and squeeze in a little lemon juice. Blitz again, until absolutely smooth. It will not look like enough dressing. It is absolutely enough dressing.

The aubergines should be ready by now – blistered and blackened and chewy and delectable – and you can toss them, while they are still warm, together with the dressing. The warmth will make the dressing go further. Let sit for as long as possible, at least until cool.

Spread the yoghurt out on a platter (I used a black slate, which looked very chic, even though it was a promotional slate for an industrial brand of Cheddar) and arrange the blackened aubergines on top. Scatter over the little scarlet bursts of pomegranate. Dollop into pittas, for Sab-*ish* (page 154), or eat daintily, for dinner parties.

Pure joy. Happy birthday, our Annie.

Beetroot Raita

The man from the Nepalese takeaway stopped on the steps, and I thought he'd dropped something, or forgotten something, so I stepped forward in case.

'Ok?' I said. I was still holding the bag of takeaway: momo dumplings, noodles, something exciting with mutton. It was warm in my hand, and heavy against my legs, and I was thinking about dinner; about Jo in the sitting room, waiting. I had made raita with an old cucumber and some mint from the garden.

But then he stood up again, and I saw that he had not dropped anything: he had, instead, been looking at the wooden tray of beetroot seedlings I had planted on the balcony steps.

'Lovely,' said the man from the Nepalese takeaway. He looked up the steps towards me. 'Lovely beetroots. Very healthy.' He stooped again, and gently took a leaf between his thumb and forefinger. 'Very strong,' he said, to my seedlings. 'Very strong baby beetroots.'

'Thank you,' I said. I was absurdly pleased. I smiled at the takeaway man, and he smiled at me; I hadn't talked to a stranger about something that wasn't the end of the world in weeks. 'Thank you,' I said again.

'You will have a lovely harvest,' he said. 'A lovely beetroot harvest.'

'I hope so,' I said, and we did: most of them I roasted, and chopped small, and scattered with dukkah for Sab-*ish* (page 154) and sandwiches, but some I kept for this raita. It is addictive. It is even quite nice if you hate beetroot, although I think I'm unlikely to convince you.

My friend Danny sent me this recipe (a simplified version of one from Meera Sodha's wonderful book *Fresh India*) which is the kind of thing he often does, which is in some ways – all the ways that matter – what love is: that, and a moment in a garden with a stranger. A moment about beetroots.

Serves 4, generously, but also keeps well for a few days in the fridge

200g beetroot

2 tsp cumin seeds

1 tsp mustard seeds

1 tbsp ghee or neutral oil

1 garlic clove

250ml full-fat Greek yoghurt

1 tbsp lime juice

1 tsp salt

Start by peeling and grating the beetroot. I am sorry about your hands: wash them straight away, with tons of cold water, but they will probably be a bit stained anyway. Set the grated beetroot aside.

Dry-fry the cumin and mustard seeds in a frying pan over a medium heat for 3 minutes; tip into a pestle and mortar and pound to a powder-ish.

Add the ghee or oil to the frying pan (don't bother washing it) over a medium flame, and – when warm – grate in the garlic. Stir and cook for a couple of minutes, then add the beetroot and cook for 5 minutes. Add the powder-ish cumin and mustard seeds, and stir.

Take off the heat, and in a clean bowl, stir together with the yoghurt, lime juice and salt.

August

Big Summer Sandwich

We have bought a paddling pool. It – she – is shaped like a unicorn, with a tail that would spray water if we attached a hose to it, or had a hose to attach to it. She is rainbow-coloured, and designed, I would guess, for ages five to eight. She takes a good hour to fill, carrying buckets of water down the steps from the kitchen. She takes up all available space on the patio, the old curtain beneath her to protect her soft underbelly, and still there is only just enough room, decently, for two of us. And not, perhaps, two people who love each other even a little less than we do.

And yet, when Nancy turns up – August Sunday, this blazing sun still so high – we have to push it, just to see. Nancy slides herself in, tipped onto one side to fit alongside the curve of the unicorn's mighty rainbow tail. 'There,' she says, with satisfaction. We are packed in like sardines, but it doesn't matter: the water is icy, and the cold cava is very cold. There are crisps, green olives the green all green things should be, little anchovies in a silver-blue tin and a bright yellow box with a ship on it. We play Mitski and Little Mix and Carly Rae Jepsen through the speaker, and suddenly, look, it's a party.

We are celebrating something again: the summer, I think, or maybe just the paddling pool, or the presence of the three of us in one place. The tomato vines are so heavy with fruit that we can lie in the pool and eat them straight off the plant, and there never seems to be less. There is never a cloud. Far away, on the clear air, I hear the sound of the trains – doors opening, doors closing, whistle, away – which is the sound of the world. Far away, by the sea, the blackberries will be out; the sea as cold as the paddling pool.

We talk about work, a bit, and the end of the world, also a bit, and whether we should do something for Jim's birthday this month, and whether in fact Jo – a November baby – should claim his birthday for her own. It's a funny thing, the birthdays of the dead. Three birthdays without him; three birthdays in which I'll soon be older than he ever was. Time. We pour more cava, and tuck the bottle into the pool with us, in the shadow of the rainbow mane, to keep it cool. We talk about love, and sex, and this little bit of freedom.

'It's going to get bad again in the winter,' one of us says, and Jo makes a face like, *well, what's new?* Which is true: Jo gets it worst in winter, the switched-off gloom, but all three of us need sunlight like little plants.

'Which means,' one of us says, 'that we should do things now, while it's sunny, while it's all good.'

'We should always do things while it's all good,' someone else says, and pours the end of the cava.

I wriggle out of the pool, and up the steps, to fetch more, but also – because I am feeling magnificent – sandwiches. I take the half-tin of anchovies with me, because I have a plan.

I have recently discovered two things: how to make focaccia (page 176), and the fact that there is an Italian deli on the corner of our road. A real Italian deli, run by Italians, who call you 'bella' and argue with you about cured meats. It was like being on holiday; like being somewhere beautiful and strange and new. I bought prosciutto, a big sack of buffalo mozzarella more pungent than mozzarella from a supermarket ever could be, and a hunk of Parmesan with the edges all crystalline and rough like quartz.

From the fridge I take pesto I made earlier, still sitting in the granite pestle and mortar. I ground it myself, with the sun on my back, and it tastes like sunshine and summer. It's better done by hand than in a machine, I think, and not much more work. The basil – and a pinch of mint – are from the plants on the balcony; the olive oil from the can Georgie brought; the Parmesan from the Italian shop.

I am on holiday, I think to myself, and we will get these sandwiches from a man selling them on the boardwalk, and take them down to the beach. Our garden has towels and cava glasses and empty bowls of crisps; green plants and blue sky and clear water and our friends. This is a holiday.

I slice a handful of tomatoes with the new big knife. I love the new knife: the wooden handle, the heft of the blade. It's mine; I chose it. I have never chosen a knife before.

The thing about tomatoes is that they are magically improved if you chop them randomly, textured in all ways: a slice here, a random corner there, some dice, a big bit, a little bit. I never understand why anyone discards either seeds or skins from fresh tomatoes. If this were winter, I'd give them a little balsamic, a little sugar, but these are mine and it's August and I am so grateful to them I could cry. I don't – I'm trying to be less pathetic – and instead I grab some broccoli and sauté it with anchovies, garlic and chilli flakes until it almost disintegrates. $\longrightarrow$

→ I can hear them wondering where I've gone, but not too hard. Why think too hard about anything? I slice focaccia I made yesterday, toast it warm. I spread each sandwich with pesto, and then with anchovy-broccoli. I fold over the prosciutto, generously and decadently, as though there will always be more. Maybe there will. I flip in a couple of preserved peppers, and then – why not? – most of a ball of mozzarella, whey-heavy and dripping. I drizzle over a little more olive oil, then shut the sandwiches with more toasted focaccia, wrap them in baking paper and tie them with string. We are on holiday. We are on a boardwalk. We should do things while it's all good.

I take the sandwiches and more cold cava down the garden steps, to where my friends are waiting. August, Italy. We are anywhere we want to be, and there isn't a cloud in the sky.

For 1 jar of pesto – we made 3 huge sandwiches, and had some left for gnocchi (see note at end of recipe)

1 peeled garlic clove (*do not use more, I don't care what the internet says about garlic*)

1 tbsp flaky sea salt

Big bunch of basil, around 80–100g

50g pine nuts

35g Parmesan or pecorino, finely grated

150ml extra virgin olive oil (*the nicer the oil, the nicer the taste of this pesto, and because you aren't cooking it, it really is worth it, I think*)

- - - - - - - - - - - - -- - - - - - - - - - - - - - - -

The crucial thing about this is, don't worry too much. People worry too much about pesto. You can use different proportions, miss stuff out (goodbye, pine nuts! no thank you, lemon!) and still have something extremely delicious. It is hard to write a recipe for something I literally always just wing. I have total faith in your ability just to wing this, so let's say that all the quantities above are pretty much approximate.

I use less cheese than some people, because I love the taste of the pine nuts so much: taste it, test it, see how you feel.

See also: I use one garlic clove when others use two, and the whole internet is dedicated to telling everyone to double the garlic in everything. This is sort of nice if you want everything to taste overwhelmingly of garlic. This is not nice, and is in fact sort of burn-y and bad spicy, if you are eating the garlic raw, as here. One clove. The flavours will develop in the fridge. It will become more garlicky with time.

You need a pestle and mortar, heavy and soothing in the hand – you can do it with a food processor but it's not as much fun. If using a food processor, use the smallest bowl, whizz it all together, done. If using a pestle and mortar, start with the garlic and the salt. Use the salt to help pound the garlic into a smooth paste. It will get there surprisingly quickly.

Basil leaves, bit by bit. They, too, will get there surprisingly quickly. Pound them smooth, which you don't think will happen, but it will. There will be bigger flecks of basil leaf, but that's ok. That is very delicious.

Then the cheese – pecorino is traditional but Parmesan is often cheaper – and then, slowly, the oil. Keep pounding and twisting the pestle in the mortar until it all sort of comes together. It will look – of course it will, but still! – like the fancy pesto in tubs from supermarkets. Taste it. More cheese? More salt? I trust you.

Assemble sandwiches, holiday-style. Cheese. Meat. Slabs of ripe tomato. Lettuce. Mysteries from the fridge. Maybe olives. I don't know – it's your sandwich. Everything is optional except generous swipes of this pesto. Maybe more olive oil, maybe salt. Probably pepper.

This pesto is also extremely excellent with packet gnocchi and the seared lamb steaks on page 126, and you can do it all in one pan: marinate the lamb; add lamb to frying pan, cook for 2 minutes; add gnocchi and asparagus to frying pan, cook for 5 minutes; toss everything with pesto; scatter with edible flowers. Just saying.

Focaccia

This is the kind of bread where if you tell someone at breakfast you're going to make it for dinner, you both have a better day. In consequence, I make it quite a lot.

It's high and light and tearable, with the kind of flaky olive-oil crust that – to speak completely frankly – takes months, if not years, of testing. I cannot tell you how much time I have spent talking to people about this crust. I cannot tell you how many better bakers I have demanded examine this recipe and explain to me how it could be improved.

Georgie and I, on the phone on loudspeaker in our respective kitchens, have talked about it every day for months. How long to bake it? How hot to bake it? How many times to prove it, and how long for each prove?

The first thing I did at the start of the summer, when it was allowed again, was to walk the four miles to the bakery to ask the baker what I was doing wrong. The baker told me; I figured it out; I had an iced coffee and a cardamom bun. The bun tasted like home, and Nancy broke off a bit of bread for the dog while I did flour maths in my head.

Baking is maths. There is no way around it, and so I fill notebooks with these awful scribbled numbers and attempts and ideas. Baking is maths, and faff, and often it sucks. I wish more baking recipes acknowledged how much making bread mostly sucks: *breadmaking mostly sucks, and you end up, after a lot of time and effort, with bread that tastes objectively less nice than bread from a shop.* If this sentence means nothing to you, please turn the page, or possibly several pages. If you're inclined to argue with me here, I'm not talking to you; I'm talking to my people, the people who really do *try*, but also, the people who know that breadmaking is so often this weird chemical mystery: one where you have to wait hours, or just one hour, or forty minutes, and then another hour, or four hours, and people talk about hydration and percentages and rise, and it is both daunting and boring (the worst possible combination). Daunting, boring and takes ages – but takes ages in a way where there is a lot of waiting around and no tasting, which is I think why it feels so qualitatively different from the rest of cooking, and also why I have never really done it much.

And yet – in this weird year when we've all had more time to tend to loaves and doughs and hydration percentages – I feel I've finally cracked it.

Which is why we have focaccia for sandwiches, focaccia for dipping in soups and swiping through sauces, focaccia for toast. Have it toasted in summer, with more olive oil and a squashed tomato from the garden; in autumn and winter I suggest you dip it into literally every soup you can think of – a classification that here includes anything with any kind of sauce, gravy or melted cheese. Also, it turns out to be extremely easy.

I wish Turkish eggs for you in spring; but I wish focaccia for you in summer, focaccia that you can bake as you like, fitted in around your life – real and important and full of things, big things and bad things, and good things and new things. ⟶

Makes 1 slab of focaccia

For the dough

500g strong white bread flour
(*not one gram more; do not
even think about it*)

7g instant yeast

400g tepid water

40g olive oil + 20g really nice
(*like extra virgin*) olive oil for
the topping + extra for hands

10g salt

For the brine

50ml water

Huge pinch of salt

For the topping

Sprigs of rosemary

Flaky sea salt

- -

Everything for the dough is weighed with an electric scale, even the liquids, because bread is *science*. Big bowl; big metal spoon. Flour. Yeast on one side of the bowl, salt on the other. They don't like to touch, so you gently rub the salt into one bit of flour and the yeast into the other, because yeast can be finicky. In a jug, stir together the tepid water and olive oil. With your big metal spoon, stir the water and oil into the flour. Stir to make a shaggy, sticky dough. It will not look like dough. It will look like you need more flour.

YOU DO NOT NEED MORE FLOUR.

I am pretty sure that's the first time I've ever used an underline in a book. YOU DO NOT NEED MORE FLOUR. It is supposed to look like that. That means you, thinking, *but she doesn't know my life, God!* I do know your life, and you don't need more flour.

Clean tea towel over the top, stick it in a warm place for an hour. Easy.

After an hour, you drag it out again. Hello bread. It is probably puffy and bigger than before. It may even have doubled in size. Good. What you're going to do now is knock all the air out of it, and you're going to do that by holding the bowl with one hand, coating the other hand in olive oil, and grabbing the dough with your oily hand and folding it in on itself. Your oily hand goes between the bowl and the dough, and you grab the dough and fold it into the centre. Then you turn the bowl, with your non-oily hand, and do it again. You're basically pulling it off the sides and into the middle. You'll note that you can actually grab it with your hands now, which is interesting, isn't it? Well done. Easy. Air knocked out.

Now, this is the cool part, the part that took me and Georgie and the baker to figure it out: the longer and colder this next stage is, the more you will get that perfect focaccia crust. If you can let it prove overnight in the fridge, it will be incredible. If, however, you have literally one hour and you really need bread – then fuck it, it will be pretty great. It just won't be the best bread of all time.

So cover the bread again, this time with a wet tea towel, and decide: have you got time to make the best bread of all time? Eight hours, somewhere cool. Do you just need pretty good bread, pretty fast? One hour, somewhere warm.

For your next trick, you need a baking sheet (tray, sheet, whatever). When the second prove is done, you'll notice it's much more bread-ish than it was before. It's basically a normal looking dough, isn't it? What you're going to do now is tip it out onto the baking sheet and, with oily hands, fold it again – fold it once, fold it twice, fold it three times – until it's got some actual structural integrity.

Now poke it. Poke it. Poke it all over, and with all your fingers at once, to make a dimpled and delicious top.

To make the brine, whisk together the water and salt. Pour the brine into the dimples, then cover the bread again with your tea towel. Let it rise one more time, for one hour, somewhere warm.

Whack the oven up as hot as it will go without burning your house down. The brine will mostly have evaporated by now; scatter the top of the bread with rosemary sprigs, olive oil and sea salt. Bake for 20 minutes or until golden and risen and magic.

I wish I had some right now. It is my favourite bread, maybe, of all.

Theo's Chicken

We think the kitten is going to die, and to take our minds off it we are inventing recipes.

The kitten is tiny, the size of two fists plus a tail, and the colour of honey on toast. His name is, of course, Weetabix.

'He's so small,' I say.

'He isn't going to die,' Theo says. We are on the phone again. I am sitting in the doorway of the kitchen; across town he is lying on his bed, the kitten stretched out, trembling, against Theo's heart. He sounds very certain, but I know he can't be. I don't say anything.

'He isn't going to die,' he says again, like he knows.

'You don't know,' I say. 'How do you know that?'

'I do,' he says. 'I just do.'

The kitten's eyes are enormous, but he himself is very small, and he is ill in a way that the vet can't exactly define. It all feels, to me, extremely familiar; and already I feel very afraid that I love the kitten just a little bit too much. He is so small: too small to love, surely.

Don't get attached, I think of Freddy saying; and of Nancy saying *don't fall in love, or anything*, and I worry that it is much too late for all of that. I am attached, terribly attached, both to the kitten and the man who owns the kitten.

'I'm not going to get attached,' I said, out loud. 'I'm not.' I thought of the man standing in my kitchen, leaning against the fridge, looking at the cucumber plants.

I want to know your taste in pepper mills and salad spoons so intimately that I could replace your whole kitchen from a John Lewis catalogue if I had to, he had said. I wanted him to know, too. I wanted him to be part of this kitchen of mine, with everyone else. I wanted him to know things.

After I read the text again, I leant against the fridge and stared at the cucumber plants, as if they would tell me something reassuring; as if they could tell me I'm not falling in love in the kitchen again. 'I'm not,' I said aloud to the triffid cucumber plants. 'I'm not attached, and I'm not in love. Not this time.' The cucumber plants said nothing.

The thing was really, even then, when he sent the text, it was much too late. You can't not get attached; or I can't, anyway. I'm always attached to everything: I live in the centre of a web, like a happy spider, and everything is connected, and everything is attached, and sometimes you just know. I always just know: I have fallen in love a hundred times, and every time I have just known. I would like to be able to tell you that I don't believe in love at first sight. I'd like to be able to tell you that, because love at first sight makes no sense: I can't see any rational reason to believe in meeting someone's eyes and knowing, absolutely, that they are the one.

But here we are: I've never met anybody who mattered in my life without knowing at once.

I met Nancy at a costume party my first year in London; we locked eyes and fell hopelessly in love and knew we were best friends. Danny – a work colleague of Jim, and a stranger to me – turned up an hour early to a dinner party I'd forgotten was happening; we started talking about music and pies and $\longrightarrow$

we've been doing that, pretty much, ever since. Rosa offered me a doughnut in a pub; Nora, then three, crawled into my lap at a house party, a bedtime escapee clutching a blankie covered in printed roses. Debo asked me about a (cheerfully gaudy) statuette of Catherine of Aragon in my window; I ran into Nelius's arms outside the Gare du Nord on an unseasonably warm October day; I saw Rachel in a queue and immediately texted a mutual friend to demand we be set up.

I met Jo on a rainy night in Camden a lifetime ago, and I knew I would follow her to the ends of the earth. Her face was painted very white, with cheekbones underlined in grey; and she was wearing a kind of Black Swan costume, and she was standing on a soundstage drinking whiskey and ginger. I made a mental note to order whiskey and ginger, too. Jim called her 'Boss', and she was nice enough to me; and I saw her looking at me to see if I knew what I'd got myself into with this mess of a man. I was afraid of her, and she seemed like somebody from another world, and I thought: *I would follow you to the ends of the earth.*

I am not a person who can decide not to get attached, and stay not attached. Is anyone, really? And so I go back to inventing recipes. I write: *what if we had a chicken with gochujang?* Then I write: *I am out of gochujang. And it will take a couple of days to get here if I order more.*

Miso, Theo says. *Miso and ketchup, mixed. A little brown sugar, a little chilli.*

He says it firmly, like he knows.

And he does. The chicken, when we make it, is perfect – perhaps the best chicken I know now, joint equal with Midnight: sticky and umami and charred and magnificent. It just works, is all I can tell you. It just works, whether it should or it shouldn't. It just does exactly what you want it to do.

It needed sesame oil, and the kitten needed medicine, but he was right about both. It is all all right, in the end, and sometimes nobody dies, and sometimes there's chicken, sticky and rich the night before and cold and tender the next morning. There's always a next morning, and sometimes nobody dies.

One large chicken: for 4 people, for 2 people, for 1 person alone at midnight and in need of bright, deep flavour

2 red onions

1 x 1.6kg chicken

Pinch of salt

1 lemon

For the marinade

50g miso

30g ketchup

2 tsp soft brown sugar
(*light or dark!*)

2 tsp chilli oil

1 tbsp sesame oil

2 garlic cloves (*although, this is one of the rare occasions when jarred or paste is absolutely fine, and maybe even better: 2 tsp chopped garlic*)

2 tsp chopped ginger (*ditto*)

- -

Thinly slice the onions into half-moons, and line the roasting tin with them. Set the chicken on top of the onions and sprinkle the skin with a pinch of salt: not too much salt, that's what the miso's for. This is just to dry it out a little, for extra crisp.

Whisk together the marinade ingredients, then slather the marinade generously onto the chicken; get it right into the crevices. You can leave it to marinate for a few hours, if you want, or get straight to it.

Pre-heat the oven to 220°C.

Push the lemon up its little bottom, then slide into the oven and cook for 20 minutes. Turn the heat down to 200°C and cook for a further 50 minutes. It will look burnt. It kind of is. That's the point. (Just trust me.) It will glisten and crackle, all bronze highlights and charcoal shadows, caramel and burn and shine and split.

Serve with...well, look. There are vegetables, there are salads, there are all the trappings of roast chicken – but really what you want here is a big hunk of part-bake baguette and a pickle.

Midnight Chicken Rice

Midnight feasts are the best meals; they are second only to *slightly drunk* midnight feasts.

We're too late even for the chip shop: we started the evening late, and we're ending it late; and now we're home and the kitten is chirping with joy that we're back, and I'm suddenly starving, and rummaging through Theo's kitchen cupboards.

What I want is chicken rice, but not the complicated kind. I want the kind with rice and chicken stock and eggs on top. The kind that's just a cup of rice, and two of boiling chicken stock, and a golden yolk (whites saved for friands or meringues or whatever) stirred through the bowl to cook in the residual heat. Midnight chicken rice, three a.m. chicken rice.

If this were another kind of night, I'd poach chicken breasts and use the stock for the rice, make a proper broth with ginger and garlic. If this were yet another kind of night, I'd have toast and call it good. But I need a minute before we go to bed; I need to breathe. I need a debrief, and the only way I know how to debrief is to cook rice, and stir an egg through it at three a.m.

Theo says, elbows on the table, 'That went pretty well, *I* think,' and then, slyly, 'Even though we were late.'

I make a face at him. I take the kettle off the boil, pour hot water over the rice and a chicken stock pot. I unearth two old garlic cloves and a wizened bit of ginger and tuck them in, dig through his spice cupboard for star anise. I realise as I'm doing it that I've never cooked in his kitchen before, and it feels so bizarrely natural – the whole evening feels so unsettlingly ordinary – that for a moment I think I should stop, leave, go home to Jo and my life. I should make it small again. Safe again. But my life with Jo was never predicated on smallness. It was never, really, predicated on safety. It was always death, and eggs, and so much space.

'*You* were late,' I tell him. 'I was just a plus one.'

'We were late,' he says, unconcerned. 'What are you making?'

We were late, he says: and it tumbles out of his mouth blithely and easily and makes me want to run. *Late*, because I hate to be late. *We*, because I'm unaccustomed to being part of a double act. I am not often late, because I've got out of the habit of factoring in someone else.

Jo and I work together but apart: if we happen to be going

somewhere together –both invited as our own people – and I'm late, she will leave without me. If she's running late, I'll go by myself. If someone else is late to meet me, I can get a coffee or read a book. I can go elsewhere. Crucially, it's always mine to manage: my place I'm going, my people I'm meeting.

'We're late, I think,' he said on the train there. I could barely even look at him. Sun streaming through the glass, and he like a Dutch master, all ochre and shadow. Gold, I suppose. *We? Late?*

'Wouldn't worry about it,' he said. 'We'll get there when we get there.'

He grinned over at me, and looked out of the window as if we weren't late at all, and he seemed suddenly – as he was for so long, for years, for decades! – a total stranger. *How weird it all is*, I found myself thinking, *how weird you are!*

It was a long time – six months – since I had been on a train; a long time since I'd gone anywhere I'd never been before; and yet there I am, on a train again, with this strange man who reaches across the train table and takes my hand easily, like there isn't any reason not to – and perhaps there isn't.

This transition from stranger to something else is the strangest thing I've done in years: stranger than death, stranger than any of it. It's like going somewhere without a map; or maybe more like making a map in the olden days, without satellites and sonar. Here Be Dragons. Here be ghosts. Here be tripwires and missing steps and holes in the floorboards. I am a haunted person to fall in love with, but then again – perhaps so is everybody.

This man, for instance, is a late person, and when we get to where we're going nobody is surprised at our lateness at all. They only pour more champagne; and the garden is full of flowers and cats, and more strangers than I have seen in months. It smells like charcoal and roses, like calçots and joy. They are all a little drunk already, his friends, and one of them takes me by the hand and puts a glass of something into my hand and a cat into my lap. She tucks her knees up under her in her camping chair. *Tell me everything*, she says; and then, to my surprise, I find I'm drunk and we're all dancing, me and these not-quite strangers, and it feels like an entirely new sensation. It has been a long time since I met strangers like this; a long time since I was anybody's *plus one*, a long time since I was the new girl in a gang.

'I know you *have* best friends, but shall we *also* be best friends?', says the girl who wanted me to tell her everything, at ⟶

some point when the stars are out, and I tell her *yes please*. And then we have to run for the last train, and then we're home, or at Theo's, or whatever this place is to me, but home is what it feels like when you get home late, and make chicken rice.

I put my hand out and find sesame oil and fish sauce without even trying, exactly where I expect them to be. Too easy. Too nice.

'Rice,' I tell him, and I put a lid over the pot, and sit down next to him. I lean against him, the kitten climbing onto his lap to show me who matters most. The kitchen has the deep, soft scent of chicken, of clean rice and the pungent depth of fish sauce.

Theo fetches bowls; I set rice into the bowls and press an eggshell into the top of each mound to make a depression, slip a raw golden yolk into the hollow left by the shell. It's perfect, so perfect, and so easy I don't know what to do with myself.

I know how I'd perfect this: know how I'd make it if it wasn't three in the morning. The proper way: shimmering pan of rice simmering away on the hob, sesame oil and butter rising in concentric rings of gold in a sea of double-strength chicken stock, and the house bright with ginger and garlic, and a fat bunch of coriander neatly shredded, waiting to go in. Two brown eggs, ready to fry; a little white bowl to put the broth in; and a whole plump lime to squeeze over, and Sriracha standing by.

And yet, you know, you don't have to do any of it. The only rules: toast the rice lightly with some good flavourful fat; twice as much stock as rice; and cover tightly. And that's it, really. But here we go anyway, with the whole thing, the real deal, the proper way.

For 2

30g ginger	Juice of 1 lime
2 garlic cloves	Small bunch of coriander
2 tsp butter	1/2 cucumber, chilled
2 tsp sesame oil	1 tsp white wine vinegar
2 chicken breast fillets	Szechuan (*or black*) pepper
1 chicken stock pot	150g rice
2 star anise	2 tsp sesame seeds
400ml water	75g Tenderstem broccoli
1 tsp soy sauce	2 eggs
1 tsp fish sauce	Sriracha sauce, to serve

Grate the ginger and garlic into a saucepan, then add half of the butter, half of the sesame oil, the chicken breasts, stock pot and star anise. Set over a medium heat, stir to melt the butter, then pour over the water: it should be enough to cover everything, but your saucepan mileage may vary; don't be afraid to add more water (you'll just have to reduce it down further at the end). Bring to the boil, then add the soy sauce, fish sauce and half of the lime juice. Reduce the heat to a simmer and partly cover the pot with the lid – sort of balance it, so that steam has a chance to escape. Cook for 10 minutes, then turn off the heat. Set a timer for 15 minutes.

Shred the coriander; finely chop the cucumber; mix together in a small dish with the rest of the lime juice and the vinegar. Grind over pepper and set aside.

When you've got 5 minutes left on your timer, melt the remaining teaspoon of butter in a frying pan over a low heat. Add the rice and toast it lightly, stirring to coat each grain with butter.

Then, measure out 300ml of the stock from the saucepan (this will probably be nearly all of it) and pour over the rice. If it steams mightily, add a splash more. Cover as tightly as you can manage (inexplicably, my Big Lid fits none of my Big Pans, so I balance it and it's fine) and cook for 15 minutes over a very low heat.

When the timer goes off, lift the chicken breasts out of the stock and place on a dish. Shred the chicken and brush with the remaining teaspoon of sesame oil; sprinkle with sesame seeds.

Pop the broccoli on top of the rice; cover and cook for 5 minutes.

Pour out any remaining broth into little bowls; fry your eggs; spoon your rice and broccoli from the pan, and top with an egg per person. Retrieve your bowl of cucumber; acquire the bottle of Sriracha.

Set your two bowls (one of egg-topped rice and a little one of broth) before you; set the dish of chicken and the dish of cucumber, and the Sriracha sauce, between you. Maybe also a little dish of extra soy sauce, for dipping the broccoli? Spoons.

Burst the yolks; watch the tacky gold drip down into the grains of glossy rice. Bit of smoky, papery sesame chicken; cold, almost-floral sharpness of the cucumber; clean, pure salty broth. Sriracha kick. Done.

Yuzu Meringue Sunshine Bars
(Supper in the Park)

They say grief is like a shipwreck. There are a lot of analogies that people tell you, when you're first grieving. Grief is like a shipwreck. Grief is like a circle. Grief is like an earthquake. Grief is like a ball in a box with a button in it. Some of these are helpful; some are mad; some are helpful one day and worthless and trite the next. So let's say it: grief is like a shipwreck.

Grief is like a shipwreck; let's say, actually, trauma is like a shipwreck. You're clinging onto the door, like Rose in *Titanic*.

(A memory: Nancy and I, curled up on the sofa, a few months before the end. 'There isn't room for two,' I said. On the screen, Jack Dawson was freezing to death. 'There just isn't balance. They would both die, if she gave him the door too.'

Nancy looked at me. 'Is that a metaphor?' she said, and I shook my head, but I'm cursed with the kind of mind that makes everything a metaphor, so it was.)

So trauma is like a shipwreck, and you're there, clinging to a bit of wreckage. All you can do is float. The water is full of broken things that used to be yours, and used to be beautiful. And the storm is still raging. At first the waves are a thousand feet high, and they come every few minutes, every moment, every few seconds. Every time they wipe out the world, and you're underwater and drowning and trying so hard to float. All you can do is hang on to your wreckage.

And after a little bit, the storm starts to abate a bit; the waves are still so high, but they come less frequently. Or the waves are a little smaller, even if they keep coming. You start to be able to look around. You start to see what else there is that can be saved. The storm abates further; the waves, after months or years, are further apart and smaller still. You start to learn to read the signs that mean a storm is coming. You start to learn the ways of the waves. You learn how to live in the ocean, and how it's beautiful here, with the birds and the stars, and that phosphorescent algae stuff that glows like on *Blue Planet II* and in *Lord of the Flies*. You see the great white albatross and the great blue whale, like you never would have known if the ship had never sunk. And you're cold, and you miss land, and yet you start, too, to learn how to survive these $\longrightarrow$

great waves that come – that still come – every once in a while. You start to understand how a person could hang on; how a person could let the storm take them, and believe and trust and hope they would survive it.

You understand, maybe, how a person could learn to live in the storm and in the sea. You understand that you're a sea person now, a changed person, and you can't go home again. You can't jump in the same river twice, and you can't go home again: there's only finding where you are, and doing your best to float through it.

And so you stop fighting. You stop trying to save someone who can't be saved; stop trying to keep a house you can no longer afford. You give up; you lose; game over, and then you see where you are. You see where the tide has taken you now, and as you float past you notice. You look. You adapt, you twist, you make it work.

There seems, suddenly this summer, to be a lot to celebrate. New people. New everything. New books and new birthdays and new babies, and I'm tired of not celebrating: I'm tired of waiting for things to be perfect before we praise them. I like it here. I like this summer. I like this plague year, five summers after our lives fell apart the first time. Nancy and I sit on her balcony, Beezle begging for Dorito chips, and plan like it means something.

(It always means something.)

We invite people. We buy fairy lights; I dig out sheepskin rugs. We roast four chickens – two Midnight, two Theo – and pack them in ice; press frozen champagne bottles around them like extra icepacks; order huge loaves of sourdough from our beloved bakery, and beg very nicely for the baker to slice it for us. I make yuzu meringue bars, the kind that would – in any other world – have been a pie, and been the worse for it.

Shortbread base; vivid golden yuzu curd middles; smoky toasted-marshmallow meringue tops. They take time, these meringue bars. It's a commitment, and it is worth it. It's worth it partly because they are delicious; but partly the faff is part of it. Each moment you spend (finding yuzu, stirring curd, monitoring meringue with a beady eye) is a perfect moment: still and calm and interesting. The sea settles. The storm abates. The sun, bright yellow, peeks through the cloud.

Theo stirs curd; Nancy orders tablecloths and wooden cutlery and paper plates; Otto organises champagne; I organise vats of hand sanitiser and napkins and baby wipes, and lay out everything outside so as to give everyone the kind of space that still feels baffling. We are not used to space; we are the kind of friends who hug, hold hands, play with each other's hair, sprawl across each other. *Kiss mother*, Nancy says, when I see her, in a passable imitation of somebody else's mother-in-law. *Kiss mother.* I kiss the air; she holds out her arms in the way we do now; I am thinking all the time of the day when this will seem to me like a mad and distant memory, and I write it down to remind myself to appreciate it. *Kiss your friends every chance you get; but don't stop having supper in the park.*

It's cool out, for August. The clouds are pale grey and soft, but there's shafts of nearly-autumn sunlight dappling through the trees.

We raise our glasses to everything: to the weather holding, to the chicken, to the yuzu meringue bars. To Nancy's book. To my book. To all the books. To Jim. To the dead. To each other, to old friends, to new friends, to absent friends. The champagne is of such wildly varying quality – £3.99 fizz, Bollinger, some odd fruit-flavoured sparkling apple wine – and none of it matters at all. We sit, each on our own blanket, and drink, and tear chicken from the bones. Nancy sits with Otto; I lean against Theo and hold Jo's hand. Danny, a country away, sings through a microphone: Tom, Dolly, Jen, Tessa, Ryan, like sun through the trees, like sun through the clouds.

People trade secrets and gossip as the sun goes down; and later in the dark we sing on the steps of the *Cutty Sark*, the way we'd sing at home, if we were allowed, trad mostly. Otto sings; then Jo sings, and Nancy's brother; Nancy sings 'The Parting Glass' and the night is over, and for once in this year we have met ourselves exactly where we ought to be, and everything is right, the great ship behind us, and the River Thames rolling away forever to the sea. $\longrightarrow$

Makes 25 little squares, or 12 big bits (also, can be a very good 20cm round cake for birthdays, to serve 12 people easily)

For the base

250g butter

250g plain flour

120g rice flour

120g golden caster sugar

For the curd

100ml yuzu* juice (*or zest and juice of 3 unwaxed lemons*)

40g butter

90g caster sugar

4 egg yolks

For the meringue

200g caster sugar

$^{1}/_{2}$ tsp lemon juice

4 egg whites

- -

Start by making the base: a shortbread, basically. Pre-heat the oven to 180°C. Blitz together the butter, flours and sugar in a food processor. It will make a dry, crumbly dough that you'll press into place with your hands.

Line a 30cm x 23cm baking tray with baking paper. (I also make this in a 20cm round cake tin for birthdays.) Tip the crumbs into the prepared tin and press into all the corners. Prick it all over with a fork, then bake for 30 minutes or until golden.

In a double boiler, or bain-marie (a Pyrex bowl set over a saucepan of simmering water over a low heat – you know this by now, as so many recipes in these pages seem to require one), stir together the yuzu juice, butter and sugar until the sugar is dissolved. Patience, grasshopper. Then, slowly, whisk in the yolks. Keep whisking. You're looking for a custardy texture, and then a jammier texture still. Sometimes they say curd should 'coat the back of a spoon', which really means: *If you dipped a spoon in the curd, and then ran a finger through the sauce on the spoon, would that line hold? Would it be visible?*

We want jammier than that, though, so keep stirring. Get to spoon-coating level and keep stirring. It will thicken, I promise. It will get there. You want something that you could take a spoonful of, and it would sit proud above the level of the spoon without threatening to spill over. When it's reached this point, set it aside;

take the shortbread from the oven, and let both curd and base cool while you make the meringue.

Take the whisk attachment and the metal bowl of a stand mixer, and wash them very thoroughly. Yes, they were clean to begin with. Wash them again anyway: grease ruins meringue. For the same reason, rub the whisk attachment and the bowl with the cut side of half a lemon.

Set up (yet another) bain-marie – this time with the metal bowl from your stand mixer set over the water, and a kitchen thermometer resting in the bowl. Put the sugar, lemon juice and egg whites into the bowl, and stir. Keep stirring, using the mixer's whisk attachment in your hand, until the sugar is fully dissolved and the thermometer reads 81°C. Then, turn off the heat and take the thermometer out of the bowl. Attach the bowl and whisk to the stand mixer, and beat the meringue thoroughly for 3–5 minutes, until it's perfect and glossy. We need what they call 'stiff peaks', which is to say: *If you take a spoon of it, dip a finger in, and pull a strand up to a point – would that point stay stiff? Or would it bend itself over?*

When you achieve this – and you will – take the shortbread base and the curd. Spread the curd thinly over the shortbread, then dollop the meringue on top of *that*. Use a spoon to bring it up to a series of swirls and peaks, just for prettiness.

Turn the grill onto high (a blowtorch would be better, but I'm personally a liability so don't use one) and slide the meringue under it for a few moments, keeping a close eye on it, until it is bronzed and – in some places – delightfully charred.

Allow to cool as much as you can bear, then slice into squares with a knife dipped in boiling water, for extra ease.

*Yuzu is sometimes described as the halfway point between a lemon and a lime, which I can't see at all: personally, I think it's more like the halfway house between a clementine and a grapefruit; a sharper, puckerier tangerine; a warmer, sunnier lime. It always seems to me to be more complicated than lemon – but then again, when you buy a very fancy lemon, the kind that leaves slick citrussy oil on your fingers as you zest, I'm often surprised by how complex that is. Buy yuzu if you can get it easily; if not, buy great lemons – the bars will be delicious nonetheless.

September

Max's Chicken

The sky is bright, clear blue; and the temperature is barely below twenty-five; and the tomato vines are still bowing under the weight of their enormous bounty; and yet there's something in the air that says autumn. An imperceptible shift; invisible, except that *I know*. My birthday. The sharp pencils. The jumpers. The leaves, et cetera.

I pour the tea, and say this – more or less – to Jo. She presses down the toaster buttons and ignores me.

'Autumn,' I say, happily. 'Autumn, autumn, autumn.'

'You *nerd*,' she says. 'You knitwear *nerd*.'

She is gathering her things together for rehearsals: scripts and scores and the little blue speaker.

'Jumpers and pencils,' I say. I stir milk into the tea – ordinary for her and oat for me – and pass hers over. 'Jumpers and pencils and umbrellas.'

'I already crave the light,' Jo says, glumly.

'Candlelight,' I say, dreamily. And then, because she's passing me buttered toast and I'm feeling generous, I say, 'We'll make you some light, I promise.'

'Impossible,' she says, and I say, 'Oh, possible. Possible! I promise!' And even though it is unnecessary I switch on the SAD lamp, and it illuminates the whole kitchen with bright white daylight. Bonus daylight. Magic daylight. People daylight.

'I believe in you,' she says, drily, and stalks off to find her water bottle.

'I believe in me, too!' I yell down the hall after her, and I'm laughing as I sit down at my desk (the high counter in the kitchen) and turn my back on the window to the garden, and think about autumn, and the harvest.

I have never felt, before this year, the responsibility of the harvest: the idea that you have to use what you grow, and to throw nothing away. In an abstract way, I've always known, but when it's mine it's different. I made this from sunshine and water and soil. I knew you when you were just a flower, just a shoot, just a seed. I owe you this. What can we do with a million more tomatoes? I eat them on toast for breakfast. Jo and I lie in the paddling pool – working on our phones – eating them from the vine. Nobody leaves the garden without tomatoes. And still there are more. ⟶

$\longrightarrow$ On her way out, Jo says, 'I'll bring Max home with me?'
A question and a peace-offering: I love Max; I will give Max
all the tomatoes she can carry.

What I make, in the end, is the simplest-possible meal.
It is somehow more than the sum of its parts, and one that I know
we will eat until the harvest is done. Max is an efficient person;
a miracle of a getting-things-done person. And this is a getting-
things-done dinner. An efficient dinner, and a delicious one.
One tin; minimal washing up. The easiest meal there could be.

Tomatoes, of course: handfuls of little cherry tomatoes in
every colour and stage of ripeness, tossed into the baking tray
with olive oil and smoked salt. Peppers and onion from the bottom
of the fridge. Basil. Balsamic. Chicken thighs, bronzed and glossy,
roasted until the skin puffs away from the white flesh and the
golden fat poaches the tomatoes into a stupor. A whole ball of
mozzarella – half oozy and tangly, half crispy and golden.

And Max is there; and Jo and I are there; and we sit at the long
pine table, and I think that this is what we've been waiting for
since we moved in: the easiness of having someone to dinner for
no reason, the easiness of asking someone back after work, the
easiness of having enough.

Serves 4 people, generously

2 red peppers

1 red onion

About 200g cherry tomatoes

1 tbsp olive oil

2 tbsp balsamic vinegar

Big pinch of brown sugar

Twist of black pepper

1 tsp chilli flakes

1kg chicken thighs and
 drumsticks

Big pinch of flaky sea salt
 (*smoked, if you can get it*)

1 x 125g ball of mozzarella

2 tbsp roughly torn
 basil leaves

Pre-heat the oven to 180°C.

Chop the peppers, onion and tomatoes. Don't worry about evenness – different sizes, different shapes add texture. Be a bit careful of the onion, though, as a big piece of onion is almost never nice.

Toss all the chopped vegetables into a roasting tin with the olive oil, vinegar, sugar, pepper and chilli and shake about. Add the chicken bits and roll them about a bit so they become oily and delicious: they should land sort of skin side up, after the rolling. Scatter over the salt and roast for half an hour.

Split the ball of mozzarella in half; reserve one half, and – yanking the roasting tin out of the oven – tear the other over the top. Bake for 15 minutes more, to blister the cheese. The chicken should be golden and perhaps a little bit blackened. The peppers should be quite blackened, and everything blistered and bubbling.

Remove from the oven, then tear over the other half of the mozzarella and scatter over the basil.

Bring to the table; find some bread, for dipping. Breathe out. Enough.

Blackberry Miso Birthday Cake

And it's because of that feeling of things finally – maybe – being enough that I hold the kitten up to my face and ask him if I should have a party of my own. He is bigger than he used to be. Stronger, too, and he pushes his chin up to meet mine in a kind of happy scowl, the way cats do. 'Shall I have a party for my birthday?'

I'm lying on Theo's bed; Theo is working; the kitten (the cat, I suppose, Weetabix the nearly-cat) is washing his paws. Or he would be if I wasn't asking him stupid questions. 'Party?' I say to him. His eyes are still enormous, and he looks at me reproachfully.

By party I mean dinner party: leave the *party* parties to next year, maybe. Besides, it strikes me that on my birthday I will be as old as Jim ever was, and I don't want to anger him. Then that strikes me as odd. Grief, as far as I can see, is just a series of being stricken with things: a series of shocks, delivered periodically and without pattern. The strikes occur almost at random, triggered by something or something else again. You remember! You drown. You go on. You remember! You drown. You go on. And so on and so on and so on. Which is why, perhaps, the rhythm of the year becomes something to cling to. And why my birthday seems, suddenly, so important. A new year. A new chance.

The kitten – the almost-cat – is purring on my chest. He is the colour of honey on toast; of miso-spiked golden icing; of pastry bronzed in the oven. 'You're alive, cat,' I tell the cat. 'Did you know?' And he purrs and purrs and purrs, that old song that's meant to soothe and heal and rejoice all in one low, impossible-to-mimic sound.

I make pie, for my birthday, with a Marie Howe quotation spelled out on it in Scrabble tiles. *More and more and then more of it*, says my birthday pie, wreathed all around in vines and flowers and butterflies and bees. In the garden, the real bees and butterflies are still everywhere; I pick carrots and tiny stripy beetroot and green tomatoes to make a sharp little salad to go alongside.

And I make my own birthday cake. It's based in part on the blackberry cake I made for Jo's birthday last winter: Jo and our friend Charley rehearsing in the kitchen, the light through the window still gold and lovely. I'm remembering this, and then I add to that picture the miso mascarpone icing on the cake I made for Nancy's birthday and left at her doorstep. That was back in May, $\longrightarrow$

when it was starting to seem like the apocalypse had been both a false alarm and much more tedious than any movie had led us to believe it would be. This, of course, is the way with apocalypses: they just happen, and keep happening, and there you are in the middle of it, trying to make pastry into something pretty. You can't help being alive when things are bad, and you think that you should be able to help it: you would think that the end of any world would take up all your time, but it can't. There's always another storm coming, and also, always, these patches of blue sky in between. September blue skies are the clearest of them all: so bright and high and blue that you can't believe they are real.

And under that blue sky I gather a handful of my most precious people: Jo, of course, the centre of my world; and Theo; and Nancy and Otto and Georgie and Rachel and Luke; and Danny on the little screen. A party; a pie; another year, another season, another slow circle around the sun. Luke is wearing a three-piece suit. Georgie tells a story about a pig; Jo tries out, with some success, the techniques of a pick-up artist she's been researching for a story. She asks us all out, one by one. We all say yes. We all say yes to pie, and then yes to cake.

I have scattered the top of the cake with little fragments of bronze, and halved blackberries that bleed deep blue into the golden icing. The cake is sharp-sweet, the way blackberries should be; a little sour, the way buttermilk should be; and dense and fudgy, the crumb sweet and moist and heavy. It feels like autumn; it glitters in the firelight.

We light candles; we sing. We sing 'Happy Birthday', and then all the old songs again, even though Jim is dead and things are changed, and Theo sings too, and I fall asleep under the big leopard blanket, the taste of sugar on my lips. Happy birthday to me. ⟶

**Makes 1 x 20cm round cake – serves somewhere between
1 and 12 people**

For the cake

175g blackberries

300g plain flour

125g butter

220g golden caster sugar

2 unwaxed lemons

1 tsp vanilla extract

2 eggs

115g thick buttermilk
(*you can easily substitute
natural yoghurt*)

2 tsp baking powder

For the icing

50g butter

300g golden icing sugar
(*please, please try to get
the golden icing sugar;
it is the perfect colour*)

2 tbsp miso

125g mascarpone, chilled

For the decoration

25g chopped pistachios

Edible bronze glitter (*optional*)

6–8 large blackberries, halved
(*save the prettiest ones for this*)

- -

Pre-heat the oven to 180°C – and, at some point before the cake
goes in, you're going to have to grease and line a 20cm round
springform cake tin. For some reason I am absolutely incapable
of doing this when I pre-heat the oven. I have no idea why. Please
grease your tin and line it with baking paper. Do as I say, not as I do.

For the cake, toss the blackberries with 2 tablespoons of the flour
and set aside. This is a good trick: somehow it stops them from
sinking...I don't understand it either, honestly, but it works.

Cream together the butter and sugar – this is a proper cake, this
one – until fluffy and pale. (For the record, you're incorporating
air into the mixture: that's why it goes pale.) You can use a stand
mixer; or just a standard electric cake whisk thing.

Zest the lemons (directly into the bowl, why not?) and beat
it in, then stir in the vanilla. Add the eggs, beating to incorporate,
then the buttermilk, beating again. Gently fold in the rest of the
flour and the baking powder. (I turn the mixer to the lowest speed,
but it's probably technically better to do it by hand with a big
metal spoon.)

This is probably the best-tasting cake batter I know. I know you're not supposed to eat raw eggs, but honestly? It's cake batter. I can't help it. This cake batter tastes like cake batter in a movie. This batter is white and fluffy and kind of luminously light-tasting. You are not supposed to eat the cake batter. Do as I say, not as I do.

Pour half of the cake batter into the prepared tin and scatter over half of the flour-dusted blackberries. Then add half of the remaining batter, followed by the rest of the blackberries, then the last of the batter. So it's like:

> *half of the batter*
> *half of the berries*
> *quarter of the batter*
> *half of the berries*
> *quarter of the batter.*

This doesn't have to be exact, obviously: it just means you'll get a more even distribution of berries throughout the cake.

Bake the cake for about an hour, but it could need up to 75 minutes. Start checking it after an hour: you want a skewer, jabbed into the centre of the cake, to come out clean (unless you've pierced a blackberry, but you'll be able to tell the difference).

When it's done, let the cake cool completely in the tin (this is so important; do not skip; do not hurry).

While the cake is cooling, make the icing. This is very easy: beat the butter and icing sugar together, then beat in the miso; fold in the mascarpone.

If you want to make the cake a day in advance, it will be fine out of the fridge before it's iced, but not after; so do do it that way round. If you see what I mean.

When you're about ready to serve, dollop on the icing. You're going for a kind of rustic effect, nothing too neat.

Scatter over the pistachios and bronze glitter (if you have it); stud the halved blackberries around the edges. Candles on top. Fire for the autumn, fire for the fire god.

Serve immediately; be praised.

Furious XO Stir-Fry Beans

It has been a perfect day. Mid-September, not a cloud in the sky. Theo has meticulously planned a late birthday surprise (treasure hunt; train; boat). Everything is perfect: there has been champagne, and dragonflies, and swans.

We are on our train home when I start it.

And I do start it.

'It's so late,' I say. It's the end of the afternoon. 'I'm so hungry...'

'You're hungry?' Theo looks at me. 'God, I forgot about lunch.'

I already know this isn't about food. I'm hungry, sure. But I could wait, and the station isn't far, and I could have said something before, when we were at the lovely pub by the lovely river under the blue sky.

'Yeah,' I say. 'You did.'

'Shit,' he says. 'We can get something at the station, I guess. Or just when we get home.'

I turn my back on him and look out of the train window.

We have never had a fight before, and it takes Theo a little while to realise what's happening. 'Are you...mad at me?' he says, reasonably, and baffled. He is still holding the train tickets and the sun is still warm on our shoulders.

'No,' I say; but I am.

'You are *being* mad at me, though?'

'I can't believe you didn't bring a picnic,' I say.

'We can get food at home,' he says. 'Or we can see if there's food on the train? You didn't say anything earlier?'

'I didn't want to be ungrateful,' I say, meanly. I am being ungrateful and I know it, but I don't know why.

'If you'd have *said*,' he says.

'I shouldn't have to *say*,' I say; and we go on like that, me upping the ante with every declaration, until I am furious, and Theo is – well, Theo is at best mildly irritated. He is preternaturally calm for someone who is dealing with such an ingrate. *He is so calm*, I think. Why is he so calm and nice? Why is this so calm and nice?

Suddenly all I want is to pop Theo's little bubble of niceness. *Life isn't like this,* I think. *Life isn't rivers and trains and treasure hunts. Why doesn't he know that?*

I am overwhelmed, suddenly, by everything. It's all too nice.

The sky is too blue. We're all too soft. If something bad comes –
when something bad comes – we will not be ready. We have –
I have – been lazy in my happiness; in my stupid hopefulness.
I have been the grasshopper who sang all summer. This isn't
life: I know life, and it isn't this. It can't be this. If it's this, what
have I been doing all this time? And why should I have it, and
not somebody else? Why should I get to be here, out drinking
champagne in the sun with this nice man? It makes no sense:
none of it makes sense, and I stare out of the window and wish
I were still in the dark.

At the station, Theo and I part ways. He kisses me a trifle
warily, as if I'm a stray cat that might scratch. Which is fair.

'I'll call you tonight,' he says, and I nod, and he says, cheerfully:
'Eat something, won't you?'

And I want to hiss like the cat again. He waves as if nothing
is wrong, and gets on the bus for the long ride back to his.

When I get home, I slam into the kitchen and start dragging
things out of the fridge. How can this be a meal? Sausages. Green
beans. There's potatoes, but I don't want mash. I want bright and
fierce and sharp. I want something to cut through this feeling: this
something. I want to break something, and so I break into a jar of
XO sauce I have been saving for something special.

XO sauce is neither a sauce, nor made with XO: it's dried
shrimp and cured ham and chillies and garlic and that red rich
oil that stains everything it touches. I want to stain things and
break things. I turn the heat up high; put the skillet over it until it
smokes; stab the sausages down the middle like a serial killer and
squeeze out their soft, pork-mince insides. I want to sizzle things
until they nearly burn; too much garlic, too much ginger. I want
sour and char and salt. Bite and fury.

'What's eating *you*?' Jo says, as I bang the dishes down on the
table. We eat, and I tell her; and then I burst into tears, and we sit
like that for a long time, Jo tucking the leopard blanket around my
shoulders, the velvet cushions (pink and teal and gold) propping
us up, with her hands stroking my hair.

'If it helps' she says, 'this is very delicious...'

And she's right: it is, and it does. $\longrightarrow$

For 2

350g fine green beans

2 tsp sesame oil

4 garlic cloves

10cm ginger (*a big bit! you need about 2 tbsp grated*)

3 shallots

3 tbsp XO sauce

2 tbsp fermented black beans (*Lao Gan Ma brand is easy to get and very delicious*)

200g pork mince (*if you want to use sausages, remove the skins and crumble the meat*)

2 tbsp Shaoxing rice wine

2 tbsp soy sauce

Sesame seeds, chopped chives and chopped spring onions, to serve

The trick here is in the heat of the pan. I use a basically dry skillet, to get the beans to shrivel and blister and scorch. A wok would be perfect here, if I had one, or if you have one.

Start with the beans: take your skillet (or, as I say, your wok) and a splash of sesame oil. Set it over a very high heat. Turn on your extractor fan and open the window – which is always sensible when stir-frying. I used to hate stir-frying, for reasons unknown, but this really sold me on it.

When the oil is so hot it's practically jumping, add the beans. Shake, shake, shake, until they're coated in the oil; turn down the heat to medium and cook for 15 minutes (stirring occasionally to sear each side against the hot pan) or until tender.

While the beans are cooking, grate the garlic, ginger and shallots on the fine side of a box grater. Not the mad tiny one that nobody knows how to use, but the next one up. Set aside.

When the beans are tender, tip them out into a bowl and return the pan to the heat. Add the grated aromatics, and the remaining sesame oil, and fry until just golden. Watch it: it will want to burn.

Stir in the XO sauce and fermented black beans, and fry those too. Turn up the heat, add the mince and fry until it is very brown and even a little crispy. Add the rice wine and soy sauce, and let them cook off until the pan is fairly dry.

Beans back in. Stir, stir, stir. Serve: sesame seeds, chives and spring onions on top.

Fish Pie

I wake up afraid.

It's been a long time since I woke up afraid like this: afraid of the blue sky outside, afraid of the heavy tomato harvest still tumbling from the vines, afraid of everyone and everything. The news isn't bad, exactly, but it's going to be a hard winter; and I'm afraid of that too.

So I cook. It's been a long time since I woke up afraid; and a long time since I cooked like this, therapeutic and absorbing. Mostly I cook for fun now, or because I'm hungry – but today I'm cooking for the rhythm of it, and the comfort of it at the end. I cook because it's my home: it's my safe place.

I make fish pie, which my mother used to make a lot when we were kids; and I make it fancy because I can. Thinking about fish pie is always soothing, and as I plan it through in my mind I feel better already.

Think about buttery mashed potato, crisped under the grill until browned, the cheese on top bubbling; think about soft white fish, flaking off the fork; think about tender morsels of salmon and the tiny little treat of a prawn. Think about the green wisps of spinach and tendrils of leek twirled around a fork, and rich, savoury white sauce. Think about how much better you'll feel for a good meal; think *nourishing*, think *soothing*, think *safe*.

I poach the fish – some smoked, some white – in milk infused with clove and shallot; the trimmings from the fennel and leek thrown in too. The rest of the fennel and leek softened in butter with more shallots. I steep a pinch of saffron in some of the milk; melted butter and flour, thickening together, with the poaching liquor and cheese beaten in to make a rich, salty, savoury, sauce. A little white wine, if I have it. Everything folded back into the sauce, gently, gently, in the tray I'll bake it in: sometimes a round copper pan, but today I think two little blue and white enamel dishes, one for now, and one for later; and on top potatoes mashed to creamy perfect smoothness with butter and mustard. More cheese for the top, then into the oven until all the little points of potato bronze and bubble. It's contentment, this. Just thinking it through is good; and eating it is even better. ⟶▷

Serves 8, or 4 hungry people who would like leftovers and seconds

3 shallots

5 cloves

1 fennel bulb

1 small leek

500ml milk

Big pinch of saffron

2 tbsp butter

200g spinach (*not baby leaf, if possible, as it wilts less nicely*)

50ml white wine (*if you have it*)

500g mixed fish (*I literally just buy fish pie mix*)

150g peeled prawns (*cooked or uncooked*)

2 tbsp plain flour

2 tsp Dijon mustard (*optional*)

125g + 25g grated Cheddar

For the mash

4 big potatoes

1 tbsp butter

2 tsp Dijon mustard

25ml milk (*if needed*)

- -

Start by infusing the milk: peel one of the shallots and stud it like a pomander with the cloves. (Five is an arbitrary number, as spice measurements often are, but it's as good as any. Four, six. How clove-y do you clove?) Take the green parts of the fennel and leek, then rinse them thoroughly (especially the leek, because mud hides in leeks). Put the studded shallot and the green bits of fennel and leek, into a large saucepan. Pour over the milk and bring to a simmer over a medium-low heat, then cover the pan, turn off the heat and leave to infuse while you do everything else.

Take a teaspoon of the warm milk from the pan, and put it in an egg cup with the saffron. Let sit. (A lovely instruction. Why does nobody ever say 'Ella, let sit'? I would love to be let sit.)

Dice the rest of the leek and the rest of the fennel very, very finely. No, finer than that. Chop them down to nothing, a fine and translucent heap. Chop the last two shallots, too, just the same.

Add the butter to a large frying pan (I do have one of those, you will be glad to hear) and gently, over a low heat, melt the butter and sauté the diced leek, fennel and shallots. Sauté them very gently, until even softer and smaller and more translucent:

SEPTEMBER

20 minutes, stirring, stirring. (Have a glass of white wine here. Why not?)

Peel and chop the potatoes; and boil as usual (start from cold – it's a root vegetable!) until so soft you can smush them with a spoon. Drain, then add a full tablespoon of butter (shut up) and the mustard. Mash, mash, mash. You know how to mash. Add the 25ml milk slowly, if you need it – you want the mash to be fairly sturdy, but silky. You get it.

Add the spinach, rinsed, to the frying pan – along with a splash of white wine if you have it – and cook until the spinach has wilted down to almost nothing, and the liquid has reduced. Spinach will take up so much space if you don't wilt it ahead of time; and it makes everything else sort of watery. Doing it like this means you can reduce the water away.

Go back to your saucepan of infused milk and, with a slotted spoon, lift out the shallot, leek and fennel tops and chuck them away. Bring the milk back to a gentle simmer. Add the fish – and the prawns, if uncooked – and simmer for 5 minutes. Remove the now-poached fish to a bowl; add the prawns to the bowl, if you're using cooked ones.

Remember that egg cup of saffron? Add that to the pan of milk and stir well.

Pre-heat the oven to 180°C.

Now turn your attention back to the frying pan: scatter in the flour and stir to thicken. You don't want to see any white specks at all. Very slowly, add the milk, stirring all the time. You're making, basically, a white sauce, but one infused with vegetables and saffron and flavour. Stir, stir, stir. Low heat. It will thicken, I swear to you. Stir, stir, stir. Add the mustard, if using, and the 125g of cheese, and stir until smooth.

Gently fold in the fish and prawns, then gently spoon the whole lot into your baking vessel of choice. Top with the mash and the 25g of cheese and bake for half an hour, or until everything is bubbling through the mash like a ready meal in an advert.

Chicken Soup

When the feeling persists – the bad feeling persists – there is only one way out. The way is chicken soup.

I'm wary, now, of saying anything can be cured. I don't know if life works that way. But if anything could be cured, perhaps this soup might do it.

Make it slowly; cup it in your hands; breathe in the steam. Shred the meat from the bones, and slice your onions, and cry if you want to. It's completely fine.

No: that's a lie. Nothing is ever fine. 'Fine' is just the thing you say when someone asks you how you are, and you don't know how to tell them that everything is beautiful and everything is terrible and everything is happening all at once.

What I mean, I suppose, is that you are allowed to cry while you make this soup. It might even be encouraged.

You start (again you start, where else is there to start?) with a carcass.

A **chicken carcass**: you start with a roasting tin full of bones, you start with the end of the meal before.

You don't get a clean slate, or a blank canvas here: nobody does. All you can do is work with what you have.

What you have is bones; what you have is a body.

What you have you can use.

You fill the kettle as high as it can go, and set it to boil. You take a big enamel casserole, or some large pot with a lid, and set it on the hob over a low heat. You put some butter in it: not too much, not too little. **A piece of butter**.

You rummage through the fridge, find **an onion and a bendy carrot and some yellowing celery**. One carrot, no more; two carrots make it too sweet. You chop them as fine as you can, and throw them into the butter. Stir, stir, stir. Do you have some **rosemary**? Some **thyme**? Maybe you inexplicably have a **bay leaf** and you put that in too, even though nobody really knows if bay leaves do anything or not. $\longrightarrow$

→ You stir the vegetables in the butter for a moment or two. Grind over a **little pepper**. **No salt**.

The kettle bubbles fiercely and clicks off, to show it's done. The chicken bones you tip into the casserole. The boiling water you pour, carefully, into the roasting tin, and you scrape it with a spatula to free the caught-on, sticky, charred bits of fat and flesh.

You then pour the water, shimmering with oil like a beautiful dirty river, from the roasting tin into the casserole, where it hisses at you. It does not cover the bones.

You pour more **boiling water** into the roasting tin, and you scrape again, and you pour again into the casserole.

You do it again; you do it for the third time, and this time the water is almost clear and barely shining at all.

You throw in any **Parmesan rinds** you have.

You cover the casserole, and you leave it for a long time on the heat: you let the stock simmer, rise, come together for hours. You listen to the rain and the sound of somebody else's fingers typing.

You listen to the dishwasher churning away. You notice how the rain hits the kitchen window on a diagonal, and barely hits the window by the sofa at all. From the sitting room you might not notice it was raining at all. There are orange roses in the mug on the coffee table; last night's candles are short and squat with burning, and there is a little pool of set wax around their bases – and if you were another kind of person, you might worry about how to get it off the table. But you're not, so you don't. And the steam that fills the room is of chicken and onion and thrift and butter; and the steam that clouds the rain on the kitchen window is of making something out of nothing, the way it used to be in the old house, when it was another someone typing long ago; and the whole house smells like someone trying to make something better: like somebody making a home.

Take your tea to the sofa, and sit there, and try and say the right things. *It might be ok? It might turn out all right? Next year, next year*, you say, like the old rhyme. *This year, next year, sometime, never*, and just hope against hope that it's not never. *Next year in Jerusalem*, like Zelda says. Next year, it might be ok. Outside it's getting dark. Outside, all across the world, people are talking like this. In every house someone is crying, or wanting to cry, and what can you say? What can you even say, except that you're lucky, in the grand scheme of things, because you're still here, and – thank God for that – the chicken soup is simmering on the stove?

After four hours, maybe, you dice another **onion and a couple of garlic cloves, another carrot and another rib of celery**, more carefully this time. You cut **a couple of potatoes** into little cubes. You shred **a little leftover chicken**, if you have it, but not if you don't. You pull the **soft parts of some wilting, ancient kale** from the tough ribs and shred that, too. You drain **a tin of the smallest white beans you can find** and tip them into a bowl.

You cook, in a little saucepan, **a handful of pasta stars**. You think this is ridiculous. You know this is ridiculous. But to cook the pasta separately gives the soup a golden clearness that you can't resist: a kind of magic. And you're doing magic, here. You're making something from nothing. You're making something to make something better.

And you drain the pasta and add it to the beans. You sauté the onion and garlic and carrot and celery and potatoes for ten minutes, or twenty minutes, until tender. A big saucepan.

You strain the stock from the casserole, and it's golden and beautiful. You add the beans and the pasta, and the chicken, to the onion and garlic and carrot and celery and potatoes. You add, maybe, a few **flecks of thyme; a twist of black pepper**. You add **salt** to taste. You add it all to taste. You add the torn-up kale.

You pour over the stock, and let it simmer for two minutes.

You ladle into bowls; you dot in a little butter, grate over a little **Parmesan**, grind a little more pepper.

And the rain is still falling outside the kitchen window, and you take the bowls of soup to the sitting room, where somebody is still writing, and you both eat it in almost silence, because what could you possibly need to say that isn't in the soup? What could you possibly try to say that would be more than the soup?

October

Apple Crumble Custard Cake Doughnuts

I'm walking through the park (corner shop, yellow church, green hill, pretty hill, heath, wall, rose garden, avenue) and I realise that it's really autumn. While I have been indoors, being afraid of the blueness of the sky, summer has given way entirely overnight. The blackberries that come so early to the coast are also here in London now, and there might be game in the shop, and there is. September slides into October, and the garden is all bronze and deepening green, tomatoes that will never turn to red. There are still little leeks, to be eaten like calçots; still carrots and beetroot. But the courgettes are over; the tomatoes are over; the cucumbers are over.

I am thinking about apples; and that next year (next year! the hope of it!) I'll buy an apple tree. You can't get good apples in London, and this is peak apple time. It's easy in a city supermarket to forget what an apple should taste like, what an autumn should taste like. Sometimes you get that smoke in the air, and remember what things should be; and sometimes you stumble across a farmers' market and pay far too much for an apple that tastes of apples, and remember how things should feel.

I am remembering, this year, how things should feel. How life should feel, even in the strangest of times; how it feels to be alive, and how it feels to be a person, vulnerable and afraid and *attached*. I am attached to my garden; I am attached to Jo; I am attached to Mitski, transient nameless neighbour cat that she is; and I am attached to Weetabix, the kitten with the fastest heart in the world; and I am attached – stupidly attached, dangerously attached, all-in attached – to Theo. *Don't fall in love, or anything –* but how can anyone help it?

And so – because of all this, the autumn, the apples, the falling in love – I make doughnuts.

I make these with apple cider, like American funfair doughnuts, and with custard creams, and Bird's custard powder (pink, chalky). Things that feel silly and good and easy, and even though there are several steps to these doughnuts, the whole thing feels silly and good and easy too.

Start with a doughnut: baked not fried, and cake batter instead of yeast dough (because I hate deep-frying, but don't – these days – mind baking). You'll need doughnut moulds, but you can get them quite cheaply, and they're worth it. You could, I suppose, make these in muffin tins, but it really would miss the point: the feeling of autumn, the feeling of magic, all the fun of the fair.

Beat custard powder into the batter, a trick inspired by the magnificent Benjamina Ebuehi, who was inspired by custard tarts: an *Inception* of pudding, a babushka of dessert. Reduce cloudy apple juice to something almost like American cider, fresh and sweet and sharp – something like an essence of an apple, something like *distilled* – and beat that in too, loosening the batter and sharpening it down. Make a brown-butter custard glaze and a smashed-biscuit streusel-style crumble; dip the doughnuts into the former, then the latter.

'It tastes like autumn, if autumn wasn't my enemy,' Jo says, looking out at the rain, her cup of tea in her hands, and I agree with her.

Makes 12–14 doughnuts

200g butter

For the crumble

60g plain flour
15g light soft brown sugar

For the doughnuts

2 large eggs
240ml cloudy apple juice
250g plain flour
75g golden caster sugar
75g light soft brown sugar
2 tbsp custard powder

2 tsp baking powder
$\frac{1}{2}$ tsp bicarbonate of soda
$\frac{1}{2}$ tsp grated nutmeg
$\frac{1}{2}$ tsp ground cinnamon

For the glaze

150g golden icing sugar
3 tbsp custard powder
1 tsp ground cinnamon
1 tsp grated nutmeg
1 tsp vanilla extract
50ml milk

Start by melting the butter to make 145g brown butter. Weigh out 45g of the brown butter for the crumble and the glaze.

Make the crumble now, so it's done: 30g of the weighed-out brown butter, plus the flour and sugar. Rub together to form crumbs. Crumble. You get it. Tip onto a baking sheet and put aside for now.

For the doughnuts, pour the remaining 100g of brown butter into a bowl and let it cool slightly, so it won't cook the eggs. Add the eggs and beat together.

Measure out the apple juice into the same buttery pan, then simmer to reduce by half and get 120ml of...strong apple juice.

Pre-heat the oven to 180°C.

Mix together all the dry ingredients, then add the reduced apple juice and the buttery eggs and mix to a smooth batter. (Stand mixer, or strong arms plus wooden spoon.)

Pour into silicone doughnut moulds – be generous! – and bake both the doughnuts and the set-aside crumble for 20 minutes, until a skewer comes out clean from the doughnuts and the crumble is golden. (You may have to break the crumble into crumbs, which is fine.)

Set the doughnuts on a cooling rack. It's important that they are cool before you glaze them – which is great, as it gives us time to make the glaze.

In a bowl big enough to hold a whole doughnut, whisk together the icing sugar, custard powder, cinnamon and nutmeg. Add the vanilla, and stir; add the last 15g of brown butter, and stir. Very slowly, add the milk: you might not need it all – you're looking for a thick, shiny, doughnut-glaze-y consistency.

When the doughnuts are completely cool, dip them slowly into the glaze, one at a time. One half – the bit you hold – stays plain. The glaze goes on the top. If you sort of twist your wrist as you do it, like when you're opening a jar, it will make you feel like a professional. A professional...doughnut glazer. Also, it gets rid of the excess glaze and adds a nice flourish. Dip the glazed doughnut into the tray of crumbs. Repeat with the rest of the doughnuts. Autumn, but nice.

Quadruple Carb Soup

Are chickpeas carbs? They might not be, but they feel like carbs in my soul. This soup has pasta, potatoes and chickpeas in it. If you serve it with warm bread, which you should, it's a quadruple carb. Lean in. Lean all the way in. It is about half carbs, half very best olive oil, and if that doesn't float your boat, I don't know what to tell you. There's some stock in there, too, and also a Parmesan rind for extra flavour. It's rich and deep and complex, and not even that much faff to make; it's the kind of soup you can give to people who don't love soup and they will love it.

It is, essentially, a variant on *pasta e ceci*, pasta and chickpeas. This is technically a classic Italian dish – or would be if it wasn't so inauthentic. Whatever that's supposed to mean.

This recipe is properly made with dried soaked chickpeas and fresh pasta. You know I will never be the kind of person who can both remember to put beans in to soak *and* take them out again. For me it's tins all the way. Tins, plus lasagne sheets, wrapped in a tea towel and smashed on the kitchen surface, act as *maltagliati*: a pasta shape perfect for this soup that means, simply, 'badly cut'.

You do need a blender of some kind, but other than that it's just oil, aromatics, potato, chickpeas, stock, oil. One pan, plus a jug for blending in. Back in the pan; pasta in to cook. A doddle. A delicious, inauthentic, deeply comforting doddle. Also, surprisingly pretty.

And so we eat this, Jo and I, in the autumn of a world that feels more impossible to plan for than ever, and it's so good.

For 4

4 tbsp extra virgin olive oil

2 garlic cloves

3 sprigs of rosemary

2 medium potatoes

2 shallots

1 rib of celery

1 tsp tomato purée

600g chickpeas (*1 tall jar!*)

1.2 litres vegetable stock

1 Parmesan rind

4 dried lasagne sheets

1 tbsp chilli oil or
 2 tsp chilli flakes

30g Parmesan

Start by warming the olive oil with the whole peeled garlic cloves and the rosemary. Gently infuse them together, in a heavy saucepan over a low heat. Lower than that. Your lowest possible. Bring them up to warm, then switch off the heat and leave to infuse, while you get on with peeling the potatoes and chopping the (now-peeled) potatoes, shallots and celery. Fine, fine, fine.

By the time you've finished dicing them nice and small, knife to the board, over and over like a little meditation, you can tip them straight into the oil, and stir. Is there a nicer smell than frying shallots? Stir to coat everything in the lovely scented oil. You might have to turn the heat up here, but not too high. A medium flame, let's say, at most. I trust you. If it seems like anything is catching, turn it down. Just watch it, and it will be ok.

Cook for 10–15 minutes, then add the tomato purée and stir. Add the chickpeas –and, if jarred, their liquid. (If using tinned, drain and rinse. I don't know why this difference occurs, but it just does.) Stir again.

Add the stock (obviously I use boiling water and a stock cube mostly) and Parmesan rind, and bring to a simmer, then cover and cook for 20 minutes.

Are the potatoes soft now? Bingo. Decant half of the soup into a jug, fish out the Parmesan rind, and – using a hand blender – blitz the jugged half into a fine, smooth purée. (You can chew on the Parmesan rind, in the kitchen, in private. It is so delicious and mildly shameful.)

Reintroduce the blitzed soup to the rest of the soup in the pan and stir to combine. Warm some bread, or make toast; wrap the lasagne sheets in a clean tea towel and smash them vigorously with a rolling pin or your hands. (Do not be tempted to use your bare hands on dried lasagne sheets, because it actually hurts quite a lot.) Smash to shards; add the shards to the soup. Cook for 10 minutes.

Decant into bowls. Drizzle over the chilli oil, or sprinkle over the chilli flakes, and grate with Parmesan.

Jacket Potato Garlic Soup

Jo wants to know if jacket potato soup is even a thing.

It's a thing, I tell her; and then, when we're eating (deep and smoky, salty and soothing; toasties on the side) she's silent for the whole time. She doesn't even turn the telly on; even when I ask. Silence, from Jo, is the greatest compliment she can pay a meal.

'How did you even *think* of this?' she says, slowly, afterwards, her bowl perfectly clean.

And it's kind of a long story, this one, but I tell her anyway: it's raining, and we've got nowhere else to be.

There was a time in my life when I was not really seeing many of my friends.

This was when Jo was living far away; and we were different to each other then anyway.

I was seeing Nancy, but mostly at midnight (climbing into bed beside her; letting her feed me snippets of takeaway) – and almost nobody else. Otto and Beezle, too, of course. Danny had gone to Scotland by then. Rosa had just had a baby. Georgie came to the hospital once; Hazel once, too; Freddy a few times; a few others once or twice. Jim was not himself by then, and I was very lonely. The drama of Jim's dying had faded into a kind of long-term, slow decay that was hard to help; and hard to watch.

Occasionally somebody I loved would turn up and drag me outside for some air, and I would say nothing of interest, and then they would go away again. I assume this is what happened: they remember it, my friends, but I have only hazy memories. Trauma is sometimes self-cleaning, like an expensive oven: and I remember almost nothing of this bit.

What I do remember, however, is this soup. I remember this soup, and the person who brought it to me: she was a barista, at a café called Ask For Janice in Farringdon, and she had a face I found very soothing, and she was also very soothing generally. I would turn up nearly every day, and cry on the big leather sofa there, under a heat lamp, like an ailing plant. And after a while I would order soup, and she would ask me small gentle questions, and it would be the only time in my whole day when anybody would talk to me. Oh, other people would say things to me, or to a person who looked like me, but nobody was talking to me: they were talking to a person who was managing a *crisis*, a person who was *handling it all very well, all things considered,* a person who was – in some ways – not real. They were talking to (alternately) a problem, or a solution: they were talking to a tedious and tricky part of their professional lives unaccountably in the shape of a person. They were not talking to me.

I didn't mind this, you know? It wasn't anyone's fault. I didn't have anything to say to my real people; and nobody had anything to say to the pretend person I was being. It was just how it had to be for a bit. But it was lonely.

And then I would go and order soup. It was a roasted garlic soup, and it came with a Gruyère toastie, and a tiny little tin with a sliding lid, and in the tin was smoked salt. I would order my soup, and I would talk to the barista. For the sake of this song, let's call her Janice, after the name of the café: I would talk to Janice, often about her clothes, which were very good. I would talk to Janice, and Janice would talk to me, and sometimes we'd talk about the reasons I was crying on a leather sofa in a café, and sometimes we wouldn't, and then I would eat this soup, smoky and buttery and unbelievably comforting. I would dip the toastie in it.

It was the grey end of the year. I remember it rained a lot that year, but maybe that's just pathetic fallacy; and I'd talk to Janice. I don't know how long this went on: not long. Six weeks? Eight weeks?

After that I stopped being in Farringdon so much, and I found a new place to have a lot of feelings. It was a church café, and there was no Janice at that one. There was an earnest vicar, which I liked less – but there were jacket potatoes. There is nothing so perfect as a jacket potato, except possibly an egg. A small bit of God is not so high a price to pay for a jacket potato.

And the other thing was that at least the vicar was talking to me. It was a very bad year, and it was a long time before I talked to my own friends again. Like I say, I didn't have anything human to say. Nothing from the world I'd once loved so much seemed to translate into the world I was now living in, and that was what was so interesting about Janice, and the vicar, and the woman at the church café who made the jacket potatoes: they got through. They said things, and I heard them, and they heard me. And I ate my potato, and my deep, smoky, salty garlic soup, and drank my coffee, and cried in public; and after a while things changed again, and after a while things got better, and I never saw anybody in this story again. I found my friends again, or most of them. ⟶

I found my voice again. I started talking to my real-life people instead of strangers.

And yet they mattered: the vicar, and the jacket potato woman, and Janice especially. They mattered enough that I wanted to tell you about them when I told you about this soup I've been making: this jacket potato garlic soup. I put a lot of butter in it.

I make the toasties, too, but you know how to make a toastie. Use Gruyère, for stringiness. This is the most soothing recipe in this book of soothing recipes, and it turns out to be incredibly easy. It takes time, is all. It takes time. (There's a metaphor for you.)

And if you're ever in Farringdon, you should go and see if Ask For Janice is still there. They were very kind to me once, a long time ago, in a different life.

And that's what I tell Jo, basically, more or less, although she already knows some parts.

'Thanks, Janice,' she says, when I'm done. She clears away the empty bowls; makes two cups of tea; and then she puts *Project Runway* back on, the blanket around us both.

For 4

2 large potatoes	1.5 litres vegetable stock
Olive oil, for drizzling	1 Parmesan rind
Salt	30g grated Parmesan
1 garlic bulb	Black pepper
2 leeks	Few chives
2 shallots	2 tsp smoked sea salt
50g butter	

You know how to make jacket potatoes: rub with oil, salt on the skin, prick with a fork, into a very hot oven, 220°C, 45 minutes. Turn the oven down to 180°C. Slice the top off the garlic bulb, drizzle with oil and wrap in foil. Add the garlic to the oven with the potatoes and cook for a further 45 minutes.

Rinse the leeks well, then cut into tiny papery squares. Slice the shallots into curls. Melt the butter in a biggish saucepan over a low heat. Add the leeks and shallots and fry gently for 20 minutes. Pour in the stock, add the Parmesan rind and bring to a simmer.

Grab the potatoes and garlic from the oven, and – carefully – split the potatoes open, so they will cool slightly.

Squeeze the roasted garlic cloves out of their skins into a food processor, and – using a slotted spoon – add the leeks and shallots. Blitz to a purée, adding the stock a little at a time, then return to the saucepan. Do not attempt to food-process the Parmesan rind. Do not attempt to food-process the potato, it goes disgusting (like glue). Scoop out the soft insides of the potatoes (saving the skins for later) and, using a balloon whisk, stir gently into the soup. If you keep whisking by hand, they will become so smooth and lovely, like the best mash.

Drizzle the potato skins with olive oil, scatter with the grated Parmesan, and return them to the hot oven for 10 minutes to melt the cheese and crisp everything else.

Plenty of black pepper on everything. Chop the chives with scissors, for garnish, and add a splash more olive oil. Smoked salt. Cheesy potato skins as a bonus.

Danny's Bean & Fennel Bake

Danny texts me the recipe for a bean and fennel bake, and I make it instantly, this evening.

I make it instantly for two reasons.

First, because it's perfect. The fennel softens and caramelises a little bit. (Is *caramelises* the right word? It catches on the skillet, the edges of it brown and golden. Let's say *caramelises*.) The beans and the cream make a smooth, rich, buttery sauce, cut through with sweet garlic; and the Parmesan on top is crispy and brittle.

Second, because when Danny tells me I'll like something I always know I will.

There is this very specific joy in having someone who only sends you things you'll like; something they have in their life that they know ought to be in yours. Someone, I suppose, who knows you the way you know yourself, no matter how far away they are, no matter how long it's been. Someone who understands you; which is to say, someone who knows you; which is to say – in this circumstance, anyway – someone who loves you. Family, is what I'm driving at. Real family.

Some families are born; others are made. All of mine have been made.

They say that blood is thicker than water, but the saying really goes: *the blood of the covenant is thicker than the water of the womb*. The promises we make to each other are more than the things we were born into; the people we make things with can be more to us than the people who made us; the thing that keeps us together is choosing, every day, to choose each other. I come from a family made by choice: my father, only a little older than I am now, looking at two small girls and agreeing *forever*. An adoption, a marriage, a choice, and like an adoption and like a marriage, I chose my friends: Jo and Nancy and Otto and Danny. We held on, through the fire, through the storm. We saw death up close in a way we were too young to see, and now we are family.

This is a metaphor, I suppose, but I don't know how else to talk about these love stories without it. 'Friend' doesn't carry the kind of weight I have needed it to bear – it doesn't carry the heft of the burden at all. It doesn't carry the duty, the responsibility, the care. It doesn't carry the love. It's hard to write about this in a way that doesn't feel fragile or melodramatic or saccharine: we don't have the language.

My Jo, whatever she is. Nancy: my sister, my wife. Danny, our collective 'wayward nephew': easier, that way, than explaining the complex intricacies of our gentle co-dependence. A collection of 'aunts', sending hampers and cards and love. Mark, our 'London dad'; and Rosa, who mothered me and fed me fish fingers as she fed her own small daughter. The small daughter – our fairy godchild – drew pictures. 'Maybe you will be worried about being alone now,' she wrote to me carefully, after Jim died. 'But, you are my family and you do not have to be!' This part was underlined twice, in red pen, with a ruler.

The last time I wrote anything, it was a love story. So is this. Every day I cook, and every day I write, the October sun streaming through the glass door onto the kitchen lino, I ring Georgie; kiss Theo; walk with Nancy. Danny texts me from Scotland. *I know you'll like this. You will love this. This is for you.*

I send him a song back, and take dinner through to Jo, the way we do every night; and she sticks on *Project Runway*, the way we do every night, the spoons on the bowls again; and we are – I think– perfectly content. A family; a home; a household. ⟶

For 4

6 garlic cloves

2 sprigs of rosemary

1 lemon

2 tsp fennel seeds

100g breadcrumbs (*optional*)

4 tbsp olive oil

2 x 400g tins of butter beans

100ml double cream

2 big fennel bulbs

100g Parmesan

Black pepper

2 tsp chopped flat-leaf parsley
(*literally just for some colour*)

- -

Finely chop the garlic – I use a very fine grater, actually – and chop the rosemary finely, too. While you've got the grater out, zest the lemon.

In a large heavy oven-proof skillet or frying pan, start by toasting the fennel seeds – and the breadcrumbs, if you're using them (you don't need them, but they are delicious and crunchy). No oil, just heat. Set aside for now.

In the same skillet, gently warm the olive oil. Stir the garlic into the oil to make a rich paste, then add the rosemary and lemon zest. Stir again, and cook for 2–3 minutes to infuse, without letting it burn. If you think it's going to burn, quickly turn off the heat.

Take a spoonful of this infused oil and put it into a food processor with one of the tins of butter beans – the liquid of the beans can go in too. Add the cream and squeeze in the juice of half of the lemon. Blitz until it is as smooth as you can get it, then set aside.

Take the fennel and separate the green fronds from the white bulbs; save the fronds for later. Slice the bulbs vertically, to give you long, chunky strips of fennel (you can kind of use the lines of the bulb as a guide). Tip the fennel into the lovely garlic-lemon-rosemary scented oil and stir to coat. Let it cook slowly, over a medium-low flame, for about half an hour, stirring every now and again – you want it to catch and caramelise a little bit, to soften and brown but still have some texture.

While the fennel is cooking, make the Parmesan crisp topping.

You need to pre-heat the oven to 180°C, and you need a baking tray, baking paper and a round loose-based cake tin with the base removed; the cake tin should be about the same diameter as your skillet. Does that make sense? You're making, basically, a crispy cheese 'lid' for the skillet.

All we do is this: baking paper on the back of the baking tray (you don't want to lift hot cheese over a lip). Cake tin, acting as a barrier, on top of the greaseproof. Finely grate your Parmesan into the circle created by the cake tin, without pressing or pushing it down. Twist all over it with black pepper, then slide the whole thing very carefully into the oven. Bake for 10 minutes, until the cheese has melted and started to bubble like very beautiful gold lace. Remove, without turning the oven off, and leave to cool.

When the fennel is ready, add the other tin of beans to the skillet, and pour over the creamy beany sauce from the food processor. Top with the fennel seeds – and the breadcrumbs, if using. Bake for 15 minutes, then remove and lay the Parmesan crisp over the top. Scatter with the green fennel fronds and parsley. Colour! Instagram! Pictures! God, I'm hungry. More wine, probably.

Pho

If I had to choose – if they made me – I would pick pho.

I would pick pho for everything; for winter cold and summer heat. I would pick Vietnamese food more generally, but pho specifically: rare beef pho, or *pho bo*, a noodle soup with slivers of rare steak and handfuls of beansprouts, hoops of red chilli, tendrils of coriander and Vietnamese basil and mint, a wedge of lime. I find it to be the purest comfort there is. I feel it in my bones – collagen-rich stock, a glossy layer of golden fat on the surface, noodles unfurling one from the other in the heat of the broth.

When you order it takeout, the beef cooks, a little, in the broth; you add it yourself, with the noodles, from a little plastic container. You add the herbs and beansprouts from a plastic bag, and you eat it from the cardboard tub it comes in. I order Vietnamese food for celebration and commiseration; I treat it like Madame Champagne treated champagne. Happy, sad, tired, wired, lonely, in company: there is pho.

There is nothing, it feels, that pho can't heal. I know this to be untrue – categorically and unchangeably – but I feel it nonetheless: I feel there is some magic in bones simmered for so long; in the deep, rich, gold broth there's no real shortcut toward.

And so Theo and I make this pho on the kind of Saturday where it feels like everything is in a movie: the first days of autumn, the artsy farmers' market open, the leaves, the wind. I borrow a jumper. It's thick red wool, with a kind of burnished dark underlay that makes it shine. When I was sixteen I borrowed my stepmother's Chanel nail polish and spilt it down the inside seam of my dad's denim shirt. I still have the shirt, though not the stepmother, and the nail polish – Rouge Noir – is the same colour as this jumper.

We walk along the canal, which I used to know, the way I never really know any other geography; I recognise it all like it's still, somehow, home. At the expensive butcher's I commit fully to flirting with the butcher – or rather, to the kind of expansive and intentional listening that people mistake for flirting, and is in fact a sincere desire to really *learn*. Tell me what to buy, I tell the butcher, who sells us a bag of bones, a piece of beef bigger than an outstretched palm, and two sirloin steaks. We buy onions, coriander, a piece of ginger as thick as a marrowbone. It's colder $\longrightarrow$

than I expected; last week we were still in shorts, bare legs, and now these tights are too thin and this borrowed jumper is everything. At home I char an onion and the ginger over the open flame of the gas hob; blanch the bones in cold water; toss garlic, cinnamon sticks, star anise and coriander seeds into the slow cooker. Weetabix the cat pads around me, curious, and while I'm blanching the bones I beat condensed milk, cream and kalamansi juice into a thick quasi-custard and freeze it, for ice cream later.

I stack blanched bones and shins in the belly of the slow cooker, like Tetris; turn this bone that way, and tuck the onion down between the ribs; slide the fat disc of shin across the top like a lid, voilà! Tetris! I've never played Tetris, but I've packed enough complicated suitcases to understand the metaphor. Theo plays a little riff on the guitar, and I pour cold water over the bones and set the slow cooker for twenty-four hours. I'll still be here in twenty-four hours, which is a promise, which is new. In twenty-four hours we'll spoon out this broth over noodles and the second of the two seared steaks, scatter over green coriander and spring onion and fiery little needle chillies. In twenty-four hours, we will still be here; nothing more pressing will have come upon us. No coolness will have come upon us but the weather. Tomorrow is ours: we have committed to it with this broth.

Tomorrow, pho, or some inauthentic, Googled, cobbled-together version of it I can make at home in London; and tonight, with me still wearing this borrowed jumper, we'll eat the first steak and he'll fry chips in the way that scares me. *Some things he does make me so nervous*, I think, which is nearly a line from a poem. And, as ever, when there comes a point of comparison between the living and the dead, the last and the now, the then and the here, I stumble a little and can't believe my luck: to be here, to be alive, when so much is dead. So much of my old life didn't make it to today, and yet, somehow, I did.

I used to think that poem about somebody else, long ago, in the same way I used to make this pho for somebody else, long ago. I made it in the dying days, in every sense, of a great love. And now I'm making it in these early days of this maybe, this might be; and even as I'm thinking this and writing it, I know that if I'm quoting Rebecca Lindenberg and if I'm making slow-cooker, twenty-four-hour, expensive-butcher pho; and if I'm doing it in his jumper, red as stolen nail polish, those *maybes* and those *might bes* are all just a little bit moot. For the next twenty-four hours, at least. And I find that, while I am still afraid – so frightened of this new bright hope and stupid happiness – it's easier, somehow, to be afraid in a house that's heavy with ginger and spices, where the air sings of something faraway, of star anise, and the rich gold fat we've panned for in the marrow of the bones. $\longrightarrow$

This honestly makes so much soup: 2 big bowls, and then 2 big Tupperwares for the freezer. There is no point making it in smaller portions because it takes forever. Serves, probably, 8; or rather 1 on 8 separate occasions.

2.5kg beef (*mostly brisket, some oxtail if brave, bones if even braver*)

4 black cardamom pods

4 star anise

2 cinnamon sticks

1 tbsp coriander seeds

6 cloves

1 long strip of orange peel

1 large white onion

150g ginger

4 garlic cloves

40ml fish sauce

2 tbsp brown sugar

500g dried rice noodles

400g sirloin steak (*optional*)

To serve

Coriander

Thai basil

Mint

Red chillies

Spring onions

Beansprouts (*if you like them, which I do not*)

(*Get a normal-sized bag of each thing; use as much or as little as you like. I trust you to know how much coriander you like. I like lots, he likes none, she likes some. You know?*)

- -

For this one, you'll need a big saucepan to blanch the bones and oxtail, and a slow cooker. So let's start with the blanching. Take that saucepan, add the bones and oxtail, cover with cold water and bring to the boil. Boil for about a quarter of an hour, horrible grey scum rising to the surface all the time, then drain the water, including the scum, and rinse everything else off. Much nicer.

Pack the blanched bones and oxtail into the belly of the slow cooker, and scatter over the spices and aromatics: cardamom, star anise, cinnamon sticks, coriander seeds, cloves, orange peel.

Char the onion and ginger (tongs, turn on the gas to the highest flame, hold them there until they blacken), then add to the slow cooker. Add the garlic cloves, whole but peeled. Cover with cold water, and flick the slow cooker on to low. Cover, and go away. Go away for, I don't know, 12 hours.

Taste it. How is it? Is it amazing? This rich beef stock is amazing already, but it's only going to get better, and so are you.

Slide the brisket into the slow cooker, and go away again.

Come back after another 12 hours. I don't know how to describe this moment, but it is sort of like a genuine miracle. Everything has fallen apart. Everything is nothing. Everything is glossy with fat and golden and deep and dark, and everything heals.

Use a slotted spoon to remove the brisket, and any other delicious fragments of meat. Set them aside.

Strain everything else through a sieve into a huge heatproof bowl. (Do not forget what you are doing and absentmindedly drain this elixir of a broth into the sink. That is the worst feeling of all time, I can confirm – and I have seen a person die. It's that sense of total waste; of pointless, stupid, lost time.) Carefully pour the broth back into the slow cooker. Stir in the fish sauce and brown sugar. Taste again. More sauce, more sugar, maybe.

Return the fragments of meat to the broth and add the noodles, then cook until the noodles are soft: 4–8 minutes, depending on brand (check the packet).

Chop the herbs, chillies and spring onions; rinse the beansprouts. Sliver the sirloin steak, if using, ready to slip into the hot broth and cook there.

Serve with everything: bring bowls of herbs to the table, plus the chillies, spring onions and beansprouts. Feel the collagen, the iron, the hours of time in every golden spoonful. It can't cure you of anything, this soup, but it might save you just long enough to get you to the next story in ways you can't yet imagine.

November

White Bean Soup

There is ice on the lake, and I'm glad I have soup on the way.

The day I knew the flat had to be given up – the Tiny Flat, I mean, where I lived with Jim – I walked the length of the canal down to the park. In the park was a café where I had spent a lot of time writing, on the edge of a lake, and on the day it became clear it was all over, the lake was frozen, all the way frozen.

It was half a year before Jim died, but I knew then he would never come home: no matter how much pho I made for collagen, how many little hearts I skewered and dates I simmered. There was nothing else to do. I had been in the Middle East with my parents, learning to see clearly, for six weeks. Jim had been taken by his mother to a nursing home in his hometown.

The word *home* had lost all meaning by then anyway; our household was divided, and so, I suppose, we had stopped being family. For so long we had insisted, then, even without a wedding, even without a shared tenancy, that we were united. *We are different*, we said; *we are special*. But then he had lost the ability to speak – and, with it, to think clearly – and that was that.

All we had had, for so long, was words; and then we lost those too. It made me see, all over again, the power of them. The power of saying, out loud, what it is you need; and the clear, sharp hope that someone will listen.

And then we lost them, and that was that: he was never coming home again, and I knew it. We all knew it. Which meant that the flat had to be given up, and our possessions divided, and the chapter closed. It was that night that Jo and I went out dancing; that night she came home with me to that Tiny Flat, where everything was in boxes; that night we knew we would build a life out of all of this.

And now I am waiting for Theo to finish work, and if you walk the other way from Theo's house along the canal – almost to the old flat – you come to the café. I buy a bowl of soup, and wait. I haven't been here since the worst day. This used to be mine; this used to be my home turf, my place.

They say you can't jump in the same river twice, but you can meander along the same canal some years later and find the same soup at the end of it. The air is icy, and the sun is bright, and the sky is very clear. The light is just the same. If everything fell away

– the benches, the pavilion, the people – the light would fall on the water just the same, and I find that intensely comforting. The light is not of us; it does not come from us; it exists alone, and isn't that a joy? Isn't that mad and lovely? The light remains.

My soup arrives, and – shortly after I finish it – so does Theo.

'I love this place!' he says, delighted that I love it too. He eyes my empty bowl; affects a *Withnail and I* voice. 'Why didn't I get any soup?'

There might be a time, I think, *when I could tell you everything that this place has been to me. You wanted to know everything, and maybe I could tell you.*

But instead I say, 'Buy your own soup, cheapskate.'

'Let's go home,' he says. 'Let's go see that cat.'

'Home,' I agree. Because if there's one thing I've learned, it's that home is where the heart is, and your heart can be everywhere at once. Home is what you make it, where you make it. 'I'll make you this soup sometime. If you're lucky.'

You soak the beans; you make the bread; buy two plump lamb shanks, and sear them brown and crisp, then simmer them slowly with beans and the very best olive oil, golden and glossy, and rosemary and bay, deep stock (chicken, probably, but lamb if you can get it), white wine and a whole bulb of garlic, smashed and papery and left as broken cloves, infusing, and the fats mingling into the broth, and turning it gold-spattered, like a Christmas picture. After a long time, two hours, three, the meat starts to fall from the bone into shreds and tangles; the beans are soft as butter; you toss in diced potato, and then, just before the end, cavolo nero, simmered until bright green in the broth. Crusty bread, with more oil. A little salt, some chilli flakes, maybe. A spoon, a bowl, the cold sunshine. It is, I am bound to say, even better the next day: one of those rare meals that is a joy to reheat. A splash of water. A stir. Some things take time; and some things are worth remembering; and some things are worth revisiting: a frozen lake, disgruntled coots, a bowl of soup, and the light, which is forever and unchanging.

'I'm lucky,' Theo says, very simply, and then he takes my arm and we walk back along the canal.

Home, or something like it. $\longrightarrow$

For 4

150g dried haricot beans

3 litres cold water

6 tbsp + 3 tbsp olive oil

2 carrots

1 small fennel bulb

1 leek

1 big garlic bulb

2 lamb shanks

500ml white wine
(*flat prosecco!*)

500ml double-strength
lamb stock (*I make
it from 2 stock cubes*)

2 big sprigs of rosemary

A few thyme leaves

1 bay leaf

Black pepper

250ml boiling water
(*if needed*)

The night before, soak the beans in plenty of water in an enormous pan. They will look very small in the big bowl. Do not be fooled and put them in a smaller pan: beans expand.

(Make some bread; page 96.)

The next morning, drain and rinse the fattened beans, then return them to the pan. Cover with 3 litres of cold water and bring to the boil. After 10 minutes, scoop off any horrible foam; 5 minutes after that, scoop off any more horrible foam. Add the 6 tablespoons of olive oil and turn the heat down to a simmer. Simmer for 3 hours, or until the beans are tender. Drain, then rinse. Not difficult, just long.

At some point in that 3 hours, peel your carrots. Dice them, the fennel and the well-rinsed leek. Take every clove from the garlic bulb and crush it with the flat of your knife. In a large cast-iron casserole, warm the 3 tablespoons of olive oil and gently soften the carrots, fennel, garlic and leek. This won't take so long – maybe half an hour?

Pre-heat the oven to 150°C.

When the vegetables are translucent and slippery, push them to one side and toss in the lamb shanks. Brown them against the hot iron, then pour over the white wine and lamb stock. Add the rosemary, thyme and bay leaf. Tradition! Absolutely masses of black pepper. Don't salt anything yet. Bring to a simmer, then put the lid on and put the whole thing in the oven. Forget about it for 3 hours, whereupon your beans should be ready to add.

(Knock down your bread.)

(Bake your bread.)

Add the beans to the casserole, put the lid back on and set over a low heat on the hob. Give it all a big stir to enliven all the flavours: if it's too thick, add 250ml of boiling water and stir through. Taste for salt; you probably won't need it because of the stock.

Spoon the soup into bowls. (Take the bread from the oven.) Eat.

Cabbage

To fall in love at the end of the world is a dangerous thing. To admit that you're in love, at the end of the world, is more dangerous still.

Dangerous, because it turns out that the world is a hard thing to end; and apocalypses take time. They happen, and keep on happening. The world keeps turning; and it gets better, and then worse again. Just now it's getting worse again. I should feel smug for having predicted it, but I don't. Just afraid, and angry. *Things already happened to me. I gave up so many years to the dying. Why must I now give more?*

I bring the big knife down on the cabbage and split it like a skull.

Stay indoors, stay home, look but don't touch. The same broadcast as in the spring, but without any spark of newness to it: just the winter, and the greyness, and Theo on the other side of town. Can't this bit just be easy? *It's easy if you let it be easy*, Jo says, and I'm trying, but it isn't my fault if everything is hard.

I split the cabbage again, into halves; and then into eighths. It's satisfying, and the inside of the cabbage is lacy and intricate and lovely. There is a poem by my friend Amy Key that starts: *Oh you most beautiful inside of a vegetable!* I say it to the cabbage now, and slide it onto a baking tray, and into the oven, and this – at least – is always easy.

The cabbage is cut into thick wedges with frilly little edges, dressed with honey and balsamic vinaigrette, and roasted until crispy and charred in places, and the tender white heart is slick and falling to tender pieces at the touch of a fork. Think salty and crispy and sticky and sharp and rich and deep. It's not supposed to be a meal; it's supposed to be a side dish, but we're eating it with bread and butter and sweet white wine, and that's all.

'I don't *want* cabbage to be my favourite food,' Jo says, glumly. She's looking at the last piece of cabbage in the blue bowl; it's golden-brown, with blackened edges. It looks like autumn. It smells like honey and smoke and darkness.

'It doesn't have to be,' I say. 'It's not obligatory.' We are sitting at opposite ends of the sofa under the leopard blanket, the bowl between us.

'So,' she says. I can sense the subject change.

'So?'

'So everything,' she says. 'So what are you going to do about Theo?'

'About him?'

'This bad bit is only four weeks now, but...' She gestures at the TV broadcast; the mysterious future; the who-knows-what. This apocalypse is still happening, and there will be more. I know that more than anybody. 'It could be longer,' she says. 'It could be months.'

'I know,' I say.

'So what's the plan?' she says, and suddenly I am in tears again. This was supposed to be the easy time.

'The thing is that I actually do love him,' I say to Jo; and Jo just says, 'I know, pal, I know,' very tenderly, and pushes the last bit of cabbage onto my plate: the ultimate in love.

For 4 (but really 2 will eat it all)

1 small Savoy cabbage	2 tbsp honey
2 tbsp olive oil	1 tbsp flaky sea salt
2 tbsp balsamic vinegar	

Pre-heat the oven to 220°C.

Chop the cabbage into halves, into quarters, into eighths. Eight frilly little wedges, arranged on a baking tray.

Drizzle with oil, and turn over in your hands, to coat.

Drizzle with balsamic, going lengthways (so sort of vertically along the baking tray); and then with honey, widthways (horizontally, I guess?) to form a kind of excellent, sticky crosshatch.

Shake over the salt and roast for 8 minutes. The cabbage might need turning over in the oven, but honestly I mostly don't worry about it, and it's still Jo's favourite thing in the world.

Bourride

When I was in my late teens, I lived briefly in a castle.

You can just do this, I thought; *you can just move to France, and live in a castle!*

The food in the castle was terrible, and so I managed sometimes to take the long, slow bus to Aix. I found an English bookshop there; a café that sold cheap coffee; and a restaurant that sold real Provençal food: bread, and butter, and bourride.

Bourride is a sort of half-soup, half-stew thing: rich court-bouillon (fish stock cooked slow with shallots, celery and herbs), transformed with whisked golden aioli into a creamy, garlicky, smoky, saffron-scented broth, thick and rich and shimmering; and within it little slices of potato, poached in the broth until tender, and plump pink prawns, and fat flakes of ivory cod; and the whole thing poured over a chunky, griddled slice of sourdough bread, buttered and charred, so that it soaks up the sweet, smoky oil and rich, buttery cream. More bread to dunk.

I woke up this morning and knew I wanted to make bourride. I woke up this morning with a feeling: a feeling that something had to happen, a feeling like moving to a castle, or a feeling like running away.

So I lived in this castle on a vineyard, miles from anywhere, where I slept in a dirty little attic, and I worked for a family so strange and so old that, even as it was happening, I thought: *someday I'm going to tell this story*. In the end, I ran away from the castle, to live with Nelius in Paris.

I made a life there; and then I met Jim, and moved to East London, and made a life there too; and then I met Jo, and moved to South London, and made a new kind of life again. And now there is Theo, too. Theo who – for now, for a while, forever, who knows? – is here, and alive, and in my life. I prop the phone against the toaster (Georgie's spot) and call him.

'I am sick of living so far away,' he says, by way of hello. 'I'm sick of not being able to see you. I'm sick of the cat not being able to go outside.'

Weetabix wants – desperately wants – to be an outside cat. He pushes his little honey face against the glass of the doors, twines himself out onto the balcony whenever he slips past Theo.

'Look at him,' Theo says, and holds the phone so I can see. Weetabix is chasing a spider; the spider is on the other side of the window. 'He hates this. I hate this.'

'If you hate it,' I say. I stir the soup, decide if I'm brave enough. 'If you hate it, you should move.'

'Move?' he says.

'Near me,' I say. 'Near us. Near me and Jo, so I can walk to you. So you can come for dinner with us. You should move near me.'

'I should move near you,' he says, and then, as if he's just hearing it for the first time, bright as garlic, sweet as oil: '*I should move near you.*'

'If you wanted,' I say, whisking the aioli. People think aioli is going to be difficult, but it doesn't have to be. You just have to be careful, but not cautious. You can't hesitate too much. You just have to do it.

'I think I want,' he says.

'I want, too,' I say; and I am struck again – as always – by the power of saying, out loud, what it is you want; the bright sweet joy when someone answers, and will give it. ⟶

For 4

¹/₂ white onion +
  ¹/₂ white onion

¹/₂ leek + ¹/₂ leek

¹/₂ fennel bulb +
  ¹/₂ fennel bulb

1 tsp olive oil + 1 tsp olive oil

750ml boiling water

100ml + 100ml white wine

2 fish stock pots

A few sprigs of thyme

115g new potatoes

150g smoked mackerel

150g white fish fillets

120g peeled cooked prawns

Baguette, to serve

For the aioli

3 garlic cloves

3 egg yolks

3 tbsp white wine vinegar

Pinch of salt

250ml olive oil

Lemon juice, to taste

Finely chop one half of the onion, well-rinsed leek and fennel bulb. Most cultures have a three-ingredient base that goes in most things – soffritto, mirepoix, The Holy Trinity – and this might be mine. I am addicted to the bite of fennel, the softness of leek, the sharpness of onion or shallot.

In a heavy saucepan, sauté these three lovely things in a teaspoon of olive oil for 10 minutes. Pour in 750ml of boiling water and 100ml of the white wine, then add the fish stock pots and stir. Thyme in too. This is, basically, an approximation of a court-bouillon, which I know is not the proper way to do things, but I can't get my head around boiling fish heads in a shared flat. So here we are. Let it simmer for perhaps an hour, 90 minutes if you've got it.

For the aioli – it sounds complex but couldn't be easier – grate the garlic into the bowl of a food processor and add the egg yolks, vinegar and salt. With the motor running, gradually drizzle in the olive oil. A little lemon juice, to taste. This is, literally, it: a perfect garlicky mayonnaise that keeps well and can be used for everything you would use mayo for. (We are going to use some of it to thicken the broth, and some of it on bread, for dipping.)

Finely chop the other half of the onion, leek and fennel and sauté them with the other teaspoon of olive oil in a saucepan until soft, about 15 minutes. Add the remaining 100ml of white wine and reduce down by half. This will take about another 15 minutes – and in this time, you should chop the new potatoes into pieces the size of a fingertip.

Strain the fake court-bouillon into a bowl (be careful not to accidentally pour away the precious liquid; you want that!), then pour back into the saucepan. Chuck away the strained-out bits.

Bring your fake court-bouillon to a simmer and add the potatoes. Cook for 5 minutes, then add the fish and prawns and cook for 10 minutes more. Have bowls ready.

Divide the fennel, onion and leek between the two bowls; with a slotted spoon, lift out the fish. Flake the fish (throw away the skin), and divide between bowls. Lift out the potatoes, and divide those between the bowls as well.

A baguette, probably. (Almost certainly a part-bake, given this year.)

Here's the only tricky bit: you need to whisk half of the aioli with all of the broth. The trick to it not splitting is to whisk the broth into the aioli, and not the other way around. So. Put half of the aioli into an empty saucepan (probably the one you sautéed the vegetables in?). A little at a time, and whisking constantly, add the hot broth. A spoonful of broth; whisk until smooth. Repeat, repeat, repeat.

Pour delicious garlicky broth over fish and potatoes in bowls. Spread remaining aioli on hot baguette. Remember a castle, a long time ago, and a story that got you out of there, and a story that brought you here, and brought you home.

Zelda's Stuffing

I have a friend who lives in Norwich, in a tall thin house with a blue door, and coming home to her house is exactly like coming home from boarding school. I have never come home from boarding school, but I imagine it's just like coming home to Julia's: stepping off the London train and into a taxi and through the blue door and into a bath, and a clean nightgown, and crumpets. The nightgowns at Julia's are long and white and cotton, with lace at the neck and the wrists; and the crumpets have honey on them and you eat them in front of the fire, and there is a long, lithe dog like in a medieval painting; and if you're sleeping in Julia's study there is a fire in there too, and books up to the ceiling; and if you're sleeping in the garret there is a little table with a jug of hyacinths, and a little white cat asleep on a horsehair armchair. There is no time at Julia's house: it isn't now, but who knows when?

One year – when? – I went there for Thanksgiving, and I was thankful: confit turkey legs, and a roast turkey crown, and little hot rolls, and clean white napkins, and two kinds of stuffing. I knew about English stuffing, but I did not know about American stuffing, which is – as far as I can see – a kind of unbelievable *pot of stuff*, with many textures and flavours, and I liked it so much I ignored everything else and just ate that. Which is saying something, when you think about how rare and delicious a confit turkey leg is. It's a rogue handful of people that Thanksgiving: Zelda and Teddy from Paris, Georgie from the countryside, me. There are so many absences: Jim, for one; but also Jo, and Nancy, and Nelius, and so many others.

Julia makes drinks; Georgie confits turkey. Zelda makes American stuffing, and says – lifting her glass as she cooks – *Next year in Jerusalem!*

It is a Jewish saying traditionally for Passover, and has a very specific religious and cultural meaning. But when Zelda says it, though, she means: next year it will be ok. Next year we'll *all* be here; and next year we'll all be home again.

This is Zelda's stuffing. It has sausages in it, and also bread, and also apples, and fried sage, and onions, and chicken stock, and eggs. It is sort of soft and fluffy inside, and crispy and sticky and chewy outside. It has every single flavour you want. I cannot imagine how this could be a side dish, ever: it's a main meal, it's a whole dinner all in one. I also cannot imagine how anyone restricts themselves to eating it only at Thanksgiving. Zelda – she who hates *Desert Island Discs* for 'imagined scarcity' – certainly never does.

So now I make Thanksgiving stuffing with Zelda's Passover saying ringing in my ears; and Jo lays the table even though it's just us; and Theo sends me houses where Weetabix could go outside, and Theo could walk over to join us for dinner any night we wanted him to be here. Next month; maybe next year. Soon.

And so that is how I make this stuffing now, thinking of my friends who are so far away – Georgie Julia Zelda Teddy, Nelius Nancy Otto, everyone else besides – and I hope that when I next make this we'll be together again, making stuffing not over Zoom but over the kitchen table at Julia's house, and we'll say *Next year in Jerusalem* whether it's Passover or Thanksgiving or Christmas or whatever occasion we can dredge up from our collective cultural consciousness to celebrate nothing more than being alive, than being here, than having got home somehow. *Next year. Next year in Jerusalem.* $\longrightarrow$

For 4, as a main (not a side)

1 small sourdough loaf

2 tbsp olive oil

Big pinch of salt

1 x 180g packet of pre-cooked
    peeled chestnuts

100g butter

1 Bramley apple

1 big white onion

4 garlic cloves

500g pork sausages
    (*about 1 packet*)

4 sprigs of rosemary

Handful of fresh sage leaves

Black pepper

2 tsp chilli flakes

2 tbsp dry sherry

2 eggs

500ml cool chicken stock
    (*make it up in advance;
    don't do the kettle-stock-cube
    thing or you'll cook the eggs*)

- - - - - - - - - - - - -- - - -- - - - - - - - - - - - - - - - - -

You're going to need a simply enormous bowl. I don't usually list equipment, but really, get a bigger bowl.

Start, first, by tearing your sourdough into chunks. When I say tearing, I mean use a bread knife, because sourdough, as Jo says, is just too sharp. Bite-sized chunks, tossed with the oil and salt, in a roasting tin in the oven. Turn the oven on to 150°C, slide the bread into the oven and let it dry it out while you do everything else.

What happens next here is pretty easy: everything needs chopping, frying in plenty of butter, and putting into that huge bowl. I'm going to give directions, but also, honestly, you don't need me. I'll be here, but you don't need me to be.

Start with the chestnuts: chop them roughly. Melt a bit of the butter – about 15g, for reference, just enough to stop stuff sticking – in a large frying pan. Medium-low flame. Slide in the chestnuts and cook for 4–5 minutes, stirring sometimes.

Peel and chop the apple, next. Tip the buttery chestnuts into your big bowl. Add a little more butter to the same frying pan and fry the apple for about 5 minutes.

Peel and chop the onion, and the garlic. Tip the buttery apple into the big bowl. Add a little more butter to the frying pan and fry the onion and garlic: 10 minutes, maybe? Try not to let the garlic catch, but you can always add more butter and you can always stir some more.

You might want to check the bread here. Is it toasty-looking? Is it a little gold? Grab it out, and add it to the bowl too. You see why it needed to be such a huge bowl.

Roughly chop the sausages next; don't worry too much about their skins. Chuck away any bits of skin that come off, but don't stress about it. You just need to run your knife down the belly of the sausage once, and then chop it into chunks. Some will stay like meatballs, some will disintegrate. It's fine.

Tip the buttery onion and garlic into the big bowl. Add a little more butter to the frying pan and fry the sausage bits for about 10 minutes, until brown, stirring sometimes. You know where this is going: big bowl.

Strip the rosemary leaves from the stems.

This time, add a more generous bit of the butter to the frying pan (big bit!) and let it melt and foam. Turn the heat up, just a little. Add the rosemary and sage leaves – they will sizzle – and cook for 3–4 minutes, letting the sage get a little crispy. Very delicious.

Add all of this to the big bowl, along with lots of black pepper and the chilli flakes.

With the pan still on the heat, add the sherry to deglaze the pan: the steam of the cold booze hitting the hot metal will dislodge all the delicious little burny bits on the bottom of the pan, and then you can scrape it all up with a spoon and tip it into the big bowl too. Do that now.

Stir everything together in your lovely big bowl. (*What a fantastic and very large bowl*, my sister Bee once said, looking at a very large and very old plastic bowl. Really the only thing fantastic about it was the size, but she was so pleased with it, it was worth saying twice. *What a fantastic and very large bowl!* And now it's full of stuffing!)

Turn the oven up to 180°C. Tip everything from the bowl into the roasting tin you dried the bread in, packing it down well. Whisk together the eggs and chicken stock, then pour evenly over the stuffing. Dot with the remaining butter and bake for 40 minutes. Be thankful the whole time. What a fantastic and very large bowl. What a lot of butter. What a year, and thank God we're all still here again.

December

Marmite Crumpet
Cauliflower Cheese

The garden is under snow, which is a grand way of saying that everything is frozen, and everything is dead.

The snow in question is a light sprinkling, like sugar through a sieve; and the herbs are indoors on the kitchen windowsill. Everything else is just tarmac and bins, and even the snow doesn't do much for it. The kitchen door is closed; the only birds are green parakeets; and even Mitski the cat has stopped coming to see us. I think she is inside with her real family. Our own real family – the friends family, the family family – are all far away.

It feels impossible to believe there will ever be spring again. And yet there is a drawer by the door full of seeds; so there must be something in me still that believes.

I string fairy lights across the fences, and wrap the compost bin up warm. I hoik up the last decaying weeds, and clear away the broken stems of summer. My hands are numb before I'm done, but it's something real. I want something to hang onto; something I can trust.

London is open, but wonkily so: we sit in the pub, and plan for every possible eventuality. The Christmas curry party, Jim's beloved tradition, is obviously out of the question. Last-Saturday-before-Christmas dumplings seems unlikely too: I've eaten dumplings with Zelda and Teddy every year since I've known them – even the years when Jim was dying, and everything else was bad. This year they can't get back from France.

And I am beginning to realise I don't want to do it, anyway. No – not that I don't want to do *Christmas*. But what I don't want to do is *do* Christmas. I don't want to make another Christmas happen in a dark time. I don't want to worry about Christmas dinner; and I don't want to do any more roast dinners, because I hate making them. I don't even love eating them. Jim loved them; and I – I realise, after a year of not making a single one – do not. And I am still alive.

And so this is how we plan: me and Nancy and Otto; me and Jo and Douglas and Georgie; me and Theo. Debo sits in the frozen garden and yells up the steps to us. Nora, brand new phone and newly into double digits, FaceTimes me to show me her novel plan, her Pony Club rosette, her scholarship letter. My family on Zoom. Zelda on Zoom. My grandparents on the end of the phone. Everyone on the end of the phone. Theo trudges from estate agent to estate agent after work, in the dark. It all feels very precarious, but then there's me and Jo, under the leopard blanket; and there's this garden, waiting, ready.

I come inside, and want warmth: easy warmth, easy comfort. Also, I am starving.

What I actually want is crumpets, but the crumpets are stale, and besides, we have to have *something* proper. We need a vegetable, and dinner, real dinner, on the table by eight. So I make this, instead: cauliflower cheese, but fancy, with a rich evaporated milk béchamel, spiked with Cheddar cheese and laced with a big spoon of Marmite; sautéed cauliflower, crisp at the edges; handfuls of greens, folded in for health; and topped with – here's the trick – stale crumpets, blitzed in a blender, and toasted in butter. $\longrightarrow$

For 2

2 eggs

150ml evaporated milk

2 tbsp Marmite

220g Cheddar

¹/₂ tbsp cornflour

1 small cauliflower

2 crumpets (*stale is fine*)

2 tbsp butter

2 big handfuls of chopped kale (*easiest to do this with scissors in the bag, IMO*)

2 tsp chopped flat-leaf parsley

- -

Take a big jug and whisk together the eggs, evaporated milk and Marmite. Easy.

Take a bowl and grate in the Cheddar. You're going, now, to add cornflour. I know. This is a weird flex, but I promise, it is ok. It just makes everything that little bit sleeker, that little bit glossier and smoother and shinier. It's a weird magic, cornflour, and let's just lean in. (Add the cornflour and stir.)

Rinse the cauliflower and chop into little florets. Boil the kettle; I don't know how people cope without kettles. Tip the cauliflower into a saucepan and pour over the boiling water. Set over a medium heat and cook for 10 minutes, or until tender.

While the cauliflower is cooking, toast the crumpets; then, using a food processor, blitz the toasted crumpets to chunky crumbs. Take an oven-proof skillet, big enough to hold everything else too; set it over a medium heat, melt the butter in it and toast the crumbs until golden. Try not to burn them, but don't worry if you do.

When the cauliflower is about a minute away from being done, add the chopped kale, and cook for a minute, just until the leaves turn bright green. Drain them both together, then tip into the skillet to steam dry.

Don't turn off the heat under the skillet; instead, add the egg, milk and Marmite mixture, and the cheese, and stir, stir, stir, until all is incorporated. Scatter with the crumpet crumbs, then stick under a hot grill for 5 minutes, until the top starts to blister.

Scatter with parsley – for visual interest – and eat immediately, from the skillet, with spoons.

Marzipan, Sour Cherry & Chocolate Chip Cookies

I'm making chocolate chip cookies again when Theo calls to tell me that I need to come and see a house.

I care a lot about cookies; always have done, but over the course of this year, I have perfected the art. I have had a lot of time to practise.

Chocolate chip, here, is sort of a misnomer. I'm fundamentally opposed to chocolate chips: they melt evenly and consistently; the bits of chocolate are equal sized and equally textured; there is something a little bit artificial seeming about chocolate chips. The chocolate bits in this recipe are more like splinters, shavings, too-big chunks. They melt into rivers and pools and satisfying solid bittersweet knots. It's a big bar of chocolate, shattered with a kitchen knife unevenly and at random, and folded partly in while the dough is still a little warm.

The key to a perfect cookie is *texture*, which is why you a) ditch the chocolate chips and b) include the squidgy sour cherries and the fudgy little bites of marzipan.

Anyway the cookies are, yes, marzipan and sour cherry, with those pools of dark chocolate and smoked salt – and when the phone goes, I assume it's the nine-minute timer.

'Hello,' I say, surprised; and he says: 'Can you meet me in twenty minutes?'; and I'm already stepping into my shoes. I slip four warm cookies into my coat pocket; leave the last couple of baking sheets under Jo's supervision and tell her I'll be back before tea.

It's not very long before I see Theo; and only a little longer until we see the house. We both know it at once. I'm in love on sight – but then, what's new? It's a shabby Victorian terrace, like mine and Jo's, with a big bay window and a little study at the back that overlooks the garden and the birds. The garden is invisible in the dark, but we know it's there.

When we leave it's starting to snow. I shove my cold hands into my pockets and thank God for the still-warm cookies. The lights of the City – empty of workers, but still softly luminous – spread across the horizon to one side, and the stillness of the park to the other, all church towers and bare trees. *It's London, Jim, but not as we know it.*

Jim never came south of the river if he could help it: he was a Londoner of the old school, snobbish and rude. 'I came south of the river for pork fucking tenderloin?!' he said to Otto, the first time they met; and Otto never really forgave him. He told me that story the day Jim died, when we lay in each other's arms, the six of us – me and Nancy and Danny and Jo and Otto, plus Beez – and talked about how Jim had been the worst and best of us. That was Jim's funeral, really: six bottles of wine, three packets of Camel Blues, and a list of his flaws.

'He seemed like a lovely man to me,' says Theo, optimistically. Theo met him once or twice; liked him; respected him, the way people who never knew him always did.

'He was lovely,' I say. 'Lovely and terrible.'

We sit on a bench in the dark, and split a cookie.

'These are the greatest cookies in the world,' Theo says, and I say, 'So are you going to take it?' and while I eat a second cookie, he rings the estate agent, there and then; and then we kiss goodbye in the lamplight like it's a film or something.

When I get home Jo has made a dozen more cookies, as instructed, each one perfect. I don't feel like cooking, again, and so we eat them instead of dinner: two cups of tea, four episodes of telly, and the greatest cookies in the world. ⟶▷

Makes 24 cookies

200g butter

300g dark soft brown sugar

100g dark chocolate

50g marzipan

1 egg + 1 yolk extra

200g plain flour

50g unsweetened cocoa powder

$^1/_2$ tsp bicarbonate of soda

50g dried sour cherries

Smoked sea salt

- -

Pre-heat the oven to 180°C. Line a baking sheet with baking paper; find the cooling rack.

Melt the butter in a saucepan over a medium-low heat; let it foam, and just about catch on the base of the pan, so that it starts to brown; you'll notice it smells absolutely amazing.

Beat together the melted butter and sugar until incorporated – now I mostly do this in a stand mixer, but you could probably do it in a big bowl with a wooden spoon or cake beaters.

Use this time to chop the chocolate – thin slivers, big chunks, roughly and crazily – and the marzipan, ditto.

When you've done that, the butter and sugar will be ready for the egg and extra yolk. Add those and beat again, then add the flour, cocoa powder and bicarbonate of soda and beat well again. Lightly fold in the chocolate, marzipan and sour cherries. Cookie dough!

Use a teaspoon to spoon NO MORE THAN SIX cookies onto the baking sheet. More than this and they will join up when they spread, which is a horrible sentence to type but shows how serious I am. Scatter with smoked salt.

Cookies in, for 9 minutes. These are so easy to overbake. Don't do it. They will seem underdone. They are not. They will get sturdier as they cool, I swear.

Cookies onto a cooling rack. If they are burnt, or hard, try the next batch for 7 minutes. If they are significantly underdone, try 10.

Repeat until no more dough. Try not to burn your mouth by eating them immediately.

Fried Jam Sandwiches

There are a lot of things people get wrong about ghosts.

The first thing – or maybe just the most pertinent thing, here and now – is that Hallowe'en has nothing on Christmas for genuine hauntings. Birthdays are bad; and weddings; and christenings; and other people's funerals – but Christmas, if you celebrate Christmas, is a minefield of ectoplasm and sudden, unexpected jolts.

Every day is a memory, and every day is a haunting. My house is full of ghosts at Christmas. The box of ornaments alone brings out half a dozen. A straw angel from my childhood home (we each have one) and a pair of glass angels from Warsaw, where my father (estranged) lived when I was little, and before he was gone from my life. A heavily embellished glass crab, with beady black eyes, which Jo and I bought on a whim to make the Crab see that we were thinking of him. The guitar string that Danny snapped the first evening I met him. A string of beads spelling out our names: ELLA-OTTO-JO-JIM-NANCY-DANNY-BEEZLE. A bone from curry goat, from the first Christmas curry party, polished and painted and hung on a ribbon. These ghosts are medicinal ghosts: bittersweet, but bearable. Good ghosts; living ghosts, almost, in the continuity of Christmas, in spite of it all. I unwrap them from their tissue paper, and lay them out across the kitchen table.

Then there are different ghosts; worse ghosts. The tinsel Zelda brought from Paris, the year I did no decorations at all. The tiny tree that sat in Jim's hospital room, even though he no longer seemed to know what Christmas was, or who we were. These ghosts are the violent ones. The obvious ones, if you like. Think a frantic 999 call, blood on the walls, the shape of a fried egg abandoned in a skillet. The thing is, if you fry an egg in a skillet and leave it there for several days, the shape of the egg remains rusted onto the iron for a long time after; even after you've scrubbed it and scrubbed it and scrubbed it. You are not supposed to scrub cast iron, and if you do you're supposed to re-season it. But seasoning was Jim's job, not mine; and washing up was supposed to be Jim's job, not mine; and Jim was never Jim after that morning. So it never got done again, not properly, and the shape of the egg made a ghost in the pan forever. Or what felt like forever, for it's gone now. That was the sixth day of Jim's stupid

LEGO advent calendar; and is now, I suppose, the first day of the Christmas hauntings.

The last egg. The last steps, and the last real words. He had brain surgery on New Year's Eve, that year, and Danny came from Scotland with a bottle of gin and a jar of jam for making unholy cocktails; and Nancy brought tarot cards and we told our fortunes over and over, looking for the future, which is now. We made fried jam sandwiches with the end of the jam; and mourned her grandfather, who had died, and Jim, who was dying. We buttered cheap bread; dredged it in eggs and sugar; fried them – like grilled cheese – under the same heavy iron skillet that had held the ghost of the breakfast, like a kind of impromptu jam doughnut crossed with French toast. The jam was molten, the eggy bread crispy and golden, the sugar powdery and floaty and delightful. It was a ridiculous thing to eat, but death is the most ridiculous thing of all. We couldn't go out; there was nowhere I could go but the hospital, and I didn't want to go; and so we wrapped ourselves round each other and told tarot and ate fried jam sandwiches and waited.

And Jo came from Manchester to sit grimly in the pub with me, holding my hand in absolute silence. She was Jim's friend then, instead of mine, but I loved her for knowing to say nothing. And we sat, and we hoped, and we planned. We are planners. *Next year*, as Zelda says, *in Jerusalem*.

This is how you lay a ghost like this: you make libations like an ancient Greek. You throw Christmas curry parties in their honour. You toast them, with wine or with dumplings or with port. You make strangers say their names. You live for them; and this year there is none of that, and it's bleak and dark and strange. We count our dead, and cut our losses, and mourn alone.

There is no room on the kitchen counter for proper cooking; there are ghosts on every surface. Washi-tape paper chains; poem-garlands of alphabet beads and glittery pink wool; the antique glass baubles Jim bought me, reluctantly, our first Christmas together. *Do we need them?* he said; and I said *yes, yes, yes*, the way I always did. The way I do. I want, even in this haunted time, to say yes. So I dig out the jam; the eggs; the butter and the cheap white bread we keep in the freezer for emergencies.

There is so much that should be happening that isn't; and so much that should never have happened that is; and it's all so unlikely that there's nothing else to do but make fried jam sandwiches and hope. $\longrightarrow$

For 1 (repeat as needed)

1 egg	2 slices of soft white bread
2 tbsp milk	1 tbsp jam
2 tsp vanilla extract	Icing sugar
1 tbsp butter	

- -

Beat the egg, milk and vanilla together in a shallow bowl, then set aside.

Butter the bread: both sides of both slices. Put the kettle on.

Put a non-stick frying pan over a medium heat; find a heavy pan or skillet to set on top.

Spread one of the slices of bread with jam, then top with the other slice; use your fingers to press down the bread around the sides. This is why you use soft, cheap, white bread: because you can squidge it together and seal it.

Dredge the jam sandwich through the egg-milk-vanilla mixture. Get it properly sticky.

Slide carefully into the hot pan; set the heavy pan or skillet on top, to press it down. Cook for 3 minutes, and in those 3 minutes make the tea.

Lift off the heavy pan; carefully flip the sandwich, then weight it down again and cook for 3 minutes on the other side, until golden and crisp and sealed.

Dust lavishly with icing sugar; take tea and jammy delight to sad friend.

Repeat, repeat for self.

Insanity Noodles

Instant noodles, if you type it too fast on a stupid smartphone, becomes insanity noodles; and that is a better name for them. Instant noodles – as in packet ramen – are the perfect food, because chicken soup is the perfect food, except when there's no time for making soup.

The thing about instant ramen is that because it's already a meal, it takes off the pressure; which means you have the time to make it fancier, if you feel like it, without feeling that it's going to all fall apart if you do it wrong. You've got noodles; you've got broth; you're going to be warm and full at the end of it, wherever you are, however you are. So why not play with it a little? Why not make it even better? It's going to be ok whatever you do; as you are.

Why not add sliced cheese, like the Koreans do (it's true!) to melt softly across the block of noodles? Why not add peanut butter for creaminess and crunch; coriander and lime for green; fermented chilli oil for red and kick; some vegetable, like cavolo nero, kale or spring onions, finely chopped with scissors straight into the pan, for health? Some meat, maybe; some tofu. And maybe an egg. Maybe a poached egg.

Only cafés can make poached eggs, I wrote, eighty thousand words ago. *I will never try it again.* I wrote it, and I meant it, and yet here we are, a book and a strange year later, and there aren't any cafés just now, and look: two poached eggs in my insanity ramen. They are tendril-y; imperfect; they look like they are overcooked, but they aren't. I was overthinking it, as usual. I overthink so much, and I'm fond of saying *never* when what I mean is *I'm scared I can't.*

You just drop the eggs into the water, with the softened noodles, and cook them until the whites firm up, and then you pour it all into the bowl and it's all fine. It isn't even hard; it is so easy, and the yolks are golden and soft, spilling into the ramen and across the cheese, meeting and mingling with the chilli oil like fire and fairy lights.

'Do you mind that it isn't real cooking?' I ask Jo, sliding a bowl of ramen before her, and she says, without taking her eyes off *Peep Show*: 'You know we would still love you if you never cooked again?', and it goes right into my bones. And right there – eating ramen in front of the telly – I order fancy delivery food for

Christmas Day, and split the cost between the three of us, Jo and Theo and me.

And the yolks spill through the broth, salty and rich, scarlet, golden, saffron and crocus and crimson and rose, all the colours of a fire, alive and always, every minute, new.

For 2

2 packets of instant ramen

2 tsp sesame oil

2 tbsp peanut butter

2 tsp fish sauce

1 tsp lime juice

4 eggs

2 spring onions

2 tsp coriander leaves

4 slices pre-sliced cheese (*Leerdammer is perfect*)

2 tsp pickled sushi ginger

1 tsp unsalted butter

2 tbsp fermented chilli oil

You know how to do this, so let's do it together. Ramen like the packet says, step by easy step: when the noodles are soft, stir through the packet seasoning and the sesame oil. Stir in the peanut butter to soften into the broth; add the fish sauce and lime juice. Crack the eggs into the soup, as far apart as possible – think the four points of a compass – and don't turn off the heat.

Chop the spring onions and coriander finely – I do this with scissors. Watch the eggs turn white, about 3 minutes.

In each bowl, lay one slice of cheese and half of the pickled sushi ginger. With a spaghetti spoon, decant the noodles and, very carefully, two eggs into each bowl. Pour over the broth and top with – in this order – a sliver of butter, another slice of cheese, liberal quantities of chilli oil, and then last of all the green things.

Lean in. Spoon. Twirly fork.

Takeaway

No parties; no homegoing; no dumplings; so we buy two Christmas trees, instead. We carry them home as a tandem effort. We buy a huge one for me and Jo – too big to be sensible, taller than the Tall Man ever was, filling the enormous floor and the whole bay window – and a little one for Theo and the cat and their new house.

We move Theo in a week before Christmas. Weetabix yowls the entire way in the cab, cries the first night, and returns to bed triumphant the next morning with the corpse of a tiny mouse. He carries himself with the secure masculine joy of the huntsman, serene and powerful. *He was so tiny he was going to die*, I say; and Theo says, *not everything ends badly all the time*. Which is true, but hard to believe.

Easier to believe, though, when it's Christmas and the air is cold and clean and bright. Jo and I hang the tree with everything from every year before: the bones, the chilli garlands, the baubles. Debo sends a tiny rocket made of felt. Jo gets out the ladder, and stands on it to set the glass Crab among the angels again. We send a picture to the Crab; we post him little pencil-sketched decorations to hang on his own non-existent tree. Douglas fixes the lights for us; my grandfather sends a hamper; our auntie (Jo's by birth, and mine by adoption) sends champagne. We listen to Michael Bublé, the way Annie does at Christmas, because we miss her.

On Christmas Day we have champagne in the street with Nancy and Otto and Nancy's brother. Theo and Jo play Sonic the Hedgehog on the new SEGA MegaDrive; the sticky roast duck arrives (Zelda, in Paris, approves: 'So Jewish of you! The Christmas dinner of the chosen people!') and the crispy saffron rice. Christmas: *not better, not worse, just different*. For pudding, we eat more cookies and Quality Street. I don't cook a thing. Sometimes you don't. Sometimes I don't. The cat, unused to people, is wary of Jo, and hides under my legs, watching her: he wants to love people so much, the way he wants to go outside, but he's too scared yet. He gets braver every day. In the spring, I think, we can have these big windows open and he can come and go as he pleases. When I think about letting him outside, wherever, unchaperoned, I am overcome by metaphor and stop abruptly. He is so small; the world is so big. But aren't we all? Isn't that always true? And not everything ends badly all the time.

I'm not saying there's such a thing as a happy ending. But mostly that's because there aren't any endings. Every ending is a beginning, every beginning an ending. In every new love is the ghost of the old, or the core of the old, the heart of the old. Here we are at Christmas, playing Sonic the Hedgehog and eating crispy duck and saffron rice. Here we are: Jo, who loved Jim; and Theo, who admired him at a distance; and me, who worshipped him, and was made by him; and the cat, whom Jim would have adored.

He loved cats, and hated dogs. He hated having his picture taken. He hated having a body, and resented corporeality like nobody else on earth; he hated going outside; he hated pasta ('pointless'), sport ('for virgins'), sunshine ('no'), and almost everyone. He loved his friends, lardo, prescription painkillers, Nietzsche, *Still Life with Woodpecker, The Princess Bride*, drag queens, old-man pubs, pop punk, regular punk, the sea, sweaty gigs in dark basements, bread with black pepper, and me. He was wildly and unpredictably generous; he loved feeling like a patron of the arts, like the spider at the centre of a web of talent. Which in many ways, he was. He knew everyone who made anything, which was how he came to know Theo without my knowing; he knew everyone good and everyone interesting, because he made it his business to know. His morals were entirely his own. He was so sharp and so funny, and too clever by half. He was a shameless gossip and a belligerent drunk and a complete flirt, large as life and camp as Christmas. He was always the tallest and loudest and cleverest person in a room. I have never met anyone with a quicker mind. He smoked too much, he drank much too much, and he died much too young. Which (to be fair to him) he had always said he would do.

And he had loved Christmas, too, after a fashion. He had loved our friends so much; Jo and Nancy and Otto and Danny, and so many more. He had loved carrying the tree home; he had loved roast dinners, and for him I had made them; and now I wouldn't make them anymore.

We never got to have a funeral for him, for complex and distressing reasons; I never got to read a eulogy or write an obituary. There were things that my kind of love – our kind of life – couldn't manage without marriage: administrative things, testamentary things, next-of-kin things. We never got – none of us, not me, not Jo, not Nancy or Danny or Otto, or anyone else who loved him – to say goodbye. And yet, in a way, we never had to. $\longrightarrow$

→ We have never had to say goodbye, because there's no such thing as endings when you keep on living.

In his death were the seeds that became our lives; and in our lives his death becomes both the eternal catalyst and utterly immaterial. We are who we are because he was. He left me Jo; he left me Nancy, and thus Otto and Beezle the dog; he left me Danny; after a fashion, he even left me Theo. And so, too, he is responsible for the cat, the Sonic, the duck, the ornaments I made with him and without him, this story for him and about him and without him, this whole damn business: his death and our lives, twined together forever, as beautiful and whole and good as an egg. Jo washes up, the way she always does; I perch on the kitchen surface, and grin at her, all the light catching in her pink-and-golden hair. *Oh no love and all alive in the kitchen.*

I text Debo and Annie and Douglas and Rachel and Luke; ring Georgie. Jo and I text the Crab a picture of us by the sea, before it all began, before it was over, and promise we'll be home again soon, in the little white house by the edge of the cliff. I text my sisters and double-digits-new-phone Nora and everyone else besides; send stupid selfies to Nancy and Danny and Otto. They send them back. The dog, in the picture, is wearing a little party hat. Everyone is home, for a given value of home, which is all we ever get. Here the cat tips over a packing case. The new curtains are too short for the windows. Down the street my friend is falling in love; and another friend has a baby just learning to be a person; and another friend just moved in, a little way down from the house we're in right now. Across the country my mother and my grandmother hug for the first time in a year; across the ocean there are thousands of people dying, every minute, and thousands being born too into this strange wild world, and everything is terrifying and everything is strange and everything is new, but what else is there?

I plan to paint the kitchen pink. I sketch out what I'll do with my garden, and with Theo's. I decide we'll have dumplings with all our friends, when it's ok again, which it will be, because it almost always is. I look at the stories of the year, and wonder what the next one will be. It's been a strange one, but then they all are: *life just keeps on happening; every day something new happens; not better, not worse, just different. Oh no, love.* So much time, and so much space, and so much to fill it with. And so Christmas passes, without my cooking a single thing: Christmas Eve, Christmas Day, Boxing Day, and the quiet days thereafter.

Spring, After

Georgie and Jo and I have made one hundred and eighty dumplings. We perch at the counter in the pink kitchen, and roll and pleat and fold. We pause only to take a batch out of the steamer; we pause only to sit in the lamplight in the kitchen and eat them. We talk about everything that's happened, and everything that's going to happen next. We talk about the dumpling evenings that happened, and that should have happened: the dumplings we ate when we first moved in; the new dumpling place opposite Georgie's flat; the dumplings I ate the Christmas before last with Zelda and Teddy, and Douglas before he was my friend, when he was just some man in a floral shirt who seemed game for a drink and a dumpling – which is, of course, how it always starts. A doughnut in a pub, a statuette of Catherine of Aragon in a window, a whiskey and ginger, or a box of dumplings; it starts somewhere, and just keeps on happening.

When we're done eating dumplings, there's still a hundred dumplings for the freezer. Georgie drives home; and I say to Jo, a week or so later: we should have our dumpling party, and we do.

The garden is thick with green things; I have bought an apple tree, and the blossoms are already holding space for tiny apples. The cucumber plants are in the window again. Mitski is back, and the doors of our street are propped open again. The kids next door are toasting marshmallows, as if they think this is a movie.

Nancy and I buy a steamer in the new Chinese supermarket in town, and a whole bunch of other frozen dumplings for good measure. We splash sauces together: grate garlic into soy and splash it with sesame oil; swirl peanut butter with pickled peanuts and chilli crisp oil.

I start packing the steamer full of dumplings; Otto catches my arm and says, to everyone, 'This woman is not doing any more of the work!'

I laugh and pour myself a glass of wine and sit down with Jo at my right hand, and Theo on my left, and Beezle at my feet eating a stray bit of fried pork.

We take Polaroid pictures; play the music too loud; lean on each other. We eat probably two hundred dumplings.

Danny gets the guitar out, the way he used to when Jim was alive; and we sing the old songs. We haven't sung them in a long time, and we hit all the high notes, one after the other: all the songs Jim loved, all the songs I love; and then Danny puts the guitar into Theo's hands and tells him to play. And he does. He plays; he sings; and it's like a miracle, because he knows all the songs we never knew we wanted to sing. We toast Jim; we toast me; Theo, for playing; and each other.

The night air is warm and full of promises; full of nearly-summer. The trains go by on the line into town, and from town, to everywhere else too: to my sisters, to our friends, to the sea. The world is there still. Changed, sure, but it's always changing. This has looked like a story about grief, but really it's been a story about change. Grief transforms you, as cooking transforms, as writing transforms, as reading transforms. As love transforms.

I dredge a dumpling through the chilli dip, and I don't know whether it's one of mine or one from the shop, and it doesn't matter. It's perfect, whatever it is, and whoever made it: plump and pleated, and translucent around the prawn. It's the moment that matters, and life – maybe always – is just a series of moments worth living for. A series of moments, and a series of miracles. This year of miracles – but perhaps all years are, in the end. ⟶

Love & Dumplings

You have to make miracles (or buy them from the Chinese supermarket), and this is ours. I think it was worth the wait. It always is.

Makes 40–50 dumplings, enough for 4 normal people

Readymade dipping sauce, to serve

For the wrappers

180g plain flour

Pinch of salt

80–100ml boiling water

For the filling

6 spring onions

25g chives

100g raw peeled prawns

10g ginger (*about 1 tbsp grated*)

2 big garlic cloves

400g pork mince, 20% fat (*fat is flavour!*)

2½ tbsp Shaoxing rice wine

1 tbsp sesame oil

1 tbsp light soy sauce

Big pinch of salt (*yes, you've used the soy, but you don't want to add any extra wetness*)

1 tbsp white pepper

- -

You can buy wrappers extremely easily; but you can also make them way, way more easily than you would think. Jo did it; and she does – as you will probably have gathered by now – very little in the kitchen. If she can, you definitely can. It's just flour and water, basically: flour in a big bowl, salt stirred through, and then the boiling water added slowly. You bring it together – with a fork, please, it is very hot! – and then knead. You knead either in a stand mixer on medium speed for 6–8 minutes, or by hand for 10.

If you knead by hand, you will find it an extremely lovely task to do: the dough is warm and supple, and comes together unstickily and sort of densely in the hands. It smells like salt dough, which is what it sort of is: like being a kid, like playing, homely and satisfying and reassuring in the hands. Knead for maybe 10 minutes: you'll know it's done when a finger pressed in leaves a dent that bounces back a little. It's not springy like brioche, but you'll feel a certain elasticness to the dough that feels just...ready. I trust you. You'll know.

Roll the dough into a log, about 15cm long and 4cm wide. Cover with a clean tea towel and leave to rest for an hour while you make the filling.

The deal here is that the filling gets cooked inside the dumpling, so everything goes in raw: raw pork, raw prawns, raw vegetables. This also means that everything has to be chopped so, so finely. This isn't difficult, it's just time-consuming. Big knife, chopping board; tiny, tiny, tiny little pieces of spring onion and chive and prawn. Smaller than that, actually.

Grate the ginger and garlic into a bowl, and mix with the pork mince; Add everything else and mix well. A useful thing to do here is to fry off a little ball of the filling in a splash of sesame oil over a medium heat – make yourself a tiny little burger. Taste to check the seasoning. Imagine making fifty dumplings that aren't as delicious as they should be. More salt? More pepper? More soy sauce? Your call. Edit as needed.

Time to compile. Television on, music on, or some excellent chatting companions.

Here is the vibe: shake a little flour onto two large baking sheets. (They won't go in the oven, so you can also use roasting tins, plates, trays, or whatever else. It's just to transport the dumplings to the steamer when done.)

Take a sharp knife and the log of dumpling dough. Slice off a piece about the thickness of a ten-pence coin from the roll; roll it up with your hands into a ball, and out with a rolling pin into a disc. You want it slightly thicker than, say, the cover of a paperback book, and about the diameter of a mug. The bigger the wrappers are, the easier they will be to fold, so if you go a little large to start off, don't worry too much.

Put a teaspoon of filling in the centre of the wrapper. Dip your finger in a glass of water and run your wet finger around the outside of the circle, then fold in half. Do not do anything else yet. $\longrightarrow$

→ This is not difficult; it might take you a minute to get the hang of; I have dyspraxia and I can do it. You have a semi-circle of dough surrounding the filling: SEMI-CIRCLE, FILLING, SEMI-CIRCLE.

Pinch the two semi-circles together at the top, so they are stuck together there, as shown in Fig. 1.

Without moving the semi-circle closest to you, fold the other half in towards the centre point on both sides – see Fig. 2.

Pinch those pleats closed. Repeat the pleating, still keeping the side closest to you flat, as in Fig. 3.

It is lucky to get fourteen of these pleats into each dumpling. Georgie can do fourteen. I can do ten if I am trying really hard. Six will keep it shut. Aim for six, then up them as you get more confident. Each dumpling should look like the one/s in Fig. 4.

Lift the dumpling onto the baking sheet (or whatever). Repeat until there is no more filling and no more dough.

How many dumplings do you want to eat? You can keep any you don't want in the freezer, then steam them from frozen: slide the whole baking sheet of dumplings straight into the freezer, and when thoroughly frozen, decant into a freezer bag.

Steam the dumplings in a bamboo steamer (very cheap, very easy to use; buy online or in a Chinese supermarket). This is basically foolproof: boiling water in frying pan; steamer in frying pan; lid on steamer. Steam for 8 minutes, then cut one open to check they are cooked – the filling will have changed colour, like the little patty we fried earlier. It may need 2–3 more minutes, but you'll be able to tell.

(Pot-stickers are advanced-level dumplings, but they are easier to get wrong: a little sesame oil in a lidded non-stick frying pan, big splash of water, medium heat, and cook until the water has evaporated and the bottom of the dumplings is crispy and brown.)

Jar of dipping sauce, because life is hard enough. Eat in the kitchen, standing up, as each batch comes out of the steamer. Steamed dumplings; steamed-up windows; the dark at bay and the people indoors. Love and dumplings, as my friend Kiran once wrote to me. I wish you love and dumplings.

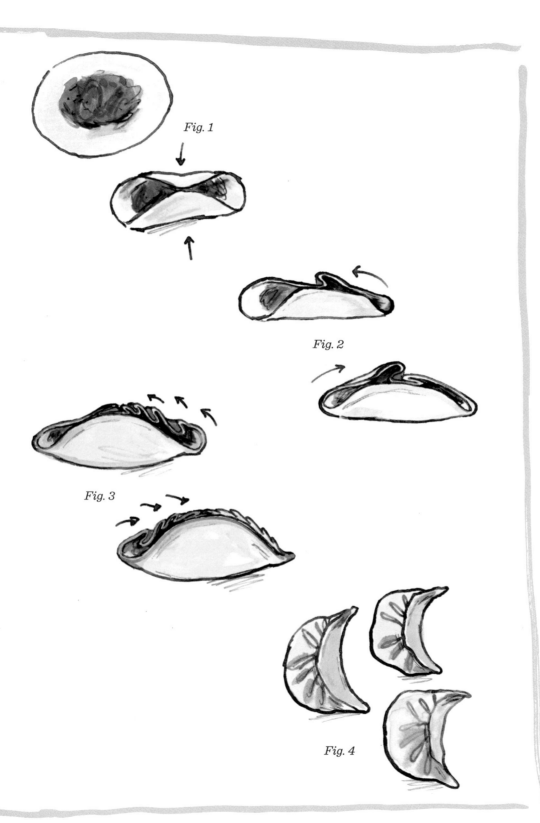

Fig. 1

Fig. 2

Fig. 3

Fig. 4

Acknowledgements

All books are a team effort, particularly this one, and so I make no apology for the length of this acknowledgments page. If it helps, there are no horrible twists halfway down this one.

First, this wasn't the book I intended to write. This means that my first thanks are to Xa Shaw Stewart, Rowan Yapp and the Bloomsbury team for their patience and understanding that the cheerful dinner-party cookbook they had commissioned was now a hungry little grief journal about falling in love at the end of the world.

To Daisy Parente, always. Without you I would make much worse books. If I made books at all. If I made anything at all.

To Elisa Cunningham, illustrator extraordinaire; and to Anita Mangan, genius designer: that this book is beautiful is down to both of you. Thank you for your remarkable talent and endless (endless!) patience.

To the many writers who have influenced this book, directly and indirectly. In particular, thank you to Diana Henry and Nigella Lawson, who have been kinder to me than I could ever have imagined when I first fell in love with their work; and thanks to the many cooks and food writers from whom I have learned so much. Being a self-taught home cook, everything in my kitchen started somewhere else – and with someone else – before being translated into my life. In particular, recipes in this book owe a debt to books, images and ideas by Felicity Cloake, Benjamina Ebuehi, Claire Ptak, Yotam Ottolenghi, Niki Segnit, Meera Sodha and Kate Young. I am so grateful for their work.

I am also grateful to the poets quoted and misquoted in these pages – Hera Lindsay Bird, Heather Christle, Marie Howe, Amy Key and Rebecca Lindenberg – and to the many other poets and writers who have shaped this work into what it is. (Reading lists provided on request.)

Thank you to my funny, wise and patient therapist, K.H. Making unbridled trauma into a narratively satisfying cookbook has been a long and difficult process, and it would have been impossible without your (extremely reasonably priced) help. Thank you.

Thank you to my friends, my family, and the friends who are my family: you know who you are, and I love you. Thank you for agreeing to change your names; thank you for letting me use the names you always secretly wished you had been called. It is a mark of...something, certainly, that three of you wished to be called Zelda.

Thanks are due to all of you, but in particular thank you to everyone who gave me recipes for this book; thank you to everyone who made me keep writing it; and thank you above all to those people who were extremely tolerant of how horrible I became while trying to make this book happen. This book has happened because you loved me enough to let it. Thank you.

Particular thanks to Harry Harris; to Gavin Day; to Sylv; to Andy Goddard, Prince of Fish; to Cornelius Prior and Klaussie Williams; to Fiona Zublin and Joe Pearson, in memory of Smitten and with love to Bleue; to Sarah, Rob, Margery and Janey Perry; to Lettie Graham; to Alice Cadwgan;

to Geoff Burnhill; to Lydia King; to Tessa Coates; to Joel Golby; to Janina Matthewson; to Zoe 'Bob' Roberts, David Cumming and Spit Lip ensemble; to Katya Herman and Ben Ashenden, my time travellers; to Lily Daunt and family; to Leila Abley; to Ellie Carr; to Ellie Cowan, Mike Harcus, and Freddie H.H.; to Kiran Millwood Hargrave for providing the last words of this book (love and dumplings!) and TdF; to everyone else I said I'd have for dinner and then the war got in the way; to everyone I couldn't put in this book by name, or even pseudonym, but who matters just the same. To my sisters, who would have featured in this book substantially more if the world hadn't collapsed; to my parents and grandparents, who taught me about love. Thank you for everything, you gorgeous bunch of weirdos. You are like miles of snow to me.

Thank you to Kay Ralph and Rob Hodgson, for their creativity and their generosity and their home: it seems amazing that the same people should be responsible for maybe the best place in the world, and maybe the best person (but it's true!). Thank you both, so much.

Thank you to Caroline O'Donoghue, my truest colleague and daily companion: without you this book would not exist at all. (And maybe nor would I.) Thank you to the Tub, the heartbeat of my day.

Thank you to J.M.U., who gave me my life. I really hope this counts as a suitable epitaph, and I hope that wherever you are, there are Djarum Blacks with honey in the filters and nobody ever counts calories. We will always miss you, I think.

Thank you to Kate Young, for always answering the phone when I get stuck (or bored). Thank you for your recipes, your wisdom, and your endless love. Family.

Thank you to the Crab, half of my heart, a third of the greatest paranormal detective agency on God's green earth, and a ninth of God: thank you, Adam Clery.

Thank you to Richard Wallace (and Rocket!), who waltzed into my life just as the world ended. Thank you for more things than I know how to write, but mostly, thank you for letting me write a book about falling in love with you and dedicating it to somebody else. Thank you for knowing everything without ever having to be told. (Thank you to the Mags, collectively, for knowing everything about this household without ever having to be told.)

And so, to Tash Hodgson, to whom this book is dedicated: thank you. 'When it's done, I want you to write, this book is dedicated to Tash Hodgson, who put up with this book for one million billion hours, all the crying and all the bloody rest of it.' It would have been for you even if you'd never asked for it. There is nobody I would rather cook for. There is nobody I would rather live with. Thank you for knowing the difference between the truth and a tragedy, thank you for knowing where the matches are; thank you for never, ever, being afraid to burn.

I can hardly believe this
I can hardly believe this life
Every time I knock, you let me in.

Index

BLOOMSBURY PUBLISHING
Bloomsbury Publishing Plc
50 Bedford Square, London, WC1B 3DP, UK
29 Earlsfort Terrace, Dublin 2, Ireland

BLOOMSBURY, BLOOMSBURY PUBLISHING and the Diana logo
are trademarks of Bloomsbury Publishing Plc

First published in Great Britain 2022

Commissioning Editor: Xa Shaw Stewart
Project Editor: Alison Cowan
Designer: Anita Mangan, anitamangan.co.uk
Illustrator: Elisa Cunningham, elisacunningham.com
Indexer: Vanessa Bird

Printed and bound in China by RR Donnelley Asia Printing Solutions Ltd

To find out more about our authors and books
visit www.bloomsbury.com and sign up for our newsletters